Langton's C

to

the

OFFA'S DYKE PATH

The Dyke heading North across Llanfair Hill
(between Knighton and the village of Newcastle)
Photograph by Van Greaves

Langton's Guide
to
the
OFFA'S DYKE PATH
A coast to coast walk

Andrew Durham

LANGTON'S GUIDES

ACKNOWLEDGEMENTS

The author gratefully acknowledges the information and assistance provided by various individuals and organisations in the preparation of this guide. In particular:

Dr D H Hill and Mrs M Worthington who briefed me on Manchester University's research into the Dyke.

Their generous assistance does not mean that they proofread this Guide. Any mistake is the author's not their's!

The author wishes to draw attention to the invaluable work of the Offa's Dyke Association.

This edition first published 1996 by Langton's Guides

See Section Five "Update" for details of the free updating service

Expedition Planning maps are based on the 1:250,000 Ordnance Survey Travelmaster series 1993. Location maps are to a scale of 1:63,360 and are based on the 1:50,000 Ordnance Survey Landranger series 1992 - 1995. Routefinding maps are to a scale of approximately 1:21,000 and are partially based on the 1:25,000 Ordnance Survey Pathfinder series and the Landranger series 1992 - 1995. All are with the permission of the Controller of Her Majesty's Stationery Office © Crown Copyright

ISBN 1 899242 02 3

Cover Photograph: Looking North along the Dyke as it descends to the River Lugg between Kington & Knighton. Photograph by the Author.

Typeset by Langton's Guides
Pre-Press by Briarwood Graphics of Mansfield
Printed by J R Ward ColourPrint Ltd of Dewsbury

About this Guide

This Guide is in five sections:

Section One - Introduction to the route and historical background.

Section Two - An expedition planning section with advice on planning your walk, safety, and a section on transport to/from the Path. Featuring 1:200,000 planning maps which provide an overview of the route and nearby accommodation & campsites.

Section Three - Featuring maps of the route in two scales, a 1:63,360 "Location" map and a large-scale "Routefinding" map at approximately 1:21,000.

Location maps (monochrome reductions of the 1:50,000 OS Landranger) pinpoint accommodation and are overlaid to show the facilities available on or just off the route. The detail on those facilities/services is shown below the map. Note that this information is Updated annually (see Section Five).

The section of route covered on the adjacent routefinding map is indicated on the location map.

Routefinding Maps are accompanied by detailed route directions. To enable rapid reference, the essential route directions are in **bold** typeface whilst "confidence" directions are in normal typeface (e.g. **"D" - Hall Road T-junction. Turn right** and pass the Church and Post Office on your left.

Additional information on the local area and points of interest are given separately in *italics*.

Section Four - Contains essential information on the Langton's Guide, a user's guide that you ignore at your peril!

Section Five - Contains details of Langton's Guides' unique "Update" service, further reading, useful addresses and information for the walker (including the full addresses and telephone numbers for the accommodation listed in the guide).

Preface

In line with our policy of improving each guide, this guide, the third in the Langton's Guides series on Long Distance Paths, reflects changes arising from the replies to our questionnaires and from the many letters from walkers who, appreciative of the earlier guidebooks, wrote to offer constructive suggestions. In particular, the new expedition planning section should make the task of planning each day's walk easier and give an even better overview of the route.

In introducing photographs to the guides, my policy has been to restrict them to just enough to give a flavour for the Path and to indicate the type of terrain along which you will walk. A surprise view is no longer a surprise if you have seen a photograph of it!

Some walkers have requested colour maps. Full colour printing quadruples the pre-press process and requires the use of more sophisticated equipment. Obviously the greatly increased costs involved could be partially offset with a larger print-run, but that is not compatible with a format that includes so much date-sensitive material. Nevertheless, we hope to start introducing some colour into future guides.

There are several other guidebooks to the Offa's Dyke Path and whilst each has its own approach to the subject, the sight of some walkers using two different guidebooks to find their way served as a reminder that certain essentials must be covered.

This a <u>walker's</u> guidebook! Its priority is to get you from one end of the walk to the other without losing your way. Its second priority is to enable you to find accommodation and facilities with ease. Lastly, it aims to aid your appreciation of the surroundings through which you will pass. If I have done my job properly, your Langton's Guide will become an invaluable companion to you on your walk. A practical guide that you will come to take for granted; but hopefully, <u>not</u> so much for granted that you forget its strengths when you come to buy a guide to your next Long Distance Path!

Andrew Durham

Contents

About this Guide   5
Preface   6

INTRODUCTION TO THE OFFA'S DYKE PATH   9
The Route   10
Historical Background   13
    The Dark Age & The Rise of Mercia   15
    King Offa   17
The Dyke   18
    Physical Profile & Research on the Dyke   19
    The Purpose of the Dyke   20
    An Absence of Dyke   23
    Manchester University Research   25
The Future of the Dyke   27
The National Trail   28

WALKING THE OFFA'S DYKE PATH   31
Expedition Planning   32
    Which Direction, When to walk, Planning the Walk   32
    Maps & Waymarks   33
    Safety   34
    Transport   35
Planning Maps   38

THE OFFA'S DYKE PATH   45
Location Maps & Routefinding Maps   46

GETTING THE MOST FROM YOUR
LANGTON'S GUIDE   197
Maps & Directions   198
Facilities Information   200

ADDITIONAL INFORMATION   205
Update & Tourist Information Centres   206
Additional Reading   207
Welsh Placenames   208
Accommodation Addresses   209

The Path rejoins the Dyke at Carreg-y-big near Oswestry
Photograph by the Author
"The (defensive) dyke would normally be topped by a thorn barrier or wooden palisade" ..... a modern fence illustrates the principle.

Section One
Introduction
to
The Offa's Dyke Path

The Route

The 285-kilometre (177-mile) Offa's Dyke Path National Trail is a coast to coast walk that stretches from Chepstow on the Severn estuary to Prestatyn on the coast of North Wales. Comparison with other National Trails or Long Distance Paths is not particularly helpful, for there is no doubt in my mind that the Offa's Dyke Path is in a class of its own. It has all the elements that combine to make a superb walk; variety of terrain, beauty of scenery, surprise, intrigue, history, a theme for continuity, and it has them in abundance.

The contrast between river valley, rolling farmland and open hill makes the Offa's Dyke Path a delight to walk. Even the up's are seldom so long or steep as to spoil one's progress, yet you get high enough to enjoy glorious views across the borderlands. The Offa's Dyke Path is not about rugged mountain scenery, with sharp contrasting rock; it is a more seductive beauty of gently rounded hills clad in soft greens and of panoramic views that are so full of interest that it takes some time to assimilate them. Other views come upon you quite suddenly and literally stop you in your tracks. An early taste of things to come is the sight of Tintern Abbey and the Wye Valley from the Devil's Pulpit.

Tintern Abbey viewed from the Path at the Devil's Pulpit
Photograph by the Author

Much of the route is over rolling hills, and the intimate valleys that lie between them only offer up their secrets at the last moment; perhaps an exquisite oak-beamed farmhouse or a tiny church caught in a time-warp.

It is a coast to coast walk that crisscrosses borders; not just the English/Welsh border, but a border with predominantly lowland to the East and upland to the West. Above all, it is a border between quite distinct cultures. This is an area that has been fought over for centuries and the many castles along the way testify to that struggle; ranging from the great castle at Chepstow to the fine example of a motte and bailey castle at Longtown.

But it is the Dyke that makes this Path unique. A massive earthwork attributed to Offa, the 8th century King of the Mercians and ruler of Saxon England; in places it is a huge bank with a deep ditch, in others it is a low mound that is barely distinguishable. Of the 129 kilometres (80 miles) of known Dyke, the Path either follows or keeps company with it for almost 96 kilometres (60 miles). For much of that distance the walker is actually on the Dyke but even where the Path parallels it, the walker gains from the new perspective.

An imposing testament to a man about whom we know so little, the walker cannot fail to be impressed and intrigued as the Dyke forges its way relentlessly across the countryside. In sharp contrast to that other great border work, Hadrian's Wall, nobody is really sure what the Dyke was built to achieve. Part of the fun in this walk is that it is something of a mystery tour.

Whilst mere statistics cannot convey what a Path has to offer (no pun intended), the long distance walker will want to know that approximately 72km's (45 miles) is open hill-walking, 160km's (100 miles) is on footpaths/tracks and 50km's (31 miles) is on tarmac, although most of that is on very minor roads and usually for only a short distance. The rest of the Path is over stiles, there are said to be 650 (hardly any of which have dog gates)!

Starting on the cliffs at Sedbury and the Severn estuary, the Path initially hugs precipitous cliffs along the Wye Valley and follows the Dyke north to the Naval Temple on top of the "Kymin" hill overlooking Monmouth. It then uses an opportunity, offered by a break in the Dyke, to take the walker across to the Black Mountains for a marvellous ridge walk to Hay Bluff and then

Looking across Hay Bluff to the Black Mountains
Photograph by Van Greaves
"Whilst potentially one of the highlights.. a very long day if the ground is soft"

down into the historic town of Hay-on-Wye. The Path then crosses hill and dale before descending off the Hergest ridge (423m)(1388ft) into Kington. Just beyond Kington the Dyke reappears and together you forge north to Knighton, the "town on the dyke".

Knighton is the recognised halfway point and although it is a "short" half, it is the most convenient point from which to get public transport off the Path. From high above Knighton the Path follows the Dyke along one of its most impressive and well-defined sections before descending from the ancient Kerry Ridgeway to the Plain of Montgomery.

The line of the Dyke across the plain comes as a welcome relief from all the up's and down's of the previous section, but the Path soon leaves the Dyke to ascend to the Iron Age hill-fort of Beacon Ring (408m)(1338ft) overlooking Welshpool. It then flirts with the Shropshire Union Canal before briefly rejoining the Dyke on Llanymynech Hill. However it isn't until Carreg-y-big that we are properly reunited with the Dyke on a grand scale as it makes its approach to Chirk Castle.

Shortly after Chirk Castle the walker bids farewell to Offa's Dyke and by then you will have seen it in all its various forms, crossing very different types of terrain. So much had I enjoyed following the Dyke that I found myself reluctant to leave it and started searching the map for further sections along which to walk. Alas, although there are small segments of Dyke to the West of Wrexham, there is no viable route north of the Shropshire Union Canal and so the Path briefly follows that before taking the walker along the Clwydian Hills to the coast.

I imagine that in writing-off the "Offa's Dyke" part of the Path at the canal, I risk the criticism of many Dyke devotees who will point to small sections of dyke that are attributed to Offa as far North as Gop Hill (just outside Prestatyn). The fact is that there is a lot of controversy about the Dyke beyond Treuddyn (nr. Mold). One thing is for sure: after the canal and the River Dee at Llangollen, the whole nature of the Path changes. Rather than view the final section of the Path as finishing off the Offa's Dyke Path, I think you will find it more satisfying if you regard it as a new chapter in your journey from coast to coast.

To position for the Clwydians, the walker first heads West to take the scenic "Panorama Walk" above Llangollen and thence to the aptly-named "World's End". Having found another world at the other side of World's End, the grateful walker descends to Llandegla for a rest in preparation for the hills ahead.

The Clwydians offer open hill-walking with magnificent views over the Vale of Clwyd. In clear weather you can see Cader Idris and Snowdon over 30 miles away. If time permits a diversion, the quiet charm of Ruthin has much to offer before the final section into the bustle of Prestatyn.

Historical Background

It is inevitable that as you walk the Dyke you will wonder why it was built, why it takes the line that it does and you will want to know something about the man who ordered its construction.

The difficulty presented by many modern histories is that they are too preoccupied with being "correct". The result is often a series of facts, dates and events which finally emerge in such a qualified and bland account, as to give no feeling at all for the events they describe. This situation is exacerbated by the fact that due to a lack of written history, the period with which we are concerned is aptly-named "The Dark Ages".

If the Dyke itself provides physical evidence of its existence, here was a King known for his Dyke but little else is on record. Some histories rely for information on letters to Offa from the court of the Emperor Charlemagne; but that is a bit like relying on official letters that end, "I remain Sir, your obedient Servant", the writer doesn't always mean it, nor should you rely too heavily on it.

Writing from St. Pauls School London in 1761, a detailed account of Offa and the Dark Ages is given in "A New History of England" by William Rider A.B. (formerly of Jesus College Oxford). I have decided to call on his account because not only does he provide a colourful and fascinating insight into the times, he isn't coy about questioning the motives of some of the clerics on whom so much of our history of this period is based. Although Rider's account agrees with much of the modern history, the fine detail would be considered unreliable by today's standards. Nevertheless, it provides a context for what was going on and I consider that preferable to the sanitised and colourless alternative.

Standing Stones on the Hergest Ridge above Kington. Gladestry Hill in the background. - Photograph by Van Greaves
"a seductive beauty of gently rounded hills clad in soft greens, and panoramic views so full of interest that it takes time to assimilate them"

The Dark Age

The Romans finally left Britain to fend for itself in AD446. An earlier withdrawal of troops in AD383 had provided a foretaste of what was to come and the Scots and Picts, finding themselves virtually unopposed, generally lay waste to the North of England. A British chief, Vortigern, invited over a Saxon army to help push the Scots and Picts back across the border into Scotland. The Saxons thought what a nice place England was, and stayed. Within 200 years they had expanded from a foot-hold in Kent to the extent that there were seven Saxon kingdoms (The Saxon "Heptarchy"), Northumbria, East Angles, Essex, Kent, South Saxons (Sussex & Surrey), West Saxons (Wessex). The seventh kingdom was Mercia, situated in the middle, and although it originally comprised what was later called Staffordshire, Derbyshire, Nottinghamshire, North Warwickshire and North Leicestershire, by the time we come to the period of Mercian history that interests us, its border was formed by the rivers Humber in the north, Severn in the west and Thames in the south. East Anglia and Essex formed the eastern border.

Although the Heptarchy was comprised of separate kingdoms, it is better to regard it as an uneasy alliance of Saxon chiefs with, at any given time, the dominant chief at its head. It was united by a need to fight off common enemies; the Saxon pirates (and later the Danes), the Britons (pushed by conquest into Wales) and the Scots/Picts (across the border in Scotland). Although intermarriage for the purpose of alliance was common, as was the practice of collecting tribute from weaker kings, this was a period of plot and counterplot, of poisonings, murders, putting eyes out and throwing your rival's offspring down wells! It is against such a background of brutal infighting that we must view Offa and his actions. Before focusing on Mercia in the 7thC and 8thC it is worth mentioning that by now Christianity and the Church had a powerful, if at times tenuous, hold on the Heptarchy and its moderation frequently prevented internecine squabbles getting completely out of control.

The Rise of Mercia

Now let's turn to Mercia and don't forget that we are only looking at one kingdom amongst seven. If the pace of conflict seems to get a bit too much, bear in mind that the other six were at each other's throats as well. Mercia rose to prominence in AD633 when Penda of Mercia, in an unlikely alliance with the British (Welsh) King Cadwallon, attacked Edwin, King of Northumbria, defeated and killed him. Cadwallon later met his fate at the hands of Edwin's successor, King Oswald of Northumbria, who later still, met his fate at the hands of Penda at Oswestry in AD642. Penda expanded into Wessex and in AD654, he again invaded Northumbria but this time lost the battle and was either slain by Oswio of Northumbria or he was murdered by his own wife. Mercia now came under Northumbria's rule although Penda's son, Peada, was allowed to rule some of Mercia by Oswio (Peada was after all his son-in-law). Peada was murdered by his wife and was succeeded by Wulfhere (a brother). Inside three years, Wulfhere (sounds vicious and he was) threw Northumbria out of Mercia, expanded his border from the Severn to the Wye and invaded Wessex and the Isle of Wight. He lost a battle to Northumbria and had to forfeit some land, attacked Wessex again in AD675 but died shortly thereafter (of exhaustion no doubt!).

Wulfhere was succeeded by Aethelred who, in AD679, recovered the lands Wulfhere had forfeited to Northumbria. In AD704 Aethelred did the only thing a king could do if he wanted to die peacefully in his bed. He resigned, and went to live as a monk (several kings tried this but it didn't always work). Aethelred passed Mercia to Coenred, son of Wulfhere, who reigned for only 5 years before he resigned and went to Rome (safer bet). Ceolred son of Aethelred took over but was poisoned (not before battling Wessex in AD715). Aethelbald (distant relation of Ceolred) came to the throne in AD716 and although he restored Mercian domination south of the Humber, his reign saw a slow decline in Mercia's influence. Aethelbald's court became so infamous for its sexual depravity that Pope Boniface sent him a stiff note pointing out that their indulgences had previously been punished by a particularly nasty form of capital punishment. There were more invasions etc. until, in AD757, Aethelbald met his death in a mutiny. One Beornred, who had started the mutiny, seized the crown but was so distasteful a fellow that the Mercian nobles dethroned him and crowned Offa, descendant of Eowa (Eawa) who was a brother of Penda.

It would be wrong to paint a picture of total anarchy during the Heptarchy for, within their kingdoms, some of the Saxon kings were very able administrators and even popular with their subjects. Unfortunately those that were best-loved usually came to a nasty end or were perceived to be weak by their neighbours and were invaded.

King Offa

Rider doesn't mention Offa's first campaign, against the East Angles, he starts Offa's military ventures with an attack on Kent and mentions Offa's inability to capitalise on his victory due to the need to return to Mercia to defend it against incursions by the Britons. Offa then attacked Northumbria (weakened at that time by a civil war) and by AD779, he had invaded Wessex (which had supported Northumbria against Offa). The 10thC "Annales Cambriae" record Offa attacking the Britons in AD778 and AD784.

The incursions of the Britons into Mercia posed a rather different threat to Offa than that presented by his fellow Saxon kings. Within the Heptarchy there was an underlying order and whilst squabbles were bloody, they were relatively short-lived and limited in scope. After all, there was no point in decimating a kingdom that could provide tribute and manpower for further campaigns. This limited warfare is evidenced by the number of times that one king successfully invaded another's territory only to find himself being repulsed a few years later by a descendant of the defeated (and usually slain) king. There was no standing army as such and each king raised the necessary extra manpower by pressing men into service for a particular campaign. This made it difficult to sustain a presence in a subjugated territory.

The Britons had a separate cultural identity, were fierce fighters and didn't submit to defeat. Frankly it was easier and more profitable to attack fellow Saxons than take on the Britons. How then was Offa to deal with these incursions? Rider states that, as Offa prepared to attack the Britons, they proposed a treaty. Offa used the peace to fortify his side of the border. The works were quickly put into effect (circa AD782 onwards) and the Britons watched as a great dyke was thrown up "from the mouth of the Dee to the Wye near Bristol". Access across Mercia was controlled at set crossing points and for a short time the uneasy peace continued. However, the Britons were incensed by the dyke and one King, Marmodius, under the guise of gathering everyone for a Christmas party (Christianity was established in Wales before the Saxons were converted), attacked the dyke which was destroyed in several places and the ditch filled in. Once more the Britons rampaged across the border. Offa was incensed, he threw the hostages he held as part of the treaty into slavery and gathering an army, set off on a long, brutal but successful campaign against the Britons. Quoting the Ligger book of St. Albans, Rider says that it was ten years before he returned to his own kingdom, "neither elate with success, nor assuming any additional titles on account of his conquests" (but did he repair the dyke?).

Unfortunately we do not know the time-frame for the sequence of events around the construction of the Dyke, but a 10-year campaign seems unlikely. We know that in AD787 Offa held a synod at Cealchyth to which Papal envoys were welcomed and at which the Bishopric of Lichfield was established with Papal blessing. Offa took this opportunity to have his son crowned as a joint ruler. Also around this time, Offa joined with his son-in-law in a campaign by Mercia and Wessex against the Danes, who had started to mount raids on the Saxons.

Offa died in AD796 and according to some, he died at Rhuddlan during a campaign against the Britons to secure the northern line of the Dyke. However this is almost certainly a mistake in later histories. Rider has Offa handing over to his son and making a journey to Rome, where he is said to have obtained the Pope's agreement to the canonization of St. Alban and an absolution for his own sins (the murder in AD794 of Ethelbert, King of the East Angles, must have been on his mind!). He is said to have returned to end his days as steward of the monastery of St.Albans (of which he was the founder).

Whatever the truth, we know that Offa encouraged trade with the continent, that he introduced the gold dinar and revised the silver coinage, that he was on good terms with the Church and that he was respected by the Emperor Charlemagne. There will more about Offa but let's move on to the Dyke.

The Dyke

If the Dyke itself provides something tangible to study, that doesn't appear to have enabled historians to reach a consensus on what it was for, or even its full extent. The walker will come across various books, guidebooks, leaflets, noticeboards and even exhibitions that "explain" the Dyke. Unfortunately, I have come to recognise common sources of differing information cropping up again and again. I have therefore attempted to summarise the debate that has surrounded the Dyke and to introduce the ongoing archeological research. If the prospect of ploughing through so much background at this stage is too daunting, skip to Section 2. I have a feeling that you'll want to know more about the Dyke once you have walked a few miles of it.

Physical Profile

In its full glory, the Dyke consists of a deep ditch along the west side of a steep bank created with the spoil from the ditch. Turf and stones were used on the face of the bank to support a steeper slope than could otherwise be achieved with loose earth. In places the height of the top of the bank from the bottom of the ditch exceeded 7 metres (25 feet). Today the combined height seldom exceeds 4 metres (13 feet). Occasionally, a lesser ditch on the east side was needed to obtain extra spoil for the bank or for drainage purposes. Where the slope down to the west was very steep, a shelf alone was cut into the side of the hill.

Research on the Dyke

The Dyke has been the subject of comment by a number of historians, particularly in the 19thC. In 1857 an astute account of it was written by an Anglo-Saxon scholar, John Earl. However, the authority most often quoted today is "Offa's Dyke: A Field Survey of the Western frontier-works of Mercia in the seventh and eighth centuries AD". It was published in 1955 and based on the work of Sir Cyril Fox who surveyed the Dyke over 6 summers, from 1925-30, whilst working for the National Museum of Wales.

Acclaimed by contemporaries of Fox, it became the definitive work on the Dyke and is used as a standard reference to this day. It is frequently quoted and many of the "Offa's Dyke" notations found on modern OS maps derive from Fox's survey.

If Fox's work is invaluable for its meticulous record of the physical state of the Dyke in the earlier part of this century, it also had the effect of slamming the lid shut on what little subsequent research might have been directed towards it. Sir Cyril Fox was held in high regard, he had examined the Dyke, pronounced his findings and that was that! The Dyke lay dead across the countryside, eroding, overgrown, open to abuse and generally ignored.

Fox's work was reviewed by Mr Frank Noble MBE who founded the Offa's Dyke Association in 1969. Part of his detailed research, for his MPhil thesis for the Open University, was published in 1983 at the request of the Offa's Dyke Association. Unfortunately Noble (deceased) was unable to complete his review. In his thesis he only got as far North as the crossing of the Severn (below Oswestry).

Noble challenged many of the planks on which Fox founded his view of the Dyke and although his work didn't add greatly to our knowledge of the Dyke itself, its effect was to prise open the debate and breathe life into a corpse. His contribution stands as David before Fox's Goliath and he awakened interest in the Dyke. Noble's work can be recognised in many Offa's Dyke Association booklets, in the exhibition at Knighton, and his early guidebook to the Offa's Dyke Path became a source for others.

Creeping into more recent guides to the Path have been references to "recent research" by Manchester University. The walker may be surprised to learn that this "recent" research has been ongoing since the early 1970's! If Noble forced the lid on a debate screwed down by Fox, perhaps it's time to give some air to research that has a more scientific foundation.

For the truth is that earlier research on the Dyke suffered from a lack of resources and, in particular, archeological excavation. Fox dug only 6 sections to confirm his findings, believing excavation to be of little value in his surveys of the Dyke. Noble was restricted to the ad-hoc opportunities that arose from time to time (eg. a new road crossing the line of the Dyke.). In his thesis, he cautioned that excavation was essential to establish the veracity of both his and Fox's findings. The team from Manchester, under the direction of Dr. D H Hill (assisted by Mrs M Worthington) has dug over 160 sections, used aerial photography and utilised equipment not available to Fox in the 1920's.

The Purpose of the Dyke

Given the lack of excavation, it is perhaps not surprising that the individual perception of those studying the Dyke led them to reach quite different conclusions as to its purpose. It has been variously attributed to being:

- A boundary marker on the border between Mercia and the British.
- A control on trade, people and animals crossing into and out of Mercia. Access through the Dyke being limited to manned crossing points.
- A defensive line against intrusion and even invasion.

A Boundary Marker

Much of the debate has centred on whether the route of the Dyke formed the actual boundary between Mercia and the Britons. Fox thought that it was the border and represented a line agreed by negotiation and treaty. This view was based on, amongst other things, the names of the places either side of the Dyke.

Fox's assertion called for some very attractive territory to be ceded by Offa to the Britons. Noble found no support for this, nor for a withdrawal of the Mercians from the natural border afforded by the Wye in the South or the Severn further North. Place-name evidence, whilst useful, wasn't conclusive and in any event he found examples of changes of name at various times.

The idea of a grand boundary marker designed to impress the Britons, doesn't seem credible if the Dyke didn't mark the actual border and a border can be much more simply marked than with a dyke of the proportions of Offa's Dyke.

Across Buttington and the Severn valley on the descent from Beacon Ring.
Photograph by the Author
"Fox thought these gaps had no dyke because none was necessary"

21

A Control

If Fox thought that the Dyke was a boundary marker, Noble thought it was a barrier to control trade and rustling. He suggested that the Dyke was strong over remote areas to act as an obstacle to unseen incursions, forcing cattle and men through set control points.

A Defensive Line

For almost all of its identifiable length, the placement of Offa's Dyke suggests a desire to achieve and maintain a tactical advantage over the Britons. As its physical profile suggests, this points to a defensive purpose. The ditch and bank (or "dyke") had been used for defence for centuries before Offa. The many Iron-age hillforts still testify to its use to slow an enemy's approach and enable a defender to use the advantage of height, thus enhancing the range and effectiveness of his limited weaponry. The dyke would normally be topped by a thorn barrier or wooden palisade.

The Roman Army were expert in the use of the dyke and it has been said that the legionnaire's entrenchment tool won more battles than his famous short-sword. In Offa's time, and only 300 years after the Romans, the dyke was still the most effective solution when it came to a defensive work.

Nevertheless, Fox and Noble both rejected Offa's Dyke as a defensive structure (although much later, Noble had second thoughts). It worried them that there were marked differences in the Dyke's construction. The sudden changes in its form that would occur along the Dyke, from a massive bank to just a low mound, seemed inconsistent with the notion of a defensive earthwork. Such changes in form were taken to be different interpretations of the building requirement by various local construction gangs.

Supporting this view were instances where the route of the Dyke seemed inconsistent with a defensive line; although Noble did not readily accept Fox's attribution of some illogical right-angled bends in the Dyke to misdirected work gangs meeting in the middle of woods.

Although the consistency in both the form of the Dyke and its line points to a central plan, their inference was that having ordered the building of a dyke, its construction was then left to local interpretation. However, excavation shows evidence of marking-out ditches along the line of the Dyke, suggesting that it was laid out some time in advance. It seems inconceivable that its construction would then be abandoned to local interpretation. Puzzling though the odd failure to utilise the best tactical route might seem, it would be unwise to use the odd exception to disprove the whole. In any event, where such anomalies occur, the tactically "blind" areas appear to be covered by the adjoining stretches of Dyke.

None of the above considerations necessarily makes the Dyke an equivalent of Hadrian's Wall! That other great border defence was permanently manned by a large force of professional troops and had communications, mile-castles, and supporting forts. It had highly-organised troops ready to rush reinforcements to any point on the wall, along roads built for the purpose. It also had layered defences in anticipation of a failure of troops to hold the wall in certain places. In comparison with a standing Roman army, the Saxon army was an ad-hoc rabble. There is no evidence that Offa's Dyke was manned in such a way.

If Offa's Dyke wasn't permanently garrisoned, the best that it could achieve would be to hinder the passage of horses and carts and show evidence of an intrusion. Centuries before the invention of barbed wire entanglements, the dyke would have been an effective substitute. If it is to be viewed as a security fence, was it patrolled? The problem is that whilst it is likely to have been easier to walk or ride on the Dyke (or alongside it) than it is today, there is no evidence of a communication road running along it. If a lookout did spot something, how was he to report and how were reinforcements going to get to the remoter stretches of dyke?

Although history has repeatedly shown the folly of reliance on fixed lines of defence, it is possible that the intention was to provide a line behind which the Mercians could retreat before turning to repel invaders; thus halting an advance whilst reinforcements were rushed to the Dyke.

An Absence of Dyke

If the purpose of the Dyke proved contentious, its absence was even more so; for there were gaps along the route where no trace of the Dyke was to be found. Fox thought that these gaps had no dyke because none was necessary; due either to dense and impenetrable forest or to where a river served as a natural barrier. Noble considered that Fox had become fixated by the idea of forests, finding them where no evidence of such extensive forestation existed only 300 years later at the time of the Domesday Record. Furthermore, Noble considered that the older and bigger the forest, the less it would have presented a barrier at ground level due to the lack of sunlight, and thus vegetation, below a dense canopy. Whilst Noble was prepared to consider the use of a river to fill a gap, he found traces of dyke that had been ignored or missed by Fox in these supposed "forests".

However, the biggest problem was the absence of Dyke over a large lowland area and especially around Hereford, an important centre in Offa's Mercia. If Fox fell back on impenetrable forests, Noble thought that there might have been just a palisade or that a buffer-state of independent but friendly Britons rendered the Dyke unnecessary. He even postulated that the people around Hereford were disaffected and putting a dyke round them might be enclosing potential enemies (although Noble himself conceded that such political considerations were only slightly better founded than Fox's forests)! Nevertheless, Noble may have had a point. Sir Francis Palgrave's "History of the Anglo-Saxons" (1876), makes the observation that the political subjugation of Powys and adjoining kingdoms, did not necessarily lead to the expulsion of the Britons. Although under Mercian rule, the whole area, including Hereford, remained essentially "British" until as late as the reign of King John.

If Noble found traces of Dyke missed or ignored by Fox, he doesn't explain how those isolated sections near Hereford fit his theory on buffer states or hostile natives. A case of no dyke at all being better for those theories than some. Furthermore, if it was possible to construct a huge Dyke on a mountain, what was the difficulty that made a palisade the only option on flat ground, where it would serve as a poor alternative? Despite the fact that they were aware of instances where landowners levelled the dyke, there is a puzzling degree of significance placed by both Fox and Noble on the physical form of the Dyke in modern times. Indeed, some of the "original access points through the Dyke" that were identified as such by Fox, have subsequently been excavated by Manchester University and the ditch of the Dyke has been found. The conclusion is that the Dyke has subsequently been levelled.

Both Fox and Noble's lack of excavation, and their reliance on observing the modern ground, highlights a fundamental weakness in any such survey. It seems too obvious to have passed without comment, that the best examples of Dyke exist in the least fertile areas; whilst many of the reduced sections and breaches are in areas more heavily cultivated in later times: a reasonable inference being that, like the Berlin Wall, once the purpose of the Dyke was lost, it was an inconvenience that was simply levelled by later inhabitants of the area.

The Manchester University Research

So the debate on the Dyke settled into Fox's boundary marker, with forests in the gaps; and Noble's immigration/trade/rustling barrier sitting just behind frontier settlements. Both camps supported a "something" from sea to sea and this was generally taken to be along a line from Sedbury Cliffs to Prestatyn.

The Manchester team examined the historical evidence for a Dyke running from "sea to sea". Numerous references in later documents seemed to derive from just one source, Asser's "Life of King Alfred" (written c AD893). Even there it was a passing comment, much in the vein of "and Offa, the King who built a Dyke from sea to sea".

Excavating a gap on the Plain of Montgomery at Site No. 153.
Photograph: M Worthington (Manchester University)
"Fox dug only six sections to confirm his findings, believing excavation to be of little value in his surveys of the Dyke"

Whilst suspecting that today's theories about the Dyke running along the entire Mercian/British border were fed from a rather slender root, the team looked for more tangible evidence. Although there didn't seem to be much dyke between Mold and Prestatyn, the termination of Wat's Dyke at Holywell and the undisputed presence of a dyke at Sedbury, at least offered the possibility that there might have been a continuous line from sea to sea; so the team set out to examine the physical evidence.

The isolated stretch of Dyke near Prestatyn turned out to be just that: isolated! No evidence could be found that it was part of any greater dyke. Offa's Dyke seemed to end near Mold; tantalisingly close to an anomaly in Wat's Dyke. An anomaly that might be explained if Offa's Dyke had linked with it for the final reach for the coast. Alas, the nature and construction of Wat's Dyke seemed to place it in a different period, and the missing link could not be found.

The team examined the other great mystery in the line of the Dyke; the missing section from Kington to Monmouth. Again, isolated stretches of Dyke were examined and found to be just that.

The Dyke South of Chirk (looking East) Photograph: Dr D H Hill
(Manchester University)
"aerial photographs that suggested the possibility of buried traces of dyke sent pulses racing" The team made extensive use of aerial photography in its survey of the Dyke.

Aerial photographs that suggested the possibility of buried traces of dyke sent pulses racing but, whilst eager examination on the ground validated the technique, it proved to be something else. Despite many attempts to locate more Dyke, the team has returned empty-handed from each sortie.

The team have recently turned their attention to the stretch of Dyke between Sedbury and Monmouth. With the benefit of what has become an expert eye, the team have gained the uneasy feeling that, whilst it is obviously a dyke, its construction does not match the form of Offa's Dyke further north!

After years of searching, and of hoping to finally establish the line of Offa's great dyke running from sea to sea, the Manchester team have reluctantly concluded that the reason they cannot find the missing sections of Dyke are because they do not exist! Although it might be unpalatable to some, the most likely explanation is that Offa built his Dyke to meet a specific threat from a very aggressive Kingdom of Powys. So his Dyke formed a defensive barrier along just the border with that kingdom. Even if the Dyke south of Monmouth was built by Offa, that was along the border between Mercia and Gwent, another Welsh kingdom that was territorially aggressive.

Supporting this conclusion is the fact that, whilst the Saxon kingdoms could unite to fight a common cause, there is no evidence of such co-operation amongst the diverse and independent kingdoms of the Britons. Therefore, there may have been no need for a dyke along the entire border.

The Future of the Dyke

Dr Hill's team continues its research as limited time and resources permit. Nevertheless, it does seem incongruous that Hadrian's Wall, built in a well-documented period of history, should have attracted so much archeological interest and resources, whilst Offa's Dyke has by comparison been virtually ignored.

The danger is that by the time the Dyke is given the recognition it deserves, it may not be there! One only has to walk the Path to see that it is under attack. Eroded by the elements, undermined by animals and slowly subsiding (due in part to too close ploughing), the Dyke diminishes with each year. Whilst it has to be conceded that walkers are also playing their part in its erosion, they are the very people who foster interest in the Dyke today and I do not believe, as some do, that the answer is to ban them from the Dyke. Far from it, for that would almost certainly consign the Dyke to the ignoble fate from which it was saved by Frank Noble and the Offa's Dyke Association. I would rather see it given the same recognition and funding as Hadrian's Wall. That is an ancient monument that is to become the focus of a National Trail. Offa's Dyke is already the focus of a National Trail but it needs to be properly recognised as a significant ancient monument.

Castell Dinas Bran and the Eglwyseg crags - Photograph by the Author
Nearby is the Pillar of Eliseg, named after the 8th century king of Powys it commemorates.

The National Trail

It is a sobering thought that the first people to complete an "Offa's Dyke Path" were almost certainly the military surveyors who supervised the building of the Dyke. However, it wasn't for another 12 centuries and the early 1960's, that recreational walkers fought their way along it through dense undergrowth. Their efforts and determination to create a long distance path, were finally recognised when the Offa's Dyke Path (the 4th National Trail) was officially opened by Lord Hunt (of Everest fame) on 10 July 1971.

There is a thriving Offa's Dyke Association whose members promote interest in the Dyke and who help must prove invaluable to the two full-time National Trail officers based in Knighton.

The Path joining the Shropshire Union Canal at Four Crosses
Photograph by the Author

Section Two
Walking
the
Offa's Dyke Path

Expedition Planning

This section is designed to help you plan your expedition to walk the Offa's Dyke Path. The 1:200,000 maps are there to help you decide how far to walk each day and to identify the approximate location of both accommodation and campsites along the route (use the location maps to obtain a more precise location). Before you use them, you might like some general advice on walking the Path. Lastly, the entry on transport is there to help you decide how you are going to get to and from the Path.

Which Direction?

80% walk the Dyke from South to North whilst a good proportion of the 20% that walk North to South have already walked the Path the other way. There are several reasons for this; the glorious views are best seen with the sun behind you, there are more steep climbs North to South than the other way round and the Southern half of the Path is useful preparation for the more arduous Northern half.

When to walk the Path ?

Although the general consensus is that April to June are the best months in which to walk the Offa's Dyke Path, it's a good walk at any time.

You'll have to balance the firmer going underfoot in summer (but thicker vegetation obscuring views), with the wetter, heavier, going of winter. Bear in mind that the shorter days of winter and the likelihood of poorer weather, call for more care in tackling the remoter stretches of the Path.

Planning the Walk

I do not suggest stages for a walk because a late train or bad weather can quickly put the walker out of phase with the guidebook. Furthermore, some will want to build in short days to permit visits to points of interest whilst others will press on. However there are some sections of the Offa's Dyke Path that merit special mention.

Might I suggest that you do not plan your expedition by counting kilometres (or miles) from Chepstow. Start by looking at the Hatterall Ridge and deciding how you are going to tackle it. Whilst it is potentially one of the highlights of the walk, Pandy to Hay-on-Wye is a long day; a very long day if the ground is soft (the top of the Hatterall ridge is very peaty in places!). You can split it by dropping down to Longtown or Llanthony but then you have to climb back up onto the ridge the next day. Once you have decided, work back to Chepstow and don't forget the 3km walk from the Railway Station to the start!

At a mere 30km (18 miles), Monmouth may seem a natural target for your first day; but unless you opt for the alternative route by the river between Brockweir and Bigsweir, I suggest it's too long for a first day. In which case think carefully, if you are going to build in a short day to position yourself for the Hatterall Ridge, you may as well spend the time somewhere interesting.

The section from Knighton to Brompton has been nicknamed "The Switchback" because of the number of short sharp descents and ascents. It's not a problem if you are fit and the weather is fine, but if you are starting again at Knighton after a break, or if your fitness is in doubt, I recommend you overnight at Newcastle-upon-Clun. This is one of the best sections of the Path, with views of the Dyke that give a quite different perspective from earlier sections; don't rush it.

Llandegla to Bodfari is another long section of up's and down's; not quite in the switchback league, but not a day to underestimate.

Last but not least, consider Prestatyn. It is a seaside resort but that does not mean that it is full of B&B's and Guesthouses; especially in the holiday season, accommodation may not be that easy to find.

Maps & Waymarks

The 1:50,000 Ordnance Survey Landranger Maps are No's 162, **161**, 148, 137, 117 & **116**. Most experienced walkers wouldn't dream of venturing up onto the higher sections without the OS maps highlighted in bold. Of course the best map in the world is going to be of limited use without a compass and the knowledge of how to use both.

The Path is well waymarked with the National Trail "acorn" and by finger posts with the acorn accompanied by "Offa's Dyke Path". Many of the stiles bear a waymark with an arrow indicating the direction. Signs may also be written as "Llwybr Clawdd Offa".

Although I indicate the approximate position of waymarks (except where their position is important on the remote stretches of the Path, in which case I am more precise), there will be those that I have missed and those that are missing. On any route you will find waymarks that have been vandalised, stolen or "redirected" (one on Llanymynech golf course being an example). My advice has to be that waymarks are prone to mischief; get a picture of the route in your mind before you set off in the morning and do not rely on waymarks for routefinding, but use them for reassurance.

Safety

It would be easy just to insert a standard warning about undertaking a National Trail and being fit, well-prepared and equipped. I sometimes think the only purpose such cautionary notices serve is to protect the author not the walker. The sudden blizzards and deep snow that arrived just as this guide was going to press have served as a timely reminder that the British weather and hills are not to be underestimated.

It is beyond the scope of this guide to give advice to novices, and experienced walkers will already know their limitations. What I can attempt is to give you idea of what the Path entails.

Climbing to over 700m (2300ft), the Hatterall ridge to Hay Bluff stretch of the Path is very exposed and has few distinctive features.

Whilst the remainder of the route seldom goes above 450m (1500ft), before you get to Knighton you need to be fit enough to tackle several sharp ascents and descents of about 120m (400ft) in a day.

Even on the flatter sections, you will need footwear with a good patterned sole and that supports the ankle. Some of the descents on the Path can be treacherous in the wet and some of the footpaths are very uneven.

As a guidebook author who is usually engaged in mapping a route, practised in the use of a map & compass, and with a GPS Navigator strapped to my rucksack, I feel badly placed to try and guess where someone else might get lost! One section where I feel there is that danger is along the Hatterall ridge to Hay Bluff. Coincidentally, that is a section where you could wander over a cliff!

Those walkers who are nervous of dogs will no doubt be pleased to learn that the dogs along the Path have largely got used to walkers. My advice is to walk firmly on your way and ignore them (but not those with a low snarl, bared teeth and tail down). Never run and do not shout. Keep an eye on them but avoid "staring them out" which can be construed as a threat gesture. Instead of a stick, I carry a "Dazzer", a small "black box" which emits an ultrasonic noise that dogs dislike and avoid (0171-228-2360 for details).

Transport

There is an excellent leaflet summarising public transport for the whole of Wales and the Borders, available from Tourist Information Offices. In addition, the following local authorities produce local bus and rail information, otherwise local Tourist Information Offices (see Section 5) and local PO/shops are a good source of information:

Gloucestershire - 01452 425609

Gwent - 01633 832478

Hereford & Worcester - 0345 125436

Powys - 01597 826642

Shropshire - 0345 056785

Clwyd - 01352 704035

Car. Public transport to and from the Path is likely to be more efficient and cost effective than leaving a car at one end of the route. If you travel to the Path by car, you will have to decide where to park. My advice is that you should not leave your car for more than a day in any place accessible to the public. Instead, use one of the B&B's that offer long term parking.

Rail. Rail services to/from the Path are as follows:

Chepstow: Is on the Cardiff/Newport - Gloucester (Severnside) line with 2-hourly services 6 days a week (Sundays - pm service). Newport (15 minutes away) is on the South Wales Main Line with hourly services to London. Gloucester is on the main line from Bristol - Birmingham but you may have to use local trains to link with the main services. Information - Severnside & South Wales Main Line Tel 01222 228000.

Knighton: Is on the Swansea - Shrewsbury (Heart of Wales) line with 4 journeys a day and a limited Sunday service in summer. Information - Tel. 01792 467777.

Welshpool: Is on the Aberystwyth - Shrewsbury (Cambrian Main) line with 2-hourly services 6 days a week and a limited Sunday service (pm's). Information Tel. 01743 364041.

Chirk/Ruabon: Is on the Shrewsbury - Chester line. Commuter service only. Information Tel. 01743 364041.

Prestatyn: Is on the Chester - Bangor (North Wales Coast) line with hourly services (Sundays pm, plus am service in summer). Information 01492 585151.

Use services via Crewe or Birmingham to get from one end of the Path to the other.

<u>Coach.</u> Contact National Express Tel. 0990 808080. Services are as follows:

<u>Chepstow</u>: Is on London - Cardiff route (5 services Mon-Sat, 4 services Sun). There is a regular service to Heathrow and Gatwick airports.

<u>Prestatyn</u>: Is on services to Manchester and Birmingham/London (2 services a day, extra services in summer)

Limited coach services also serve Monmouth, Kington/ Presteigne, Welshpool, Oswestry, Chirk and Llangollen.

<u>Buses.</u> See location maps for an indication of the bus service in a particular town/village. Since deregulation, bus timetables have become something of a nightmare and it is essential you check the latest timetable; especially as many country services are part-funded by the local authority. The reason I give an indication of the level of service to a particular place is because whilst companies come and go and timetables change, services tend to be influenced by stable factors such as local market days, location of secondary schools, commuter traffic, tourism etc. The underlying level of service does not change, so use the information accordingly but don't put yourself in the position of relying on a service unless you have checked. When you enquire about buses make sure you ask the following questions:

- Whether the service is a "stops only" or "hail and ride"
- Which operator is providing the service and where it is going to/from
- Which bus-stop it uses

If a local authority helpline is closed, try major operators:

Stagecoach Red & White (01633 266336) - up to Hay area

Sargeants Bros (01544 230481) - Kington area

Midland Red West (01905 763888) - Knighton area

Minsterley Motors (01743 791208) - Bishop's Castle area

Cambrian Midland Red (01691 652402) - Welshpool/ Oswestry area

Tanat Valley Coaches (01691 780212) - North of Severn area

Crosville Cymru (01970 617951) - Llangollen/Ruabon area & Ruthin/Prestatyn area

Taxis. Although we have provided the telephone numbers of taxi firms operating in the area, it is important to recognise that taxi firms in general are notorious for setting up one day and being out of business the next! Make sure that you agree a fare beforehand, especially if the taxi is coming out into the country to collect you. Alternative sources of information are: the local "Yellow Pages", Tourist Information Offices (telephone numbers are in Section Five) and do not forget "Talking Pages" which operates 24hrs a day (Freephone 0800 600900).

Taxis may be difficult to obtain between 0800-0900 & 1500-1600 due to school contract work. Be prepared to let the number ring as some are now on a through link to a mobile phone. Taxis may be more prepared to collect you from open country if you can give an accommodation address to which you wish to be taken.

Taxis are listed under the following towns: Chepstow, Monmouth, Abergavenny (page 73), Hay-on-Wye, Kington, Knighton, Welshpool, Oswestry, Llangollen, Ruthin, Denbigh, Prestatyn. Refer to the Location Maps.

Expedition Planning Maps

Most walkers will do an average of 20, 25 or 30 kilometres a day, which as near as makes no significant difference, equates to between 12, 15 or 18 miles. The distance markers have therefore been set at 10km intervals. Note that where a B&B offers backpackers somewhere to camp (see Section 4), a square and a circle have been located on the map.

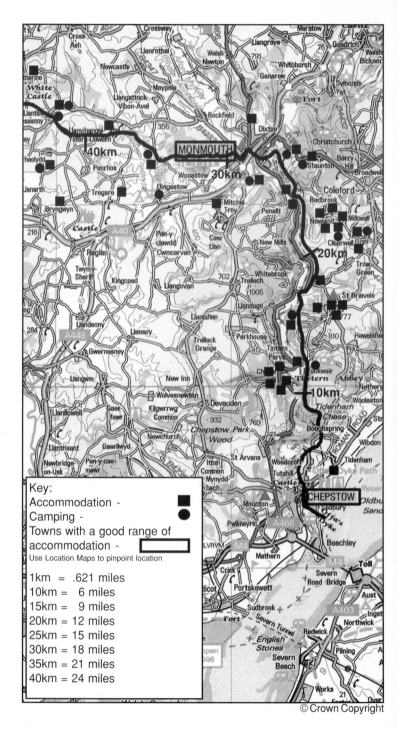

Key:
Accommodation - ■
Camping - ●
Towns with a good range of accommodation - ▭
Use Location Maps to pinpoint location

1km = .621 miles
10km =   6 miles
15km =   9 miles
20km = 12 miles
25km = 15 miles
30km = 18 miles
35km = 21 miles
40km = 24 miles

© Crown Copyright

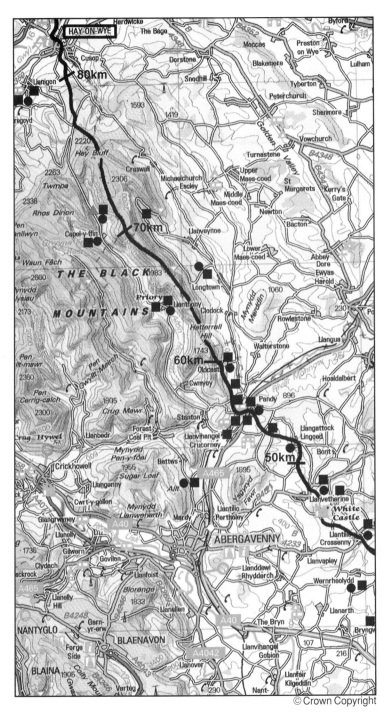

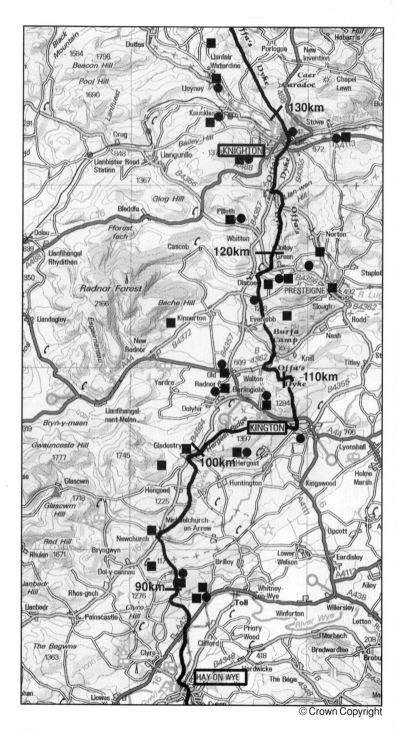

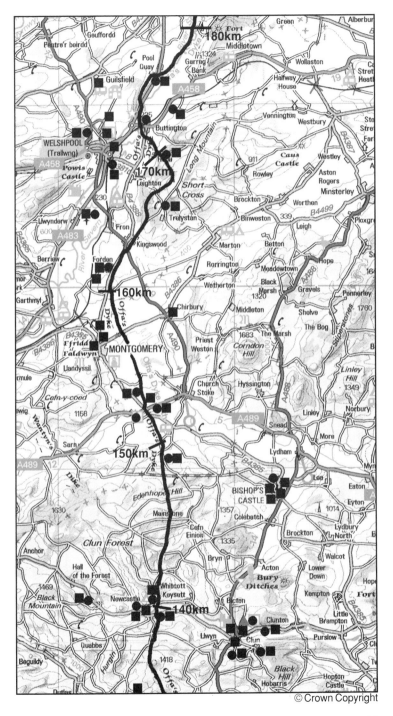

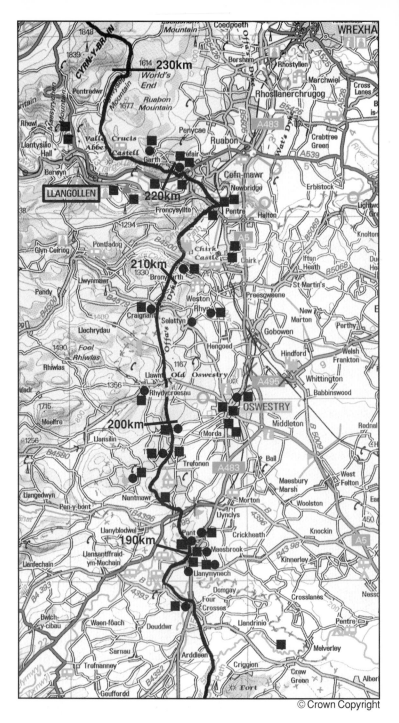

© Crown Copyright

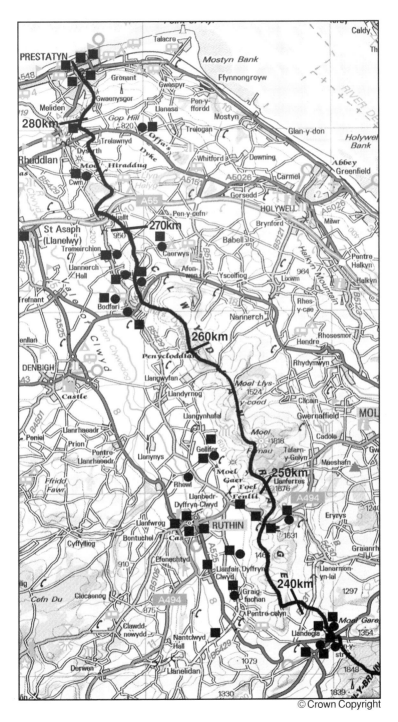

© Crown Copyright

43

Looking North - the approach to Chirk Castle
Photograph by the Author

Section Three
The
Offa's Dyke Path

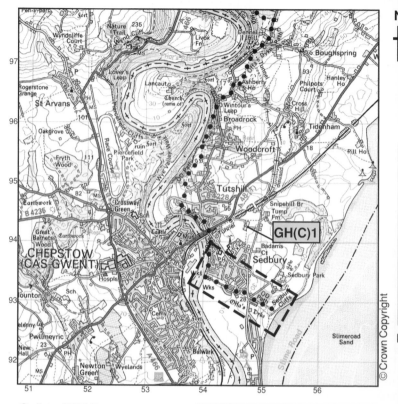

Sedbury (01291)
<u>GH(C)1</u> - <u>Upper Sedbury Hse</u>.
Tel. 627173 WTB 2 Crown
Jan-Dec Band 1/2 (2D,1T,1F)(1PB)EM
Dogs. Pk'dL. Veg. Trans. LTPkg. Bags.

Chepstow
Accommodation - see pages 48/49
Facilities - see pages 50/51

Chepstow

Founded by Normans, name derives from Old English "Chepe" and "stow" meaning marketplace. Settlements have existed here since Iron Age and the Romans built a bridge across the Wye. A busy port and shipbuilding centre in the 18th/early 19thC's.

<u>*Chepstow Castle*</u>*. Begun in 1067, with major improvements in 12th & 13thC's. First stone castle in Wales. A Portwall was added in the 13thC to encompass the town. During Civil War it was held by Royalists who surrendered it in 1645. In second civil war it again fell to Parliamentarians. After restoration it was used as a prison and Henry Marten (a signatory to Charles I's Death Warrant) was held here for 20 years until his death in 1680. Castle ceased use as a fortification in 1690.*

<u>*Church of St. Mary*</u>*. Founded 1071 as a Priory by Marcher Lord William Fitzosbern who brought over Benedictine monks from the Abbey in Cormeilles. Priory dissolved in 1536 and much stone removed.*

......continued

Sedbury Cliffs - Chepstow

See below for directions from Chepstow to Buttington Tump

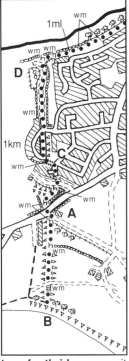

"A" - **Minor Road at Buttington Tump**. **Take the track** emerging **from NE** but after **only 10m, turn right to a stile**. Through trees to pick up hedge on your right hiding a ditch (Offa's Dyke). **Continue** with the Dyke on your right to a stile and then follow on the bank of the Dyke to the marker-stone at the start of the Path.

Unfortunately it is not easy to get a good view of the Severn Estuary from the end of the Path. However, if you look at the mud-flats between Sedbury Cliffs and the Severn Bridge, you'll see a wooden frame extending across the mud into the river. Prior to a high tide, baskets were hung on the frame to trap salmon making their way up river. The traps would then be emptied at the following low tide.

"B" - **Offa's Dyke Marker-stone**. Retrace your way back to the Minor road at Buttington Tump ("tump" meaning stone).

"A" - **Minor Road at Buttington Tump**. **Cross the road to a stile** by a gate. **Bear right** across a field and over an old railway embankment. **Over a stile** in a crossing fence and bear left to a footbridge opposite. Emerging into a cul-de-sac, continue until the first road off right.

"C" - **"Norse Way"**. Opposite Norse Way, **turn left** to take a path behind housing, between two fences. At the end of the fence on your right, **Turn right along "Mercian Way"** noting the bank on your right (Offa's Dyke again). Continue along "Offa's Close", which becomes a tarmac road between hedges, to pass a sewage works.

"D" - **Sewage Works**. Pass the works on your left, but as the road bends left, **continue to a crossing hedge and a stile to your right**. Bearing right to take a path behind housing, along a green and once more behind houses. Continue as the path swings right and emerges onto Wyebank Avenue.

Chepstow to Buttington Tump.

The most direct route from the railway station to the start of the Path, is to cross under the bypass and turn right alongside the A48. A flight of steps will take you up onto the Sedbury road where you turn right and follow the road.

Chepstow cont'd....

Norman Tower partially collapsed in 1656 and then completely collapsed in a storm in 1703. A carpet just inside door now covers the stone that bears Henry Marten's epitaph (information behind door).

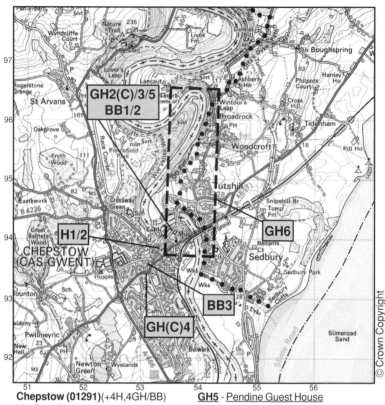

Chepstow (01291)(+4H,4GH/BB)

H1 -Beaufort Hotel
Tel.622497 TB 3 Crown Comm
Jan-Dec Band 3 (5S,6D,6T,2F)EM
Switch. Visa. MCard. Amex. Diners.
Dogs. Lic'd. PkdL. Veg. Trans.

H2 - King's Head Hotel
Tel. 623379 WTB App
Jan-Dec Band 2 (3T,1F)(2PB)
Dogs. Lic'd. PkdL. Veg. Trans.

GH(C)2 - Ashburne House
Tel. 625747
Jan-Dec Band 3 (2S,3D,3T,5F)
Dogs. PkdL. Trans. LTPkg.

GH3 - Castle Guest House
Tel. 622040
Jan-Dec Band 2 (1S,1D,1T/1F)(4PB)
Dogs. Veg.

GH(C)4 - Lower Hardwick Hse
Tel. 622162
Jan-Dec Band 1/2 (2S, 2D, 2F)(2PB)
Dogs. PkdL. Veg. Trans. LTPkg. Bags.

GH5 - Pendine Guest House
Tel. 623308 TB 2 Crown
Jan-Dec Band 1 (3S,2D,2T,2F)(4PB)
EM. Dogs. Non-Smkg. PkdL. Veg.
Trans. LTPkg. Bags.

GH6 - Hazelhurst Guest House
Tel.622266 TB Listed
Jan-Dec Band 3 (1S,1D, 1T,2F)
EM. Dogs. PkdL. Veg. Trans. Bags.

BB1 - Curfew House
Tel. 628532 WTB 2Crown HComm
Jan-Dec Band1 (1S,2D)(1PB)
Non-Smkg. Veg. Trans. Bags.

BB2 - Afon Gwy
Tel. 620158 WTB 3 Crown
Jan-Dec Band2(Band4-single)
(3D,1T/F)(4PB)
Visa. MCard.
Dogs. Licd. PkdL. Veg.

BB3 - Cobweb Cottage
Tel. 626643 WTB 1 Crown
Jan-Dec Band1/2 (1D/F,1T)(1PB)
Dogs. Non-smkg. Veg. Trans. Bags.

Chepstow - "Wintours Leap"

"E" - <u>**Wyebank Avenue (wm)**</u>. **Turn left** and follow the avenue as it bends right to the Sedbury road. Turn left, **cross above the railway/A48**. After 175m, note a high stone wall to your right.

"F" - <u>**High Stone Wall**</u>. **Opposite** the wall, **bear left down a tarmac drive** (note footpath sign). Ignore the footpath, continue past Woodbridge House on your <u>right</u> and **descend steps**. **Ascend a narrow footpath** to a road. **Turn left**, descend between high walls to a junction with a crossing road (choice of ramp or steps for the last few metres).

"G" - <u>**T-junction**</u>. **Turn right** and ascend to the **Old A48. Cross** and take the "terminated" road opposite. **As the road bends right, turn left to a stile** and continue up the field edge, initially with a fence on your right, to pass the 16thC Tutshill Tower (a beacon?).

"H" - <u>**Tutshill Tower**</u>. **Continue** as you are funnelled towards the corner of a crossing wall. **Bear right across a stile** and continue along the field edge with the wall on your left, until a short crossing wall.

"I" - <u>**Short Crossing Wall**</u>. **Turn left,** over a stile and take a path between walls to emerge onto a drive. Turn **right along the drive for 25m and turn left over a stile** to cross a field to another stile.

"J" - <u>**Stile with overhead footbridge beyond**</u>. **Turn right.** Passing under another overhead footbridge, emerge through a gate onto the **B4228** where you **turn left** until a stone arch on your sharp left.

"K" - <u>**"Moyle Old School Lane" Archway**</u>. **Turn sharp left** under the arch (note reverse) to take a path through 2 kissing gates to the "Old School".

"L" - <u>**Moyle Old School**</u>. Pass on your left, to a T-junction where you **turn left and then right** in front of the old quarry gates. Follow the path to emerge at the B4228 and Wintours Leap.

The cliffs are sheer, the fence inadequate. A safer viewpoint is on the left just after you join the B4228.

"M" - <u>**Wintours Leap**</u>. **Turn left** along the B4228.

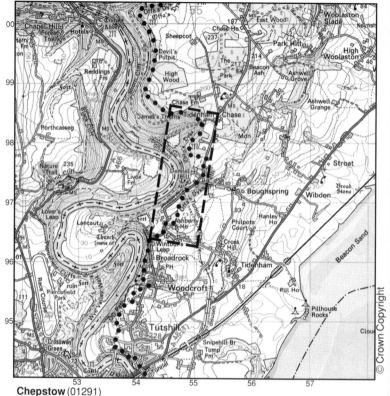

Chepstow (01291)

<u>Banks</u>. Nat West (ATM), Midland (ATM), TSB (ATM), Barclays (ATM), Lloyds (ATM).

<u>Taxis</u>. M&R 624482. A-B 625696.

<u>Buses</u>. M-Sa - Limited to Bristol, Frequent to Newport (Su - Regular), Regular to Gloucester, Regular to Monmouth.

Tintern Abbey. Founded 1131 by Walter fitz Richard de Clare for Cistercian monks from the Norman abbey of L'Aumone. The monks were known as the "white monks" from the colour of their habits. At its foundation there were probably some 20 monks and 50 "lay brothers", the latter serving under less severe rules and assisting the "choir" monks with the manual labour. The lifestyle or "Rule" of the monks was founded on austerity and hard manual work. Visitations from the mother abbey in Normandy ensured adherence to the Rule and one Abbot may have been deposed in 1188 for taking the "tithes" from churches. The Abbey Church was rebuilt in the latter half of the 13thC with the help of an important patron, Roger Bigod III, the Earl of Norfolk.

The hard work of the monks, and gifts lavished on the Abbey by noblemen anxious to save their souls, meant that by the time of the dissolution of monasteries in 1536 (under Henry VIII), the Abbey was the richest in Wales. At its dissolution there were 14 monks plus the Abbot.

Wintours Leap - James's Thorns

Some of the dangers on this bit of the B4228 are not immediately obvious. The steep bank one side with a wall on the other, between two bends, on a well-used road, is bad enough: in summer, the dense canopy of trees creates a blind alley for drivers. This is not the time to wear drab clothes.

Continue along the B4228 until a bus shelter between two driveways on the right.

"N" - Bus Shelter. Pass the shelter and the second driveway. **20m on, turn right to a stone stile** and continue along the field edge to a stile into a wood. Continue to the far edge of the wood where the **Path turns left.** Now walk just inside the E edge, to a stile and continue along a field edge (hedge on your right). Continue across 3 more stiles before joining the B4228 once again.

Don't forget to look back over the Severn Bridge before you get to the B4228.

"O" - B4228. **Turn right** along the B4228. Once past the houses of Dennel Hill, look for a stile on your left.

"P" - Stile on left. Take a path between two fences until you come to an English Heritage sign and the bank of Offa's Dyke.

"Q" - English Heritage Sign. **Turn right along the Dyke** with a steep bank off left. **Descend a series of "steps"**, cross a path, and descend more steps to a rough track.

"R" - Quarry track. **Straight across**, up a few steps, and continue on a meandering path through the wood. After a 100m or so, pick up a wall on your left and keep company with it until emerging at a **Forestry road. Cross** the road and rejoin the **Wall on your left**. The wall soon **does a right turn** in front of you and you **cross it, turning right, to put the wall on your right**. The Path bears left, with open fields over to your right, and emerges onto a green track.

"S" - Green track. **Turn right** along the green track for only a few metres before you **Turn left to mount the bank of Offa's Dyke** once more. Continue along the Dyke to the "Tintern via Old Railway - Path"

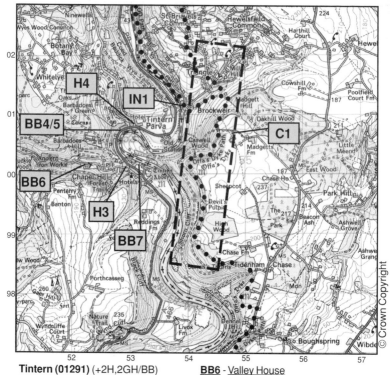

52   53   54   55   56   57

Tintern (01291) (+2H,2GH/BB)
PH's (food). PO & shops.
Buses. See Chepstow
H3 - The Royal George Hotel
Tel. 689205 WTB 4 Crown HComm
Jan-Dec Band 5
(2S,16D,14T,7F)(17PB)
All cards. EM. Dogs. Lic'd. PkdL. Veg.
Trans. LTPkg. Bags.
H4 - Parva Farmhouse Hotel
Tel. 689411 WTB 4 Crown HComm
Jan-Dec Band 4 (5 Single) (4D/
T,3D,2F)(9PB)
Visa. MCard. Amex.
EM. Dogs. Lic'd. PkdL. Veg. Trans.
LTPkg. Bags.
BB4 - Holmleigh
Tel. 689521
Jan-Dec Band 1 (1S,1D,1T)
Dogs. PkdL.
BB5 - The Old Rectory
Tel. 689519 WTB 1 Crown
Jan-Dec Band 1 (1S,2D,2T)
EM. Dogs. PkdL. Veg. Trans. LTPkg.
Bags.

BB6 - Valley House
Tel. 689652 WTB 2 Crown
Jan-Dec Band 2/3 (2D1T)(3PB)
Amex
Dogs. No-smkg. PkdL. Veg. LTPkg.
BB7 - Wye Barn
Tel. 689456 WTB Listed
Jan-Dec(excl Xmas) Band 2
(1S,2T)(1PB)
EM. No-smkg. PkdL. Veg.
Brockweir (01291) (+1BB)
Telephone. Telephone & Shop at
Triangle (500m off Path) 0800-1700hrs
(closed 1230-1400hrs) ec W.Sa.Su (Su
opens 0900)
IN1 - Brockweir Country Inn
Tel. 689548 LG Rec.
Jan-Dec Band 2 (1S,2D)
EM. Lic'd. PkdL. Veg.
C1 - Beeches Farm
Tel. 689257 LG Rec.
Jan-Dec £1.50pp pn.Toilets. Dogs.
*(Limited facilities & an uphill walk from
the pub but on the path, usually fly-free,
lots of space and the view is superb.)*

52

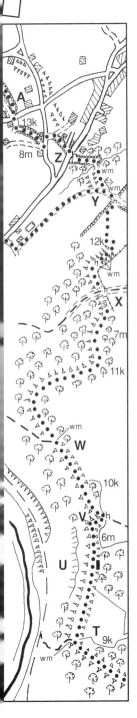

James's Thorns - Triangle (Brockweir)

"T" - <u>Tintern via Old Railway Path</u>. The Tintern path goes steeply down to your left, but you **turn right** along the bank and ascend. The Path levels at a memorial seat.

"U" - <u>Memorial Seat</u>. Passing the seat, the Path soon arrives at the aptly-named "Devil's Pulpit".

The classic photo opportunity!

"V" - <u>Devil's Pulpit</u>. Turn right with the Path. Just **Before a stile and gateway, turn sharp left down the bank**. Having lost little height, the Path resumes its journey with now a bank on your right. A marked footpath bears off left.

"W" - <u>Tintern Footpath</u>. Continue to contour along the edge of the valley until descending a series of worn "steps". Pass a chicane to cross a track.

"X" - <u>Track to Beeches/Madgetts Farms</u>. Cross the track and continue, now with a fence to your right and open fields. The fence and Path turn right. **Cross a stile** by an English Heritage Notice. Keep on the bank for **200m before bearing left** to cross the field **in a steep descent** to the bottom hedge. **Turn left** over a stile in the corner **and join a track** which passes a ruined barn on your right.

See next page for Alternative Route.

"Y" - <u>Division of Path</u>. Stay on the track to descend to Brockweir (turning right after the HAPPS stables). **OR Bear right to descend the field** and cross a stile and footbridge. Turn **left up a track and turn right over a stile** onto a minor public road with the "MacKenzie Hall" on your right.

"Z" - <u>Minor Road</u>. Turn right and take the first left turn up a driveway to pass "Sunray" on your right. The drive turns right but you continue along a green lane. Bear left as the lane joins a drive for 30m before emerging at another minor road. **Turn left along the road for 20m and turn sharp right to take a hedged track** between the road to Rock Farm and a bungalow "Alexander House). The track joins the drive of "Llynwood" as you bear right to a minor public road.

"A" - <u>Minor Road at "Llynwood"</u>. Cross the road and **take the twitchel ahead**.

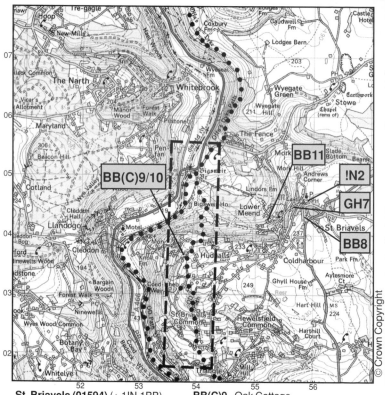

St. Briavels (01594) (+ 1IN,1BB)
Telephone. 2 x PH's (food). PO &
Shop.

Buses. M-F - V.Limited to Monmouth,
V.Limited to Chepstow (schooldays
only). TuTh - Shopper to Chepstow.
W - Shopper to Monmouth.

IN2 - The George Inn
Tel. 530228 Good Pub Guide
Jan-Dec Band 2/3 (2D,1T)(3PB)
EM. Lic'd. Veg. Pk'dL. LTPk'g.

GH7 - Cinderhill House
Tel. 530393 TB Listed Comm
Jan - Dec Band 3/4 (2D,1T,1F)(4PB)
EM. Dogs. Non-Smk'g. Lic'd. Pk'dL.
Veg. Trans. Bags.

BB8 - Ivydene Cottage
Tel. 530699
Jan -Dec Band1 (1D,1F)(1PB)
Non Smk'g. Pk'dL. Trans. Bags.

BB(C)9 - Oak Cottage
Tel. 530440
Feb-Nov Band 1 (1S,1T)
EM. Non-Smk'g. Pk'dL. Veg. LTPk'g.

BB10(C) - Tyersall
Tel. 530215
Mar-Nov Band 1 (1S,1D,1T)(1PB)
EM. Non-Smk'g. Pk'dL. Veg. Trans.
LTPk'g. Bags.

BB11 - Woodcroft
Tel. 530083
Jan-Dec Band 1 (2F)(2PB)
Dogs. Non-Smk'g. Pk'dL. Veg. Trans.
LTPk'g. Bags.

YHA - St. Briavels Castle
1995 - Feb10-Mar4 & Apr7-Oct28
(7days), Mar10-Apr4(exc WTh), Nov6-
Nov30 (exc FSaSu). Tel.530849
See YHA handbook for further details.
Page 60 for info on St. Briavels.

Alternative Route to Bigsweir Bridge.

*Bear right immediately before Brockweir Bridge to go down to the
riverbank and keep the river on your left all the way to Bigsweir Bridge.*

Triangle (Brockweir) - Bigsweir Br.

Emerging from the twitchel at a **minor road, turn left** and **then right at a T-junction**. You pass a postbox set into a wall outside "Fernleigh".

"B" - **"Fernleigh"**. **Pass** the postbox **and bear right up a track**. Pass a converted chapel on your left and **Bear left up a twitchel**. Bear left at a Y-junction of paths, up to a **Minor road; turn left** to pass a redundant stone stile with a Gloucestershire CC sign about dogs being kept on leads.

STICK TO THE PATH ON NEXT SECTION!

"C" - **Redundant stone stile**. **Continue** along the road to a **Wooden gateway**. Before it, **bear right** up to a stile in a fence, bear right **across a paddock**, to a stable where you turn left. Now descend to the corner of the paddock to go **Over 2 stiles** in a crossing wall. Continue past a barn on your right and **bear right to** cross a field to **a stile. Turn right** along the road to a "crossroads" formed by a farm track off left and the road bending right.

"D" - **"Crossroads"**. Take the very **minor road ahead** which becomes a stony path. **Join a drive** and bending right **to** a **T-junction and turn left.** Follow the road as it swings right to pass a large house on the right.

"E" - **House with balcony**. **Before the house, turn left down a twitchel**. A wall on your left ends at a crossing path, with a steep drop in front of you.

"F" - **Crossing Path**. **Turn right for a few metres before turning sharp left**. The path (indistinct at times) wends its way down through the wood and is joined by another path from the left just before a stile at the edge of the wood.

"G" - **Stile at edge of Wood**. Cross the field **bearing slightly left**, **to a stile** by a gateway opposite. **Bear left** through bracken. Now **descend** the field aiming for the Bigsweir Bridge. **Join a drive** and **bear right** to the main road (A466).

"H" - **A466**. **Turn right** along the A466 and **then bear right** up a minor road.

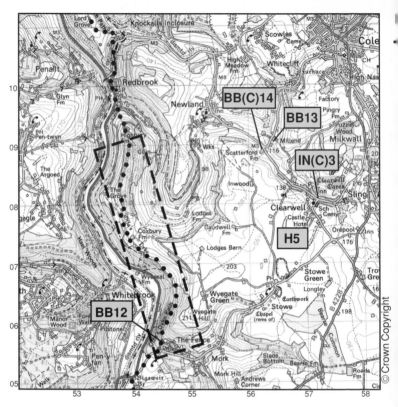

The Fence (01594) (+0)
BB12 - Offa's Mead
Tel.530229 TB 1 Crown
Mar-Nov Band 1 ((1D,2T)(2PB)
Non-Smk'g. Pk'dL. Veg. LTPk'g. Bags.

Clearwell (01594) (+1IN,1BB)
Telephone. PO & Stores (M-Sa am only)
H5 - Tudor Farmhouse Hotel
Tel. 833046 TB 3 Crown
Jan-Dec Band 3/5 (6D,2T,2F)(10PB)
EM. Visa. M'Card. Amex. Switch.
Dogs. Lic'd. Pk'dL. Veg. LTPk'g.
IN(C)3 - Butcher's Arms
Tel. 834313
Jan-Dec Band 2 (3D,1F) (4PB)
Visa. M'Card. Switch. EM. Lic'd. Pk'dL.
Veg. Trans. LTPk'g. Bags.

Newland (01594) See next LMap for more...

BB13 - Millend House
Tel. 832128 RAC 4Q TB 2 Crown
Jan-Dec (exc Xmas)
Band 2 (1D,1T,1T/D)(3PB)
Non-Smk'g. Pk'dL. Trans. LTPk'g.
Bags.
Beautifully restored 200 year old country house with modern facilities; set in a lovely hillside garden at the end of a valley, with views of Newland.

BB(C)14 - Scatterford Farm
Tel. 836562 TB 2 Crown Comm
Jan-Dec Band 2 (2D,1T)(3PB)
Non-Smk'g. Pk'dL. Veg. Trans. LTPk'g.
Bags.
Quiet 15th century farmhouse, set in large garden. Spacious oak-beamed rooms with lovely views. Within walking distance of excellent food and pubs.

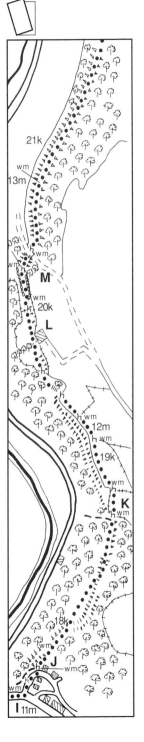

Bigsweir Br. - Highbury Fm

Follow the road up from the A466 to pass Slip Wood on your left.

"I" - **Slip Wood**. At the SE corner of the wood, **turn left up a minor road** (1st off left). Pass a stile and gateway on your left and continue to a second stile and gateway.

"J" - **Second Stile & Gateway**. **Immediately after stile bear right** along a well-defined path up through the wood. The Path climbs before levelling off and eventually descending to a stile at the edge of the wood.

"K" - **Edge of Wood**. Cross the stile and continue with the edge of the wood on your left through 3 more stiles, until a fifth stile in a corner of the wood. Re-enter the wood, descending steps and emerging once more at a stile. Continue, now with the low bank of the Dyke and a fence on your right, to Coxbury Farm.

"L" - **Coxbury Farm**. Continue, past the farm buildings on your right. Straight over a stile in a **Crossing fence ahead** and in **approx 100m, jink right and left to continue in a twitchel.** At a **Stile in the fence on your right, turn right** to cross the stile and **bear left up a twitchel**. Through a metal gate to Coxbury and Wyegate Lane (a green track).

"M" - **Coxbury and Wyegate Lane**. **Cross** the lane to a **stile opposite**. Pass an English Nature "Highbury Wood" sign and **ascend the bank** of the Dyke where you **turn left to follow the Dyke** through the wood until descending a steep spur to Highbury Farm.

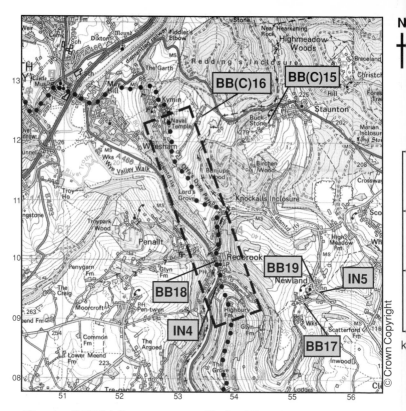

Staunton (01594) (+0)

BB(C)15 - Assisi
Tel. 836900
Jan - Dec Band1 (1S,1T,1D/F)
Dogs. Non-Smk'g. Pk'dL. Veg. Trans.
LTPk'g. Bags.

BB(C)16 - Graygill
Tel. 712536
Jan-Dec Band 1 (1D,1T)(2PB)
Dogs. LTPk'g. Bags.

Redbrook (01600) (+1BB)
Shop. Little Chef. 3 x PH's

IN4 - The FishNGame
Tel. 713612
Jan-Dec Band 2 (1F)(1PB)
Switch. Visa. M'Card. EM. Non-Smk'g.
Lic'd. Pk'dL. Veg. LTPk'g.

BB18 - Tresco
Tel. 712325
Jan-Dec Band 1 (2S,1D,1F)
EM. Dogs. Pk'dL. Veg. LTPk'g. Bags.

Newland (01594) (+2BB)

IN5 - Ostrich Inn
Tel. 833260 TB Listed
Jan-Dec Band 2 (1D,1T)
Switch. Visa. M'Card. Amex.
EM. Lic'd. Veg.

BB(C)17 - Tan House Farm
Tel. 832222 TB Listed
Jan-Dec (exc Xmas/NY)
Band 2 (2D,2T)(4PB)
Non-Smk'g. Trans. LTPk'g. Bags.
Grade II Queen Anne farmhouse.
Tranquil setting beneath the beautiful
village of Newland. Excellent centre for
walks in unspoilt countryside. Good
local Inn for dinners.

More opposite

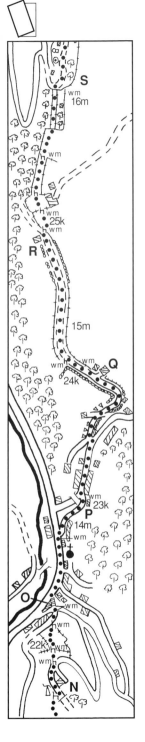

Highbury Farm - The Kymin

After a steep descent you emerge at a Nature Reserve sign and a stile. **Turn left to take the track through Highbury Farm.**

"N" - **Highbury Farm**. Follow the track to pass the farm on your right and as the **track bends right, turn left over a stile** and cross to a second stile in a crossing fence. After the **Second stile, bear left** for a few metres, **then bear right for a steep descent to a stile with steps**, to emerge onto a road at the back of a row of houses. **Turn right** and follow the road down to a T-junction where you cross to **Descend a long flight of steps**. At the foot of the steps, bear left for the A466.

See page 60/61 for information on Redbrook

"O" - **A466**. **Turn right** alongside the A466 and opposite the **Little Chef/petrol station, bear right** up a tarmac track to pass the bed of an old incline plane over the Coleford road.

"P" - **Incline Plane**. Pass the plane on your left. **Bear right along the Coleford road**. Opposite "Woodlands", a road comes in <u>sharp</u> left from "Incline Farm". **Bear off left** to take the <u>other</u> road **up the hill**. Continue as a road crosses and follow the road to Duffields Farm.

"Q" - **Duffields Farm**. As the road bends right to the farm, **bear left along a track** and continue along it to "Cockshoot Barn".

"R" - **Cockshoot Barn**. Just past the converted barn on your left, **turn right to cross a stile in the fence** on your right. **Bear left** away from the stile, cross to a stile in a crossing fence and continue over a further 2 stiles. Continue, to enter the wood through a kissing gate set in the middle of a crossing wall. A path between fences emerges through a kissing gate into the National Trust parking area.

"S" - **National Trust parking area**. **Turn right** and follow a track that bears left to pass the Naval Monument and the Kymin.

See page 60/61 for information on this National Trust Property.

BB19 - <u>Sycamore House</u>
Tel. 834895 TB Listed
Jan-Dec (exc Xmas/NY)
Band 1 (1D,1T) Non-Smk'g. Pk'dL. Trans. LTPk'g.
Bags.

St. Briavels.
Castle. Built 1131 by Milo Fitz Walter, Earl of Hereford. The Norman keep collapsed in the 18thC but the gatehouse (dating from 1275) and other buildings now house a Youth Hostel. St. Briavels was the administrative centre for the Royal Hunting Forest of Dean, the Constable of the Castle being the Warden of the Forest. The Castle has a "hanging room" and an "oubliette", a 30ft deep dungeon, into which unfortunates were cast and then forgotten!
The Castle is open daily 1300-1600hrs, 1 April - 30 September.

Redbrook.
The Wye Valley was an important centre for iron-working in the 17thC. Limestone was readily available and iron-ore was mined locally. The water-power for the furnaces and forges came from holding ponds built at Redbrook and you pass the bed of an incline plane which transported ore from the mines down to the river.

The Kymin.
Built by the "first gentlemen of Monmouth", the ostentatious Round House was opened in 1794 as an observatory from which they could look out over the local countryside and later dine in the room below. A bowling green was added and the Duchess of Beaufort had a carriage road constructed to make it accessible to the ladies. How this latter "improvement" was viewed by the men is not known! A Naval Temple, adorned with the figure of Britannia, was opened in 1801 to commemorate the Battle of the Nile and was visited by Admiral Lord Nelson and Lady Hamilton. The temple lists the naval victories of 16 Admirals from 1759-1801 and has been renovated by the National Trust.

Monmouth.
Birthplace of King Henry V of Agincourt fame and referred to by Shakespeare as "Harry Monmouth". The Castle was built by William fitz Osbern to command the crossing of the rivers Monnow and Wye. The 12thC keep is still standing and a Great Hall was added in the 13thC although this was after the town fell to the rebel Earl of Pembroke who pillaged and burnt the place. The Great Castle House was built in 1673 and in 1875 it became the headquarters of the Royal Monmouthshire Royal Engineers and is still in military hands to this day.
Another famous son of Monmouth is commemorated by a bronze statue outside the Shire Hall. Born 1877, the Hon. Charles Rolls was one of the first to own a motor car in this country. He started making cars and later founded Rolls Royce Ltd. He was an early pioneer of flight and made the first two-way crossing of the Channel without landing. He was an avid balloonist, making over 170 ascents in his own balloon.
The Path takes you through the particularly fine stone gatehouse built in 1270 on the bridge over the Monnow . It is one of only two such gatehouses in Britain.

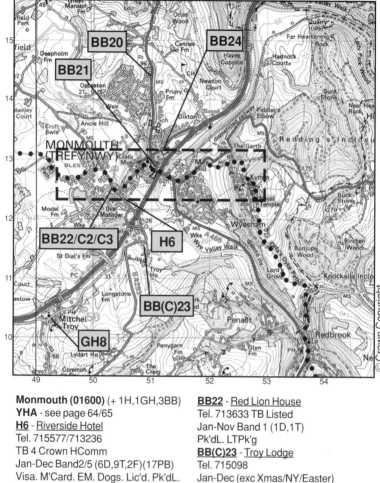

© Crown Copyright

Monmouth (01600) (+ 1H,1GH,3BB)
YHA - see page 64/65
H6 - Riverside Hotel
Tel. 715577/713236
TB 4 Crown HComm
Jan-Dec Band2/5 (6D,9T,2F)(17PB)
Visa. M'Card. EM. Dogs. Lic'd. Pk'dL.
Veg. LTPk'g. Bags.
GH8 - Church Farm Guest House
Tel. 712176 TB 2 Crown Comm
Jan-Dec Band 2 (1S,3D,2T,2F)(6PB)
EM. Dogs. Non-Smk'g. Pk'dL. Veg.
Trans. LTPk'g. Bags.
BB20 - Beacons View
Tel. 713591
Easter-Oct Band 1 (2D,1T)
Dogs. Pk'dL. Trans.
BB21 - Burton House
Tel. 714958 TB Listed
Jan-Dec (exc Xmas) Band 1
(1D,1T,1F)
Visa. M'Card. Dogs. Pk'dL. Veg.

BB22 - Red Lion House
Tel. 713633 TB Listed
Jan-Nov Band 1 (1D,1T)
Pk'dL. LTPk'g
BB(C)23 - Troy Lodge
Tel. 715098
Jan-Dec (exc Xmas/NY/Easter)
Band1/2 (1T,1bunk) (2PB)
Dogs. Non-Smk'g. Trans. LTPk'g.
Bags.
Prior booking essential.
BB24 - Wye Avon
Tel. 713322
Jan-Dec Band 1 (1S,1D,1T/F)
Non-Smk'g. Pk'dL. Veg. LTPk'g. Bags.
C2 - Monmouth Caravan & Camp Park
Tel. 714745 TB 4 ticks
Mar-Oct (15 tent pitches)
Show'r. Dogs. Shop.
C3 - Monnow Bridge Caravan Site
Tel. 714004 Jan-Dec (12 pitches)
Show'r. Dogs. Shop.

The Kymin - Monmouth

Designated Points "T" - "U". Use the routefinding map NOT OS maps!

"T" - **The Kymin**. Pass the Kymin and a garage on your left. **Turn left to descend stone steps** and after the first flight of steps, **do not take the path ahead but turn right to descend more steps**. The path descends to become a sunken path. It **Forks at a fence** where you **turn right** in front of the fence and **then bear left** to descend with the fence on your left. The Path (indistinct at times) passes through conifers and you emerge over a **Stile onto a lane.** With a house to your left, **turn right and** as the lane bends left, **cross the stile on your right**. **Turn left, down the field to a junction of paths** where you **bear right** towards a corner of the wood on your right. Past the corner, bear right **to a stile and a crossing path just inside the wood. Turn left** to follow the path down through the wood. **Emerge via a stile** where you **turn right** to a reservoir.

"U" - **Reservoir**. Pass the reservoir on your right and descend the lane until it turns sharp right.

"V" - **Lane turns sharp right**. **Straight ahead** through a kissing gate and continue along the field edge, **through a second kissing gate**, and down to metal railings and the A4136.

"W" - **A4136**. **Bear left** alongside the A4136, **Cross the River Wye and** use the subway under **the A40**. Keeping the Monmouth School on your left, leave the A40 behind and turn left. **Past the school building into Almshouse Street**. Turn right along **St.Mary's Street** and at the end, turn left along the narrow **Church Street** to enter Agincourt Square. Continue down Monnow Street to the Monnow Bridge.

See page 60/61 for information on Monmouth. See page 64/65 for facilities information.

"X" - **Monnow Bridge**. **Cross** the river to a roundabout and **turn right** along Drybridge Street. Pass the Fire and Ambulance Stations to the next road off left, Water Lane.

"Y" - **Water Lane**. **Turn left** and follow the lane.

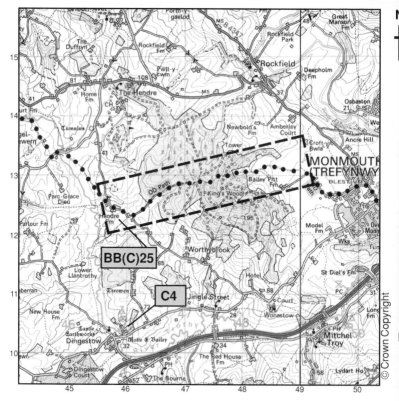

BB(C)25 - Hendre Farm House
Tel. (01600) 740484 TB 3 Crown
HComm
Feb-Nov Band 2 (1S,2D,1T,1F)(2PB)
EM. Dogs. Non-Smk'g. Pk'dL. Trans.
LTPk'g. Bags.

C4 - Bridge Caravan & Campsite
Tel. (01600) 740241 TB 5 ticks AA 3
Pennant
Easter-Oct (25 pitches)
Show'rs. Wash/Dry facs. Dogs. Shop.

Rockfield & The Hendre
Telephones. No facs.

Monmouth Facilities (01600)
YHA - Priory St.
Tel. 715116
1995 - Open 1 Mar - 31 Oct
See Handbook for further details.
Banks. NatWest (ATM), Lloyds (ATM), Midland (ATM), Barclays (ATM).
Nationwide with Link.
Nelson Museum. M-Sa 1000-1300hrs & 1400-1700hrs Su 1400-1700hrs.
Castle Museum. Summer 1400-1700hrs. Winter SaSu 1400-1700hrs
Taxis. Castle Cabs - 714730, Whiteways - 716274.
Buses. M-Sa - Regular to Ross-0n-Wye, Hereford, Chepstow, Newport.
M-Sa - Limited to Abergavenny.

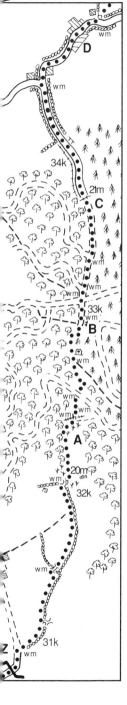

Monmouth - Hendre Farm

Note section of Path omitted.

"Z" - <u>**Water Lane bends left**</u>. **150m** after Water Lane bends left to go to Bailey Pitts Farm ahead, **turn right into a field entrance and bear slightly left** to put the hedge on your right. Ignore the stile on your right and continue along the field edge. Just after the corner **Bear right to cross a footbridge** over a deep gully. Continue, with a hedge on your right, to the next field corner where you **cross a second footbridge. Turn left** along the field edge to enter the woodland ahead.

"A" - <u>**King's Wood**</u>. After only **200m turn left over a footbridge and cross a stile** to enter the King's Wood proper. The Path bears right and ascends. **Cross a forestry track** and continue to ascend. A path joins from sharp right as the Path levels and after another 75m you pass a low "1857 Monmouth Parish" boundary stone immediately on your right. Continue as the Path bends right and briefly climbs to emerge at the end of a forestry track with a seat.

"B" - <u>**Seat at end of forestry track**</u>. **Continue ahead** along the forestry track which eventually emerges through a metal barrier at the edge of the deciduous wood on your left.

"C" - <u>**Metal Barrier**</u>. Continue along the lane to join a road. Bear right to pass "The Cidermill" on your right as the road bends right to Hendre Farm.

"D" - <u>**Hendre Farm**</u>. **100m past the farm** and just after a house on your left, **turn left over a stile** by a gate. Walk directly away from the gate to cross the field (path indistinct).

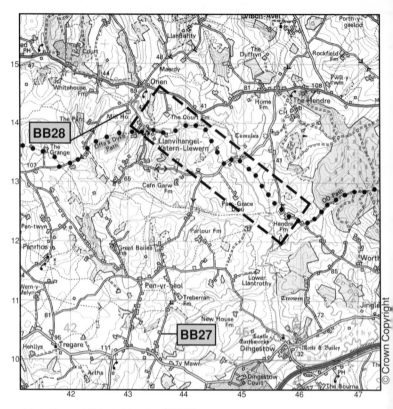

Llanvihangel Ystern-Llewern (01600)
No facs.
BB27 - The Lilacs
Tel. 740686
Jan-Dec Band 1 (2S,1D)
EM. Dogs. Pk'dL. Veg (by
arrangement). Trans. Bags.
BB28 - Mill House Farm
Tel. 780468
Jan-Dec Band 1/2 (2S,1D,1T,1F)(1PB)
EM. Non-Smk'g. Pk'dL. Veg. Trans.
LTPk'g. Bags.

Onen (+1BB)
Telephone. No facs.

Llanvihangel - Ystern - Llewrn
(St.Michael's of the Fiery Meteor)

"D" continued. **Cross a stile and footbridge in a crossing hedge**. With hedge right, continue to a **Stile by a large oak**. Turn right to cross the stile and then **turn left** for only a few metres **before bearing right** across the field **to a stile** in the far hedge. **Head for a stile and footbridge in the far right corner** of a long field. Continue with a fenceline on your right. The fence turns right at a redundant stile (wm) on your right but you continue, over a stile by a house, to **Turn left along the road** to the "Abbey Bridge".

Grace Dieu Abbey. Just on your left as you approach the road is the site of a Cistercian Abbey founded in the 13thC. It was abandoned at the Dissolution and the name of the bridge and nearby cottage is all that remains to mark its presence.

"E" - <u>Abbey Bridge</u>. Continue and **Just before the entrance to "Abbey Cottage", turn right over a stile** (aim to the left of a corrugated iron barn ahead) and cross the field. Go over a stile in a crossing fence and cross to the barn.

"F" - <u>Corrugated iron barn</u>. **Cross the stile to the left of the barn** and continue along a field edge with the hedge on your right. **Cross a stile and cut the corner of a field to a further stile** where you **bear left.** At a line of trees ahead and the **River Trothy** the Path swings left to **parallel a steep bank on your left** and passes through 2 gateways to a redundant stile (wm) stuck in the middle of a field. To your left lies "Sunnybank Farm".

"G" - <u>Sunnybank Farm</u>. Head along the field, **passing the farm over on your left**, and **turn left to cross a stile** onto the access track for the farm. Turn right and **follow the track to the Church** of Llanvihangel - Ystern - Llewrn ("H").

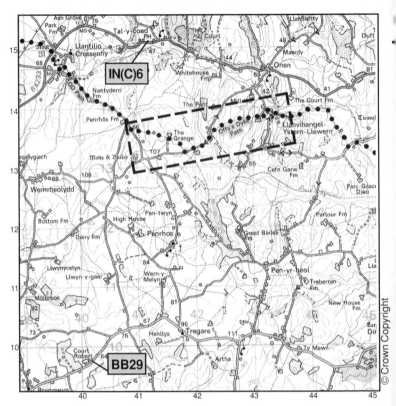

Tal-y-Coed (01600) (+0)
IN(C)6 - The Halfway House Inn
Tel. 780269 Gateway to Wales Award
94&5
Jan-Dec Band 2 (2T) (2PB)
EM. Lic'd. Pk'dL. Veg. Trans. LTPk'g.
Bags.

Rural Location
BB29 - Court Robert
Tel. (01291) 690709 TB Listed
Jan-Dec Band 1 (2D/T,1F)
EM. Dogs. Pk'dL. Veg. Trans. LTPk'g.
Bags.
Will transport from Llantilio Crossenny.

Llanvihangel (etc) - Penrhos Farm

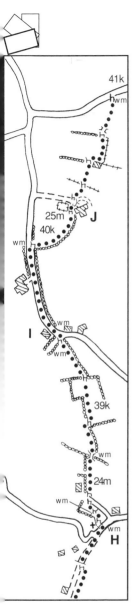

"H" - **Llanvihangel Church**. **Turn left** through the lower church gate **and bear right over a stile**. Initially with the churchyard on your left, cross the field to a footbridge, over a stile and through rough pasture to a stile leading onto a drive. **Straight across the drive**, over a stile and follow the hedge on your left down to a **Footbridge** over a stream; continue, hedge on your right, **to a stile which you cross to put the hedge on your left**. As the hedge does a left turn, Continue across the field to a stile in a crossing fence and now with a hedge on your right, emerge over a stile ahead by a farm.

"I" - **"Pen-pwll-y-calch Farm"**. **Bear right onto the road** and pass the farm on your left. Continue along the road, passing the entrance to "New House", to **Turn right over a stile** in the hedge on your right.

KEEP TO THE FIELD EDGE AND DO NOT CUT ACROSS THE FIELD TO THE GRANGE! **Follow the field edge** (anti-clockwise) round to a stile, past an outdoor riding arena, and through a gate onto the drive of The Grange.

"J" - **"The Grange"**. **Cross the drive** to go over a stile. Cross two fields to a stile to the left of the **Ruin of Little Grange; bear right** to a fenceline **and turn left** to follow the field-edge down to a stile (with a swinging bar!). Continue across a large field to a stile in the hedge opposite. Cross the stile to emerge on the **Public road** and **turn right** to Penhros Farm.

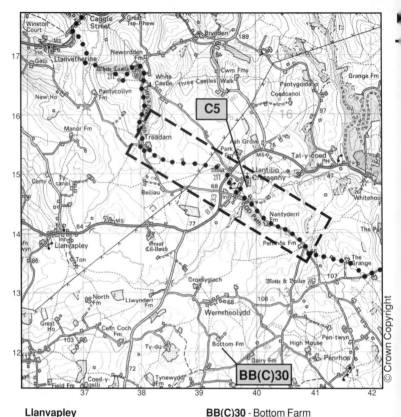

© Crown Copyright

Llanvapley
Red Hart Inn (food)
Llantilio Crossenny (01600) (+2BB)
Apart from a telephone and the 15thC
Hostry Inn, there are no facilities.
Hostry Inn - 1200-1500hrs & 1830-
2300hrs (Su 2230) (food)
A number of farms offer B&B through
the Landlord of the Hostry Inn and they
will collect you from the pub!
Buses. See Llanvetherine Post Bus.

BB(C)30 - Bottom Farm
Tel. 780216 TB Listed
Jan-Nov Band 1 (1D,1T)
EM. Non-Smk'g. Pk'dL. Veg. Trans.
LTPk'g.
C5 - Court Farm
Tel. 780288
Apr-Sep
Toilets. Dogs.

Don't forget BB29 will collect from here!

Llantilio Crossenny. The name means the Church of St. Teilo at Iddon's Cross. Iddon was a local king engaged in fighting a Saxon incursion in the 6thC. On hearing that Teilo (later Bishop of Llandaff) was nearby, Iddon asked him to pray for his victory in a forthcoming battle. Teilo raised a cross here and prayed whilst the battle raged nearby. In gratitude for his success, Iddon granted Teilo the land for the building of a church.... The church is well worth a visit. The present building dates from the 13thC with the nave, chancel and Lady chapel being added in the 14thC. The shingled spire was added in the 18thC.

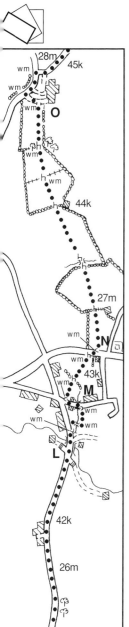

Penrhos Farm - Treadam

"K" - **Penrhos Farm**. Continue along the road, passing Nantyderri Farm to the bridge over the River Trothy at Llantilio Crossenny.

"L" - **River Trothy Bridge**. **Cross** the bridge and just after a track off right (campsite!), **Turn right through a kissing gate**. Bear left to **Cross a footbridge** over a stream on your right; **turn left** (stream on your left) to go through a kissing gate and emerge on a road by a BT phonebox.

Advance Warning - Llanvetherine Inn? Do not plan on a lunchtime drink there. It's now a house?

The 15thC Hostry Public House in Llantilio Crossenny (see LMap for opening hours) is well worth a visit but leave your muddy boots and packs in the entrance. Alas it no longer (1995) offers B&B, but the landlord keeps a list of local farms who both offer B&B and will transport you from/to the pub! He also has a wealth of stories with which to amuse you while you wait (ask about the socks on the brass bedknobs!).

"M" - **Phonebox**. **Turn left** to cross a bridge over the stream and just after a house on your right (postbox set in wall), **Turn right through a kissing gate**. Ignore the waymark, bear left across the field **to a stile** in a crossing hedge. **Bear left** across the field to emerge through a kissing gate onto the B4233.

Hen Cwrt. or The Old Court (situated just NE of the Path by the B4233) was probably the moated site of a 13th/14th century manor house belonging to the Bishops of Llandaff. Lying in the SW corner of a deer park created by Sir William ap Thomas, the Lord of the White Castle, or his son , William Herbert of Raglan. The house was believed to have been in use until the Civil War.

"N" - **B4233**. Bear right **across the road to cross a stile**. **Cross the middle of a field** to a stile opposite. **Continue**, across the next field, to cross a double stile (footbridge in between) and then across a third field to a stile just to the left of a barn. Continue over 2 further stiles. Now with a hedge on your right, go through a gate onto a **Farm access road** and **turn left** to the road by Treadam ("O").

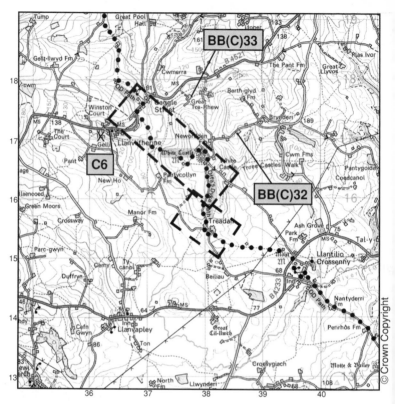

BB(C)32 - Treloyvan Farm
Tel. (01600) 780478 TB 1 Crown
Mar-Nov Band 1 (1T,1F)(2PB)
EM (booked!). Dogs. Non-Smk'g.
Pk'dL. Veg. Trans. LTPk'g. Bags.
Llanvetherine (01873) (+1BB)
Buses. M-Sa Abergavenny-LlanV-
Skenfrith Postbus 2 a day (1 via
LlanCros) (Tel. 01222 393279)
NB. The Inn marked on the OS map is
closed.

BB(C)33 - Great Tre-rhew Farm
Tel. (01873) 821268 TB Listed
Jan-Dec (exc Xmas/NY) Band 1
(1D,1T,1F)
EM. Pk'dL. Veg. Trans. LTPk'g. Bags.
C6 - Church Cottage
Tel. (01873) 821475
Apr-Sep. Toilets.
Three Castles Walk. (diversion)
BB(C)26 - Brook Cottage (nr Skenfrith)
Tel. (01600) 750319 TB Listed
Jan-Dec (exc Xmas) Band 1
(1S,1D,1F)
Pk'dL. Trans. LTPk'g. Bags.

The Three Castles.
Although the castle at Monmouth provided a secure base on a major route out of Wales, the Normans realised the need to defend the land won in their conquest of this part of Gwent, and so three fortified positions were established at Grosmont, Skenfrith and Llantilio Crossenny. The early works were earth and timber defences with wooden buildings within.
Continued on page 74...

Treadam - White Castle - Caggle St.

"O" - **Minor Road at Treadam**. **Turn right** at the minor road, past Treadam Farmhouse, and take the **First turn right** at the 16thC "Old Cottage". Follow the lane all the way until a road joins sharp right just before a fork in the road. Take the **Left fork to the White Castle.**

White Castle. (See information on "Three Castles") CADW - Summer opening from late Mar - late Oct 0930-1830hrs. Winter opening M-Sa 0930-1600, Su 1400-1600.

"P" - **White Castle**. As you round the corner to the gates into the castle grounds, continue **down a green track immediately to the right of iron railings**. Follow the lane as it bears left round the castle, past a cottage and then bears right **to a stile at a field entrance**. **Turn right** and follow the edge of the field. Just **Before farm buildings to your right, turn right over a stile** and pass the buildings to **cross a stile in the hedge on your left**. The hedge, now on your right, bears left just before you **Cross a stile to put the hedge on your left again**. Continue until the hedge bears left and starts to descend the hill. Leave the hedge and **Bear right steeply down to a stile** in a crossing hedge and continue to a footbridge.

"Q" - **Footbridge over River Trothy**. Cross and **bear left** to the corner of the hedge opposite. **Bear right and follow the hedge to a stile**, **bear left along the field** to a stile in the far right corner and the B4521 Caggle Street.

"R" - **B4521**. **Turn right** along the road to a Chapel on your left.

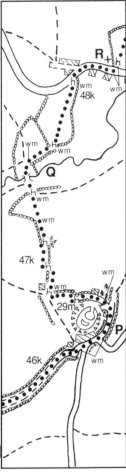

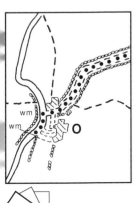

Abergavenny (01873)
Taxis. Lewis - 854140, Carlton - 850716,
Park Taxi - 858416, Graham - 857233.
Rail. Welsh Marches (South) Line.
Newport-Abergavenny-Hereford-Shrewsbury.
Hourly service (2-hourly Su) (Tel. 01222 228000)
Buses. M-Sa - Limited to Monmouth, Hereford (via Pandy). Regular to Brecon. Frequent to Newport.

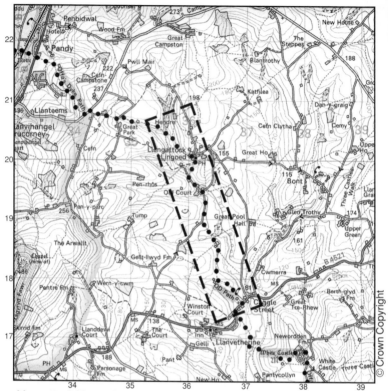

Llangattock Lingoed (+2BB,1C)
Sub-PO only. Telephone nr PH
PH - Hunter's Moon 1200-1500hrs & 1800-2300 (Su 1900-2230hrs) (food).
Buses. Check with Local Authority Helpline for TuF shopper service.
The house next to the Church advertises "Camping".

The Three Castles cont'd. An attack by the Welsh on Abergavenny in 1182, in which the Sheriff of Hereford was killed and the castle burnt down, started a programme of building using stone. The White Castle became known as such due to the plaster with which the walls were rendered.

The first half of the 13thC saw a series of improvements but otherwise things were relatively quiet. Then Llywelyn Gruffudd ("Llywelyn the last") commenced his attacks by taking Builth in 1260. The castles were quickly garrisoned in anticipation of attack. Llywelyn's attack on Abergavenny in 1262 was driven back and the Treaty of Montgomery followed in 1267. However, following the death of Llywelyn in 1282 and the conquest of Wales by Edward, the Marcher castles became largely redundant and were used mainly as administrative centres.

There was a brief resumption of the castles" military role during Owain Glyndwr's campaign (1404-05). That was the last time that the castles were used for their primary purpose; by 1538 they had been abandoned.

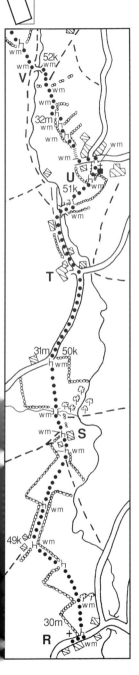

Caggle Street - Hendre

Pass the Chapel on your left **and turn left to cross a stile** by a gate. **Bear right** to where a line of oaks meets the hedge ahead and **then bear left to a stile on a hedge corner**. **Turn right** to follow the field edge (hedge on your right). Over a stile into a **Green lane** by two barns and **turn right** to follow the lane. The lane ends at a gateway and stile. Continue, over a further stile, to the buildings of Little Pool Hall.

"S" - **Little Pool Hall**. **Continue** past the derelict farmhouse and buildings **to a stile** at the end of a low wall on your right. Ignore the waymark; **Walk straight away** from the stile to **Cross a footbridge**. Continue across the middle of a field and over a stile in the hedge opposite. Emerging onto a minor **Public road, turn right** to the magnificent building of Old Court.

"T" - **Old Court**. The road bends right with Old Court on your left but you **continue** down the "No through road" ahead. Just past **Cwm Farm bear right** down a track and **over a bridge. Turn left, over a wooden footbridge and turn right**. **Bearing left, ascend** the steep bank to a stile on the corner of the hedge and the Church.

"U" - **Llangattock Lingoed Church**. Pass the Church on your right and **through the churchyard gate. Turn left at the road** and down to some steps on your right. **Turn right, up steps**, between two fences and over a stile (1) into the corner of a field. Continue with hedge on your left, over another stile (2) and **Turn left over a third stile then right**, to put the hedge on your right. The hedge bends right but you now **Bear left down the hill** to cross a hedgeline, pass a lonely waymark (!) and continue to a footbridge.

"V" - **"Footbridge over "Full Brook"**. Over the brook and **bear right up a steep bank** to a stile in a crossing hedge.

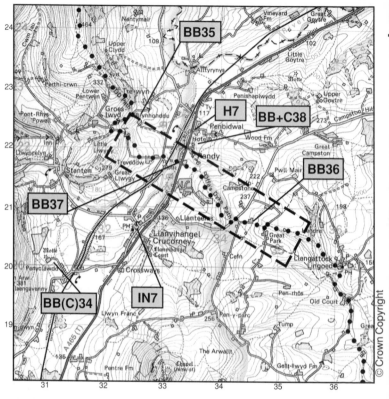

© Crown Copyright

Llanvihangel Crucorney (01873)
IN7 - Skirrid Mountain Inn
Tel. 890258 TB 3 Crown Comm
Jan-Dec Band 3 (2D)(2PB)
EM. Lic'd. Pk'dL. Veg. LTPk'g.
BB(C)34 - Penyclawdd Farm
Tel. 890591 TB Listed Comm
Jan-Dec Band 1 (2D/T)
Dogs. Non-Smk'g. Pk'dL. Veg. Trans.
LTPk'g.

H7 - Park Hotel
Tel. 890271 TB 3 Crown
Jan-Dec Band 2 (single Band 3)
(1S,4 D/T/S) (5PB)
Switch. Visa. M'Card. (+5% on credit
cards)
Dogs. Lic'd. Pk'dL. Veg. LTPk'g.
*Comfortable Country House in lovely
setting, with excellent home-cooked
Austrian and English food. Come and
just relax!*

Pandy (01873) (+1IN,1BB)
See opposite for facilities
BB35 - Brynhonddu
Tel. 890535 TB Listed
Jan-Dec (exc Xmas) Band 1
(1D,1T,1F)
Dogs. Pk'dL. Veg. LTPk'g.
BB36 - Llanerch Farm
Tel. 890432 TB 1 Crown
Apr-Nov Band 1 (1F)(1PB)
PK'dL. LTPk'g.
BB37 - Rhos Rhudd
Tel. 890703
Feb-Nov Band 1 (1D,1F)
Dogs. Pk'dL. Veg. Trans. LTPk'g. Bags.
BB+C38 - Ty-Newydd Farm
Tel. 890235 TB Listed
Jan-Dec Band 1 (1D,2T)
EM. Dogs. Non-Smk'g. Pkd'L. Trans.
LTPk'g. Bags.
10 tent pitches. Toilets. Show'rs. Wash/
Dry facs. Shop.

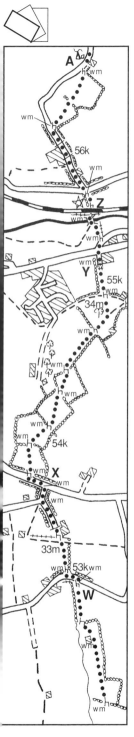

Hendre - Pandy - Treveddw

"V" continued. Bear left along the field to pass above a barn. Drop left to a stile by the stream and continue (hedge on your left) to a stile and the road by Great Park.

"W" - **Road by Great Park**. **Turn left,** after 75m **turn right over a stile** by a gate. With the hedge on your right, go **straight ahead** to a stile just to the left of Llanerch farmhouse and **Continue down the farm access road** to join a minor public road at bend. **Bear right** 100m to a T-junction.

"X" - **T-junction on Llanvihangel Crucorney Road**. **Turn left** and in **75m turn right, over a stile (no.1)**. Bear slightly left to a double stile (no.2&3) in the opposite hedgeline. Bear right to a stile (no.4) and bear left to descend to a double stile (no.5&6). Continue down to a **Stile (no.7)** in the hedge over on your left; **turn right** to follow the hedge to a stile (no.8) in the corner of the field. Bear left across a large field with a barn over to your right. **As you pass a clump of trees, bear left down a bank to a stile (no.9)** by a metal gate. Follow the hedge on your left to pass through double gates and emerge at the A465.

"Y" - **A465**. Cross to the **slip road opposite** and **turn left over a stile**. With a fence and ditch on your right, cross to a footbridge over the river, up steps, through a kissing gate and across the railway.

"Z" - **Railway**. **Up the bank** on the other side of the railway **and bear left** to follow a hedgeline to a stile and the **Minor public road**. Cross to **take road opposite**. Once **Past** the buildings of **Treveddw Farm, turn right, over a stile** and **bear gently left** across a field to a stile just below a radio mast. Cross the stile and emerge onto the road again.

Pandy
Shop at North end of Llanvihangel Crucorney (Opens "When I'm ready" Shuts "When I'm finished" - useful!)
Buses. M-Sa Limited to Abergavenny/Hereford.

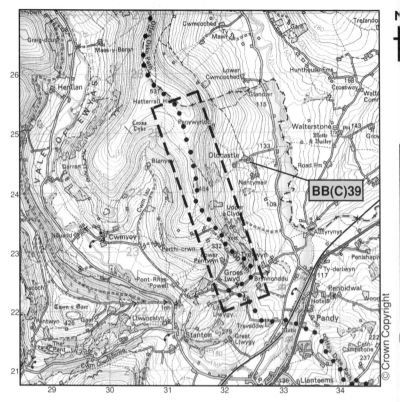

BB(C)39 - Oldcastle Court Farm
Tel. (01873) 890285 TB 2 Crown
Jan-Dec Band 1 (1S,1D,1F)(1PB)
Dogs. Pk'dL. Trans. LTPk'g. Bags.

Hill-country Routefinding.

The ascent into hill-country calls for some changes:

1. Waymarks (wm) may be more fully described and shown as (rt) or (lt) to indicate which side of the Path they are on.

2. Cairns may be shown as "cm" = cairn marker. Be very wary of over-reliance on cairns. Unmapped cairns spring up overnight and there are some kind souls bent on destroying them all!

3. Grid references (GR) are given to the nearest 100m using a 1:25,000.

4. Global Positioning System grid references (GPS GR) are frequently accurate to within a few metres but because of "selective availability" and other GPS factors, they are only rated to +/- 100m 95% of the time. They are shown with the Easting and Northing divided by a "/". The problem with GPS is that it can be spot on for one fix and then way out the next because the satellites then in view have selective availability in operation!

5. Where a path is shown with a "?", it is not obvious on the ground.

78

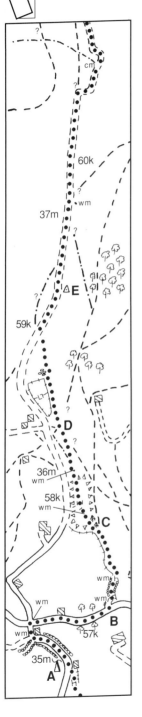

Treveddw - Hatterall Hill

"A" - **Radio Mast**. **Turn right**, along the road and at a **Crossroads turn right**. The road descends and level with the buildings of Brynhonddu over on your right, **Turn left into a field entrance**.

"B" - **Field entrance**. **Bear right,** along a track for 20m **before bearing left** up a twitchel to a **Stile** ahead, then **bear left up the hill**, with a wall on your left, to an Iron Age hill-fort.

See notes opposite on Hill-country navigation.

"C" - **Iron Age Hill-fort**. The wall on your left turns left before the outer ramparts of the fort. **Bear right to a clump of pine trees** and passing them on your right, take a path **through the middle of the fort**. Emerging through a gap in the north-west corner, follow a broad green path (with a rough track paralleling you on your left). **As the path forks, take the right fork** to the "Castle" enclosure.

"D" - **"Castle" Enclosure**. A walled enclosure used as a pen for sheep. Continue, to **pass the wall of the enclosure on your left**. The wall turns left and the Path bears right to go round a rocky outcrop. As the Path levels, a rutted green track joins from sharp left and you follow it to the OS Triangulation Point at spot height 464m.

GPS Users. On the days these readings were taken Selective Availability did not seem to be in operation. Altitude readings were -50m, PDOP typically low 2's, 5-6 sat's in view.

"E" - **OS Trig Point No. S6114 (GR 315241)**. Continue past the trig point on your right. Pass a waymark (rt. GPS GR 3147/2458) where the Oldcastle path (?) joins. In 500m **follow the track** as it bends right (see note below) then left passing a cairned footpath (lt. GPS GR 3126/2542) off left.

The official path is shown on the 1:25,000 OS map as running along a footpath that goes straight on at the bend, rejoining the track in 0.5km. That footpath does not exist on the ground.

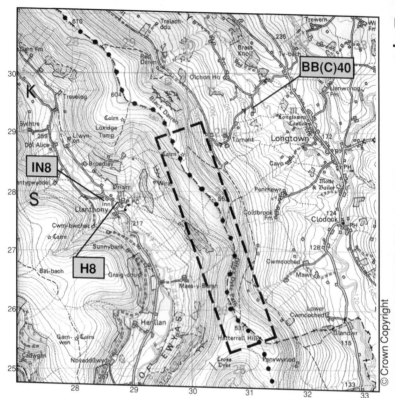

Llanthony (01873)

Telephone at road. No facs.
Nearest alternative accommodation at
Capel-y-ffin or
B&B (Gaer Fm GR297217) +
INN Queen's Head Inn at GR3122.

H8 - Abbey Hotel

Tel. 890487
Week before Easter -
W/ends only from end Oct!
Su-Th Band 2. F&Sa Band 3 per night
(NB must stay both F&Sa nights) (4D)
EM. Dogs. Lic'd. Veg. LTPk'g.
*LG Note. The requirement to stay both
nights at a weekend is an understandable
rule if the hotel is to make the most of its
limited capacity (you could always ask, if
they are otherwise empty....). The hotel
is part of a ruined 12th Century
Augustinian Priory and to say it is unusual
is the understatement of the year... what
a setting!*

IN8 - The Half Moon

Tel. 890611
Jan-Dec (exc Xmas day) Band 2
(4D,2T,1F)
EM. Dogs. Lic'd. Pk'dL. Veg. LTPk'g.
Camping. Farm adjacent Abbey allows
camping (no details) as does Farm at
GR298265.

Longtown (01873) (+1BB)

Shop. PO. PH.
Buses. M-Sa - Longtown - Craswall -
Hereford VLimited (01432 356201)

BB(C)40 - Olchon Cottage Farm

Tel. 860233 TB 2 Crown Comm
Jan-Dec (exc Xmas) Band 2 (2F)
EM(booked). Dogs. Pk'dL. Veg. Trans.
LTPk'g. Bags.

**See page 88 for more about
Longtown.**

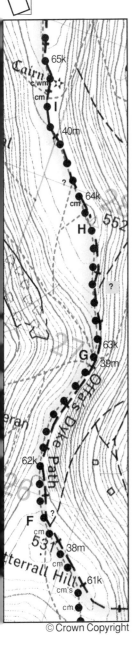

© Crown Copyright

Hatterall Hill - Black Darren

A scarcity of detail for the normal format of routefinding map prompted the use of enlarged 1:50,000 mapping (shown here at 1:25,000) but the path is still distinct on the ground. Look carefully and there is more detail than at first appears. Is it a cairn, or a waymark, or both? On the right or left of the Path? If it's a waymark, does it show just an acorn, an acorn with arrows or just arrows?

"F" - **Quarry (GR 308259)**. A cairned path joins sharp left just before a quarry hole on your right. Continue on the track.

Now could be a good time to divert off the ridge. Longtown is rather limited but the motte and bailey castle is a little gem where no expense has been spared on illustrative display boards that give an excellent idea of what it looked like when occupied. However, Llanthony Priory is probably the main attraction with both an hotel and a campsite next to the Priory.

See page 82 for information on Llanthony Priory.

"G" - **Llanthony/Longtown Crossing (GR307269)**. The track seems to end at the crossing which looks like a crow's foot as the path to Llanthony forks off left down to pick up a wall within 150m, the **Path rises ahead** and another path forks right up a low mound. The Longtown path forks off right in 10m. The Path becomes indistinct before continuing as a rutted track to the trig point at 552m.

"H" - **OS Triangulation Point No.S6109 (GR304278)**. Continue along the track to another crossing of paths.

"I" - **Path to Car Park below Black Darren (GR298285)**. A cairn (lt) before the crossing. Path off left (distinct), path off right (less distinct). Continue, to pass a low cairn (lt) with an "acorn" painted on a slab (GPS GR29916/28613).

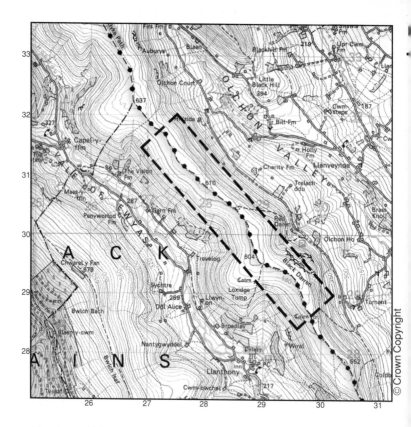

Llanthony Abbey (or Priory).

According to the romantics, in the early part of the 12thC, William, a knight of Hugh de Lacy, came across a ruined chapel in the Vale of Ewyas. He resolved to give up his life of arms and become a hermit. He was joined by a priest, Ernisus, and out of this unlikely beginning sprang the Augustinian community that was to become Llanthony Abbey. There is another version that says William sent Ernisus ahead to the valley to found a religious community.

The Abbey grew and became rich but it also became the target of attacks by the Welsh. Many of the canons were forced to flee to Gloucester where a new priory was established in 1136 that was eventually to become greater than that at Llanthony. The Abbey at Llanthony continued for another 400 years although at the time of its dissolution in 1539, it had only 4 cannons and a prior.

In 1807 the Abbey and its estate was bought for £20,000 by the poet Walter Savage Landor who had great plans for the place. Alas, he couldn't get on with either his tenants or the local society. After frittering away some £200,000 on the estate, Landor left to live abroad, a bitter and disillusioned man.

Black Darren - Trig Point 610m

Passing a cairn (rt) with a faint crossing track (GPS GR2966/2916), continue to a pile of stones.

"J" - **Pile of stones (GPS GR2953/2924)**. On your right, **a high pile of stones**, the largest on this section of Path. Continue to pass a low stone (rt), propped up with an acorn above two arrows (GPS GR2949/2945) (easily missed as there are two paths at this point).

"K" - **Circular Shelter of stones (GPS GR2933/2942)**. On your right, **with a slab against it showing an acorn**. Continue, to pass a single stone (rt) with an acorn (GPS GR2920/2949) and then, as a faint path comes in from the left, a single stone propped by others, showing only arrows (GPS GR2899/2952).

"L" - **Spot Height 604m (GR289296)**. **Marked by a large cairn** (lt) with a path in from the left. Continue to pass a stone (lt) with acorn and 2 arrows (GPS GR2864/3022). A track (from the Red Darren carpark) joins from the right at a flattened pile of stones (rt) (GPS GR2852/3042). A stone (rt) with an acorn on 3 sides and arrows on the fourth (GPS GR2840/3049), propped by stones.

"M" - **OS Triangulation Point No.S7276 (GR281/307)**. Continue and in 1km, pass four small cairns.

"N" - **Four small cairns (GPS GR2750/3154-2740/3167)**. **In quick succession**. Continue to a crossing of paths.

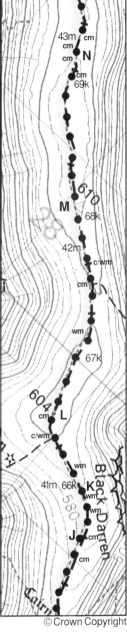

© Crown Copyright

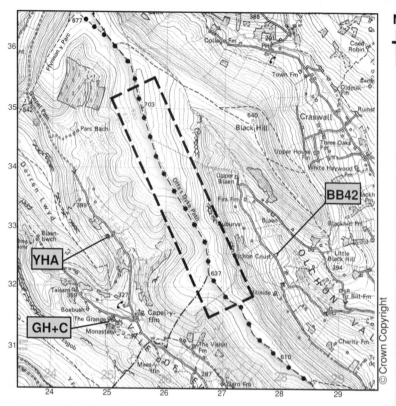

© Crown Copyright

Capel-y-Ffin (01873) (+0)
No facs.
GH+C - <u>The Grange</u>
Tel. 890215 TB 1Crown
Apr-Oct Band 2 (1S,1D,2T,3F)
EM. Dogs. Pk'dL. Veg. Trans. LTPk'g.
Bags.
Camping - Show'r. Wash/Dry facs.
Meals!
YHA(C) - <u>Capel-y-Ffin</u>
Tel. 890650
1995 - Open - Feb (FSa only), Mar (exc
W), Apr, May/Jun (exc W), Jul/Aug,
Mid-Sep/Oct (exc W), Nov (FSa only)
*LG Note - Talk about complicated!
Check your handbook for precise
dates.*

Olchon Valley
BB42 - <u>Olchon Court</u>
Tel. (01873) 860356
Jan-Dec (exc Xmas) Band 2
(1D,1T,1F)
EM. Non-Smk'g. Pk'dL. Veg. Trans.
LTPk'g. Bags.
*LG Note. Bit of a long shot if you
haven't booked but a very pleasant
place to stay!*

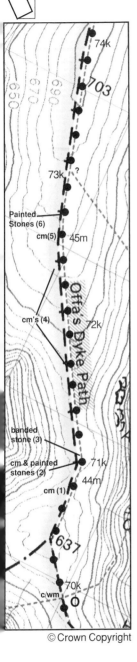

© Crown Copyright

The Olchon Path - The Highest Point

See page 86 for information on the Monastery at Capel-y-ffin.

"O" - **Olchon Path**.   The Path is well-defined at the crossing of the indistinct Capel-y-Ffin to Olchon path (GR27000/31950), marked by a waymarked post set into a cairn of stones.
Now is not the time to get lost, cliffs await you on the right!
Continue to pass:

1 - a cairn of stones (lt) (GPS GR2666/3258)

2 - a cairn of stones (lt) with yellow painted stones in it (GPS GR2673/3275)

3 - a stone set into the Path with blue, yellow & red painted bands (30m beyond 2)

As you start to climb to the highest point on the Path at 703m, the ground becomes very eroded and the peat covering has been worn down to the rock. Alas there is plenty of evidence to suggest that pony trekking may be the main culprit. You pass:

4 - a long line of 21 cairns (starts GPS GR2640/3342),

5 - a lone cairn (GPS GR2606/3401)

6 - then a cairn with stones painted red and green to its left (GPS GR2598/3407)

There is nothing to mark your passing of the 703m spot height (GR25600/35000) and you start to gently descend to the steep bank that marks the Llech-y-Lladron (Robbers Stone).

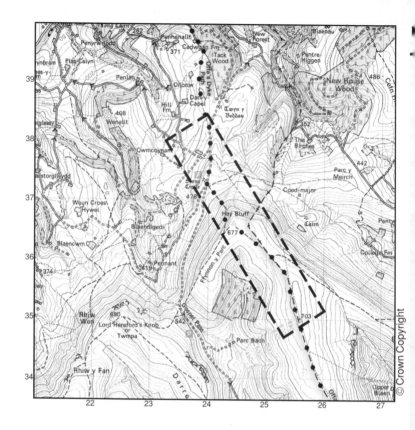

Capel-y-ffin Monastery.

There's obviously something in the water here because just up the valley from Llanthony there are two chapels and a former monastery (Capel-y-ffin means "Chapel on the Boundary").

The monastery was founded in 1870 by an Anglican Clergyman, the Reverend Lyne, and loosely followed the Benedictine Rule. Calling himself Father Ignatius, Lyne remained in charge of the monastery until his death in 1908.

Whilst Lyne was alive, the monastery was kept going on money raised as a result of his charismatic preaching in London and America. After his death, it became a dependency of another Benedictine community. That subsequently transferred to the Roman Catholic church, and the community at Capel-y-ffin declined.

Parts of the monastery fell into ruin and it was bought in 1924 by the sculptor Eric Gill. He created a small chapel dedicated to Our Lady and St. David. In 1935 the buildings became a girls' school and later a Youth Hostel. It is now privately owned.

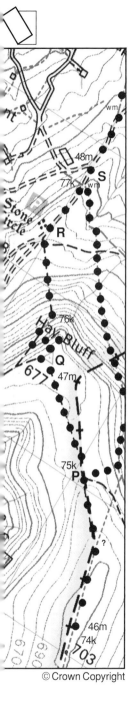

© Crown Copyright

Llech-y-Lladron - Gospel Pass Rd

"P" - **Llech-y-Lladron**. The Robber's Stone (GR25050/36050) is on your left at the top. You **descend the bank and continue** on a well-defined path to the OS Triangulation Pillar at Hay Bluff (GR24425/36625).

Alternative Route. The alternative route descends more gently than the route down the Bluff. It is not waymarked at the foot of the Llech-y-Lladron bank nor is it obvious on the ground. Turn right approximately 30m from the foot of the bank and descend bearing left so that you contour the hill above a line of gullies (known as "The Riggles") (GR25150/36400) before continuing down the hill to emerge at the Gospel Pass road.

"Q" - **Triangulation Pillar (Serial No. S5447)(GR24425/36625)**. There are a variety of paths off the Bluff. The simplest is to **head North to the point of the Bluff** (GR244/367) and **turn left to descend** on a path to an **Outcrop of rocks** where you **turn sharp right** to join a path and descend to the car park by the Stone Circle.

"R" - **Stone Circle Car Park**. **Turn right, along the road** to pass the point where the alternative route joins.

"S" - **Alternative Path joins (GR240/ 377)**. Just before a passing place with a road-salt container, a drain cover and waymarked rock marks the alternative path. **Continue**, a road joins from sharp left, as does a fence on top of an old wall. As the **Fence/wall bears left, continue** off the road to a stone waymark.

Now that you are off the hill, the routefinding maps revert to their normal format. We don't use enlarged mapping often as there is a maximum percentage of OS mapping that may appear in a guide such as this. In any event, neither the 1:50,000 nor the 1:25,000 OS maps bring out all the features, such as stiles, that are so useful to walkers in their navigation.

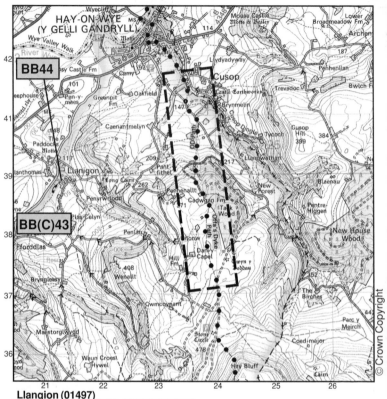

Llangion (01497)

BB44 - <u>The Old Post Office</u> Tel. 820008 TB 2 Crown Comm Feb-Dec (inc Xmas) Band 1/2 (2D,1T) (2PB) Dogs. Non-Smk'g. Pk'dL. Veg. Trans. *17th century character house set in the* *outstandingly beautiful Brecon Beacons* *National Park, on the foothills of the Black* *Mountains. Relaxed atmosphere &* *superb vegetarian breakfast.*	**BB(C)43** - <u>Lynwood</u> Tel. 820716 Mar-Oct Band 1 (1S,1D,1T) Dogs. Pk'dL. LTPk'g.

Longtown.

Founded in the middle of the 12th century when the motte & bailey castle was built by Lord of the Welsh Marches, Walter de Lacy, to replace an earlier castle nearby. It was known as the colony of "Ewyas Lacy". The keep of the castle is particularly fine and the illustrated display boards make these impressive ruins spring to life before you. (Open all times). The village green has a gruesome history. In 1808 a local man was hanged for murder and his body hung in chains on a gibbet until the smell of the rotting corpse caused villagers to plead for its removal. The "deterrent" message didn't work and the scene was repeated in 1811!

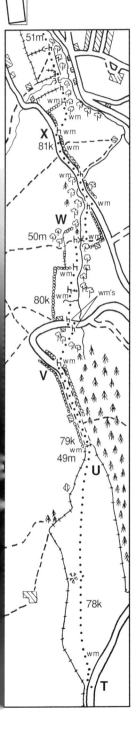

Gospel Pass Rd - Cusop Dingle

"T" - **Fence/Wall bears left away from the road**. **Bear left** at a stone waymark and head **over** the highest point of **the common** (path indistinct) to a gate in the furthest corner.

"U" - **Gate leading to sunken track**. **Follow the track** past Cadwgan Farm. The track bears left as you turn right over a stile in the hedge on your right.

"V" - **Stile in hedge on your right.** **Bear left away from the stile** and cross the field. At the bottom, bear right, **Through a belt of trees and bear left** to descend to a stile onto a road. **Turn left along the road for 20m and turn right** over a low stone stile. Straight ahead from the stile, cross a plank over a stream and **Continue** past a redundant stile to a stile in the corner of the field. Bear right to follow the field edge to a stile and footbridge on your right.

"W" - **Stile and Footbridge on your right**. **Cross and turn left**. With the stream now on your left, follow the edge of the field to its corner and a stile leading onto a public road. **Turn left along the road**, ignoring two footpaths off to the right (the second to "Cusop Dingle") until you come to a stile in the hedge on your right.

"X" - **Stile in the hedge on your right**. **Bear left** away from the stile across the field to a stand of trees where you continue **to a stile in the corner**. Straight away from the stile, with **Cusop Dingle on your right**, to a stile in the corner of the field. Descend to cross a subsidiary stream via a footbridge and **continue** up the other side, with the Dingle still on your right, to a kissing gate <u>and</u> stile in a crossing fenceline ("Y").

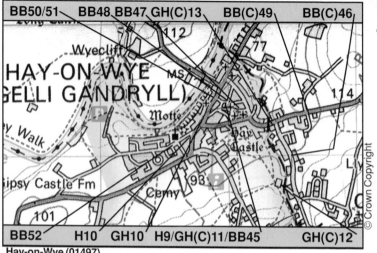

The map shows labels: BB50/51, BB48, BB47, GH(C)13, BB(C)49, BB(C)46, HAY-ON-WYE (GELLI GANDRYLL), BB52, H10, GH10, H9/GH(C)11/BB45, GH(C)12

Hay-on-Wye (01497)

(+1H,2GH,12BB)

H9 - Old Black Lion
Tel. 820841 TB 3 Crown HComm
Jan-Dec (exc Xmas) Band 2 (Band 5+
single occupancy)
(1S,5D,3T,1F) (10PB)
Visa. M'Card. Amex. Diners.
EM. Dogs. Lic'd. Pk'dL. Veg.

H10 - The Swan at Hay
Tel. 821188 TB 4 Crown HComm
Jan-Dec Band 4/5+ (1S,11D,4T,1F)
(17PB)
Switch. Visa. M'Card. Amex. Diners.
EM. Dogs. Lic'd. Pk'dL. Veg. Trans.
LTPk'g.

GH10 - Belmont House
Tel. 820718
Jan-Dec Band 1 (single Band 2) (1S,
2D, 2T, 1F) (1PB)
Dogs. Pk'dL. Veg. Trans. LTPk'g. Bags.

GH(C)11 - Kilverts
Tel. 821042 TB 4 Crowns
Jan-Dec Band 3 (1S, 6D,3T)(10PB)
Switch. Visa. M'Card. Amex.
EM. Dogs. Lic'd. Pk'dL. Veg. Trans.
LTPk'g. Bags.
*Drying facilities available. Selection of
Real Ales. Interesting & varied range of
bar snacks as well as A-la-carte
Restaurant. Live music alt Thurs. Jazz
Festival last w/e July.*

GH(C)12 - Rosedale
Tel. 820804
Jan-Dec Band 1 (2S, 2D, 1T,1F)
Dogs. Pk'dL. LTPk'g. Bags.

GH(C)13 - York House
Tel. 820705
Jan-Dec Band 2 (1D,3F)(4PB)
Vias. M'Card. Amex.
EM. Dogs. Non-smk'g. Pk'dL. Veg.
LTPk'g. Bags.

BB45 - 8 Chancery Court
Tel. 820152 TB 2 Crown
Jan-Dec Band 2 (1D,1T)(2PB)
Non-Smk'g. Pk'dL. Veg. Bags.

BB(C)46 - Fernleigh
Tel. 820459
Mar-Oct Band 1 (single Band 4)
(2D,1T)(1PB)
Non-Smk'g. Pk'dL. Veg. Trans. LTPk'g.
Bags.

BB47 - Hendre
Tel. 820439
Band 1 (1D,2T)
Non-Smk'g. Pk'dL. Veg. Trans. Bags.

BB48 - Jasmine Cottage
Tel. 821168
Jan-Dec (exc Xmas) Band 1 (2D,1T)
Non-Smk'g. Pk'dL. Veg. Bags.

BB(C)49 - Norville
Tel. 820162
Jan-Dec Band 1 (2D,1S)
EM. Dogs. Pk'dL. Veg. Trans. LTPk'g.
Bags.

Cusop Dingle - Hay bridge

"Y" - <u>**Kissing Gate & Stile**</u>. **Straight ahead** from the gate. The fence on your left bears right, **continue** across the field through a kissing gate in the crossing hedge/wall. Continue through a third kissing gate and past a redundant fourth. With the castle car park over to your left, continue through a fifth gate onto a lane and emerge onto the B4348.

"Z" - <u>**B4348**</u>. **Turn left** to pass the car park and tourist information on your left. At the **T-junction turn right**, past the clock tower and **turn left down Bridge St**.

Hay-on-Wye. A more interesting route through Hay is to turn right at the B4348 and take the first left, then bear left into the maze of little streets in the centre of the town.

"A" - <u>**Bridge over the Wye**</u>. **Over the bridge** and at the end of the railings **turn right**, down some steps. Continue (ignore the path down to the river) across a stile and follow a path **along the top edge of the wood**. The **Path bears right, down to the river** where you follow the bank, over a stile and across a meadow.

BB50 - <u>Rest for the Tired</u>
Tel. 820550 TB 2 Crown Comm
Jan-Dec (exc Xmas) Band 1
(2D,1T)(3PB)
Non-Smk'g. Pk'dL. Veg. LTPk'g.
BB51 - <u>Tinto House</u>
Tel. 820590 TB 2 Crown Comm
Feb-Nov Band 1 (1D,1T,1F)(3PB)
Pk'dL. Veg. Bags.
BB52 - <u>The Willows</u>
Tel. 820387 day, 820174 evening.
Mar-Oct Band 1/2 (2S,1D,1T)(1PB)
Pk'dL. Veg. Trans. LTPk'g. Bags.
C7 - <u>Radnors End Campsite</u>
Tel. 820780
Mar-Oct (15 tent pitches)
Toilets. Show'rs. Wash/Dry facs. Dogs.
Shop.

Hay-on-Wye (01497)
<u>Banks</u>. NatWest (ATM). Midland
(ATM). Barclays ATM.
<u>Camping Shop</u>. W L Jones (Camping
Gaz).
<u>Taxis</u>.
OD BC - Tel.821266
A2-B - Tel.847714 (& 0831 543570 &
(01374 620229) (Baggage carrier!)
<u>Buses</u>. M-Sa - Regular to Brecon,
Hereford (Su - VLimited).
Th - Local area buses.

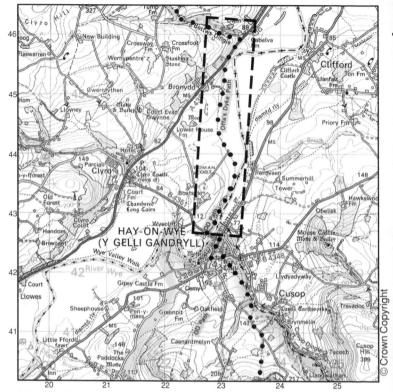

Hay-on-Wye.

Situated at a natural choke point in the Wye Valley, with hill-country on three sides and the fertile plains of Hereford and Leominster on the other, Hay-on-Wye's strategic value had long been recognised. The name Hay derives from the English word for hedge and the Welsh name, Y Gelli Gandryll, means "clipped hedge"; suggesting a hedged enclosure. The Romans certainly recognised the importance of the site for they established the large fort of "Gaer" on an area of raised ground just across from the present town.

A Norman settlement grew up in the early 12th century around the Church of St.Mary and a motte and bailey castle, just to the west of the present town. With the building of a stone castle, and later a town wall, early in the 13th century, the centre of the town moved to its present site. The tale of the castle built in a day is a tribute to one Maude de Valerie, wife of William de Braose, one of the more infamous Lords of Hay. A woman of admirable resolution, determined, brave, she is supposed to have built it single-handedly overnight! Alas, for all her legendary qualities, tact wasn't one of them. She upset King John and ended up being starved to death in Corfe Castle.

Continued on page 94

Hay Bridge - Bettws Dingle

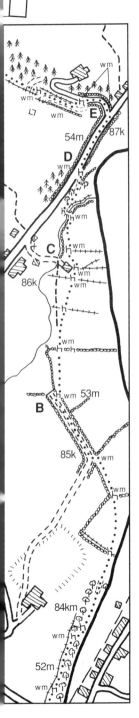

.... **continue** across the meadow, pass through the trees and alongside the river **to a stile** in a crossing hedge. **Bear gently left** away from the river **to a stile** in a crossing hedge. Keeping a hedge on your left, follow the field-edge to the **Corner of the field** where you **jink** left then right **to continue on a green lane**. At the end of the lane, come to a mileage stile on your right.

"B" - <u>Mileage Stile</u>. **Bear left** away from the stile **to** cross the **left-hand stile of two** in a crossing hedge. **Continue** over two further stiles in crossing fencelines to emerge before farm buildings and a silage clamp.

"C" - <u>Silage Clamp</u>. **Cross the stile immediately on the right of the clamp** and **bear left** across the corner of the field to a stile in a crossing fenceline. **Straight ahead** to join a hedgeline to your left **and turn left over a stile and footbridge.** Cross a stile and **turn right, then bear left up a track** to pass through trees. Bear left up to a stile and the A438.

"D" - <u>A438</u>. **Turn right** alongside the A438 and **take the first road off left** (with a "No through road"-sign). The road bends left and as it starts to bear right and descend, **cross a stile ahead at the corner of a wood. Join a track** along the edge of the wood (right) which soon turns left into fields but you **continue on a path** and over a stile ahead, keeping the wood on your right. A track joins from sharp left near "New Barn" (ruin).

Clyro (+1H)
Baskerville Arms Hotel.
Shop (M-Sa 0900-1300 & 1400-1730hrs ec WSa)
PO. Kilvert Gallery.

Clyro and Sir Arthur Conan Doyle.

Sir Arthur wrote his Sherlock Holmes story "The Hound of the Baskervilles" whilst staying in the village but it has no connection with the local Baskerville family.

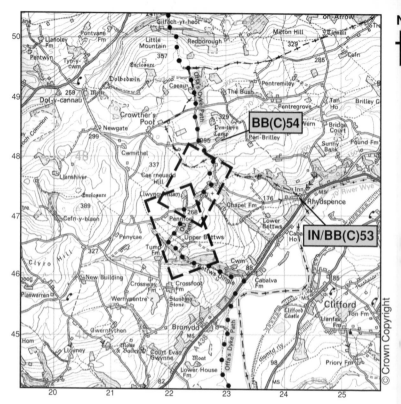

Rhydspence (01497)
No facs.
<u>IN</u> - <u>Rhydspence Inn</u>
Tel. 831262 TB 3 Crown HComm
Jan-Dec Band 4 (D4,T2,S1)(7PB)
Switch. Visa. M'Card. Amex.
EM. Lic'd. Veg.

<u>BB(C)53</u> - <u>Rhydspence Cottage</u>
Tel. 831595
Jan-Dec Band 1 (1S,1T)
Dogs. Pk'dL. Veg. Trans. LTPk'g. Bags.
<u>BB(C)54</u> - <u>Pentwyn Farm</u>
Tel. (01497) 831337
Apr-Sep Band 1 (2S,2D)
EM. Dogs. Non-smk'g. Veg. Trans.
LTPk'g. Bags.

<u>Hay-on-Wye</u>. *(continued from page 92)*
 the English and the Welsh. King John burnt it in 1216, Llywelyn razed it
in 1231, it was besieged in 1263-1265 and Owain Glyndwr sacked it in
1400.
Hay was granted a market in 1233 and is still a popular market town. In
recent years it has become a centre for second-hand books. Faced with
so many books and bookshops, the visitor might like to know that there
is a handy leaflet available in the shops. It details which shops specialize
in which books, so your search need not be random.

Bettws Dingle - Cae-Higgin

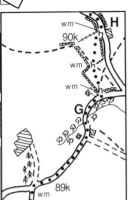

"E" - <u>Track joins near "New Barn"</u>. **Continue** on the track as it bears right, **down into the wood** and crosses a stream. **The track rises steeply and as it bends right to Upper Bettws, bear left** up through the trees to cut the corner **and turn sharp left to join a path**. The path follows the edge of the wood (left) to end at the foot of a flight of steps leading up to a minor public road.

"F" - <u>Minor Public Road near Upper Bettws</u>. **Turn right** along the road. At a **T-junction** (and with the access road to Llwyngwilliam Farm ahead) **turn right**. The road descends and bends left to cross a stream and pass another dingle on your right.

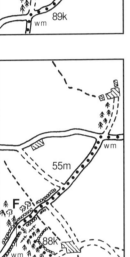

"G" - <u>Dingle</u>. Passing a drive to a house over to your left, the **road bends right** but you **continue ahead over a stile. Bear left** across a field **to a stile** in a crossing hedge/fence and **bear right** across a second field to the far right corner. Emerge over a stile onto a minor road by Cae-Higgin farm ("H").

Clyro and the Rev. Francis Kilvert.
The Rev'd Francis Kilvert was Curate of Clyro from 1865 - 1872 and later returned to take up livings in the borders. From 1870 onwards he kept a remarkable diary in which he describes his ministry. A keen walker, he travelled all around the area and evidently thought nothing of a round walk of 20 miles. The enormous value of his diaries derives from his warm narrative description of the lives of the people he met and of country life. Some of his diaries were published in 1938-40 but disaster struck when 19 of his 22 notebooks were destroyed by a lady to whom his papers had passed.

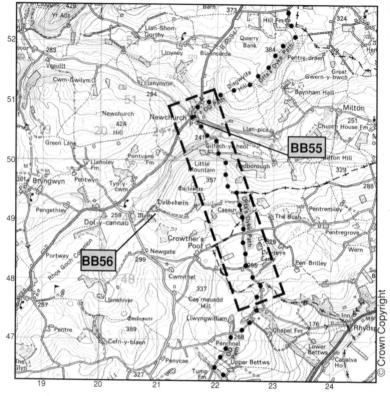

Newchurch (01544)
No facs.
BB55 - Great House
Tel. 370257
Easter - Oct Band 1 (2F)
EM. Dogs. Pk'dL. Veg. Trans. LTPk'g.
Bags.

BB56 - Dolbedwyn
Tel. (01497) 851202 TB 2 Crown
HComm Jan-Dec (exc Xmas/NY)
Band 3 (2D,1T)(1PB)
EM. Dogs. Non-Smk'g. Pk'dL. Veg.
Trans. LTPk'g. Bags.
*Grade II listed Tudor farmhouse
offering comfortable and elegant
accommodation. The imaginative menu
features home-grown and local meat &
produce.*

*Kilvert and Newchurch. It was here that the Rev Francis Kilvert visited
David and Margaret Vaughan, the local clergyman and his family.
Kilvert records how "Emeline's grave was dressed with white flowers.
How short a time it seems since, on happier harvest festival's, I saw the
lovely fair-haired child come smiling out of the porch of the little church
and walk down the churchyard path to the gate beside which her grave
now grows green". A poignant reminder of the mortality rate amongst
children at that time; the clergyman evidently lost 2 sons and 2 daughters.*

Continued on next LMap.

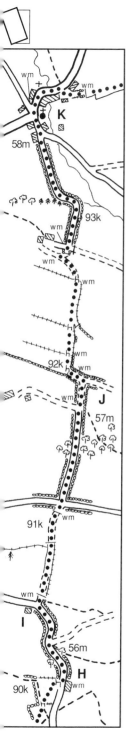

Cae Higgin Farm - Newchurch

"H" - **Cae Higgin Farm**. **Turn left** and follow the road . The road bends left for the third time, just before "Pen-y-van" (the house, not the 886m (2906ft) mountain (the highest in S.Wales)).

Langton's Guides nominates Pen-twyn Farm for the "Prettiest sign award", if there is such a thing.

"I" - **Pen-y-van**. **Just before the house, turn right,** through a metal gate and **along a green lane**. At a **Minor public road go straight across**, the road becomes a track up to a T-junction.

"J" - **T-junction of tracks**. **Turn left to the end of the lane, over a stile and bear right** to follow the fence on your right. **Continue over 3 stiles**, now on a track, **bear left** towards the buildings of Gilfach-yr-heol but **before a gate, turn sharp right and then left** to a green lane down to the road. **Continue** along the road to Newchurch ("K").

Newchurch. What is so attractive about the church is not the building itself (which is very plain), but the information in it that someone has painstakingly provided to tell you about the people who lived in the Parish.

Don't miss the picture of the 1,100 year-old yew tree which was blown down in 1990, or the epitaphs to be found in the graveyard, eg. "He fought the good fight and lost".

It may be a poor church (I hear they asked for the electricity to be disconnected because they can't afford it, or perhaps it was because they don't need it, which is subtly different) but it has a richness that isn't present in many churches that are more materially affluent.

Remember young Emeline on the way out.

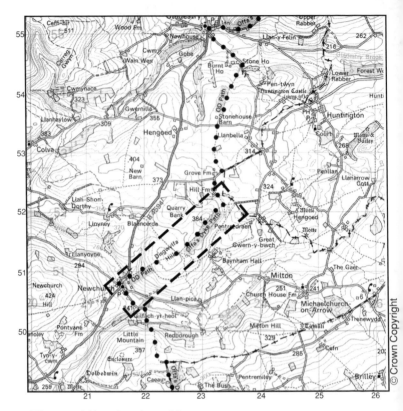

Kilvert and Newchurch cont'd.

In another entry, dated October 4th 1871, Kilvert recalls preaching at Newchurch. On finding that he had been misinformed as to the height of the pulpit, he had to lie on his side and stick a leg out in order that he could read his sermon notes. Was it the sermon or his antics in the pulpit that resulted in a record collection that Sunday?

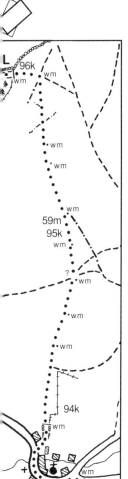

Newchurch - Hill Farm

"K" - **Newchurch Church**. Pass the Church and **bear right** along the B4594. **Cross the river and bear right to cross the yard of the former Oak Inn**. Passing the house, just on your left, **follow a green lane up the hill**, through a gate and into open pasture. **Continue** up the hill with a fence on your right. It turns right away from you but you continue over the first summit and just to the right of the second. *The crossing of paths between the two summits is indistinct on the ground but there are waymarks. Just keep going straight.*

Descending off hill 384m, a path crosses from sharp left. Then you come to a fork in the path where you **take the right fork to** descend to a waymark and **a convergence of paths** (not all marked on the map). **Bear left** to a stand of firs and a gateway to the lane leading to Hill Farm ("L").

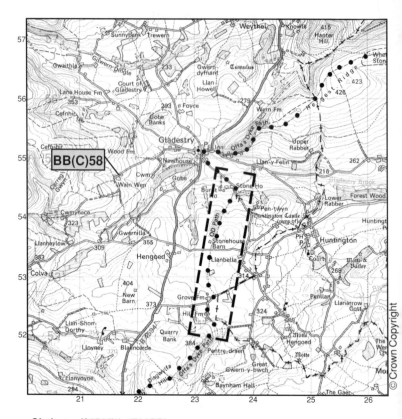

Gladestry (01544) (+1IN,2BB)
Telephone (on Path)
PH - Royal Oak (does food &
accommodation/camping)
M-Sa 1200-1400hrs & 1800-2300hrs.
Su 1200-1500hrs & 1900-2230hrs.
PO/Stores
M-Sa 0900-1730hrs (ecWSa)
<u>Buses</u>. Schooldays - am - Kington-
Gladestry-Presteigne-Kington. pm -
Kington-Presteigne-Gladestry-Kington
(Sargeant Bros Kington Tel.(01544)
230481)
Tu only - Shopper - am Kington-
Gladestry-Kington, pm return.
(Sargeant Bros)
BB(C)58 - <u>Wain Wen</u>
Tel. 370226
Easter- Oct Band 1 (2S,1D,2T,1F)
EM. Pk'dL. Trans. LTPk'g. Bags.

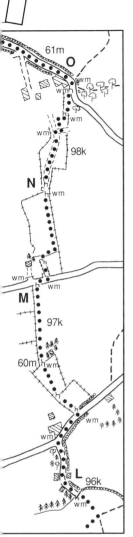

Hill Farm - Stonehouse Farm

Hill Farm. A tap has been thoughtfully made available to walkers at Hill Farm and in the hot summer of 1995, its cool fresh tasting water was most welcome. Note that this generous gesture isn't an invitation to stay for lunch!

"L" - **Hill Farm**. Follow the lane past Hill Farm and **down its access road. Turn right** along the public road, past Grove Farm for one field, to **turn left over a stile** in the hedge on your left. Bear slightly left away from the stile (ignore the path crossing the field). **Follow the field edge (fence left) to a stile** in the corner of the field. **Bear slightly right to cross the field to a stile** in the opposite fenceline. **Continue** with a fence on your left to emerge over a stile onto the road opposite the entrance to "Fairfields".

The Path used to go down the drive of Fairfields (formerly Stonehouse Barn) but it has been diverted. Just as well for it can hardly be said to welcome uninvited visitors!

"M" - **"Fairfields"**. **Turn right** along the road for approx **50m** and **turn left over a stile** and along a lane running between close fences. **Continue through a gateway into a field** and **turn right to follow the edge of the field** to a stile in the far right-hand corner. **Over the stile** to a modern silage clamp.

"N" - **Silage Clamp**. Passing the clamp on your left, **cross a stile ahead** and **follow a farm track** across an open field. As a gully appears on your right, **turn right at a junction with another track and almost immediately turn left** on a path to walk with the gully immediately on your right. The Path turns right to descend steeply to **cross the gully and bear left** (either over a stile or use the hand gate!). Cross an area of rough pasture (aiming for a barn ahead) and then turn right over a stile to emerge onto a public road by Stonehouse Farm.

"O" - **Stonehouse Farm**. **Turn left and follow the road** to emerge opposite the Church.

The road to Gladestry becomes narrow with high hedges. Beware landrovers towing trailers, there's one driver living nearby that doesn't leave any margin for error!

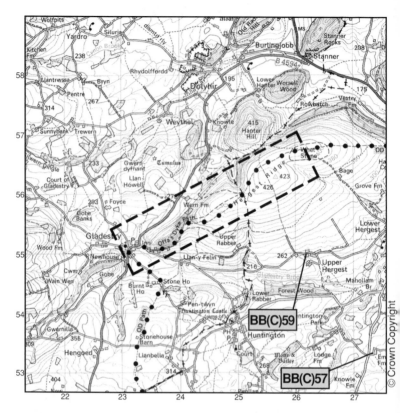

BB(C)57 - Empton Farm
Tel. 230153
Easter - Sep Band 1 (2D)
Pk'dL. Trans. LTPk'g. Bags.

BB(C)59 - Bucks Head House
Tel. (01544) 231063
Jan - Dec Band 1 (1S,1D,1T,1F)
EM. Dogs. Pk'dL. Veg. Trans. LTPk'g.

Hergest Croft Gardens

On its way into Kington the Path passes the Hergest Croft Gardens, a remarkable garden that was started in 1867 with the planting of a Greek Fir and subsequently developed into a collection of plants from all over the world. Apart from its collection of rhododendrons, the visitor can see - magnolias (May), azaleas (May/June), lilies/roses/hydrangeas (July/ August). Autumn is the best time to see the National Collection of birches and maples.

So there you have it! If you've enjoyed the magnificent views from the Hergest Ridge and still have time to spare before over-nighting in Kington, Hergest Croft Gardens offers plant-lovers an extra treat (and there's a tearoom).

Open mid-Apr - end-Oct (1330-1830hrs) Tel. (01544) 230160

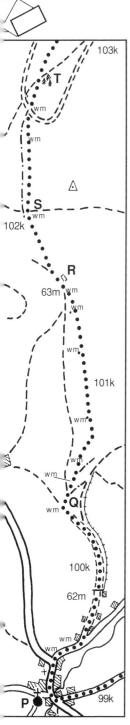

Gladestry Church - Hergest Ridge

St.Mary's Church. Founded following King Harold's successful campaign against the Welsh in the 11thC.

Note the memorial to Captain Basil Bickerton Evans who survived campaigns at Gallipoli (where he was wounded), Flanders and Salonica, only to die (aged 26) at the very end of the Great War. In recognition of his distinguished service with the British Military Mission in the Balkans, he was awarded the Chevalier of the Order of George I by the King of Greece and was buried with full military honours in Karagach Cemetery at Adrianople by the French Garrison.

"P" - **St.Mary's Church**. **Bear right along the B4594**. Past the Royal Oak Inn, **Bear right along a minor road and then bear left up a "No through road"** by "Broken Bank Cottage". Follow the road as it goes up the hill, through a gate and becomes a track then a green swathe. **On the Hergest Ridge, bear right** to continue **up the ridge** and as you round a low mound, the path divides in three.

"Q" - **Path divides in three**. **Take the centre path** and **then the left fork** as the path divides again. You are aiming to pass just to the right of the first summit and then to pass to the left of hill 423m. Having crossed the first summit, the Path bears left to pass the top of a steep cwm on your left. Other Paths join from sharp left and you pass the concrete base of a former building on your right.

"R" - **Concrete Base**. **Continue** to a four-fingered waypost which marks the crossing of footpaths.

"S" - **Crossing of Footpaths**. **Continue** on the main swathe and don't be tempted onto lesser paths. The course of the former racetrack crosses, continue to a stand of trees.

The Whetstone. A large glacial boulder deposited after the last ice-age and with various local legends attributed to it (probably best avoided at mid-day on the first Tuesday after Michaelmas). If you must visit it, turn left instead of going straight on and rejoin the Path at "T".

"T" - **Stand of Monkey Puzzle Trees**. **Continue**, passing the trees on your right.

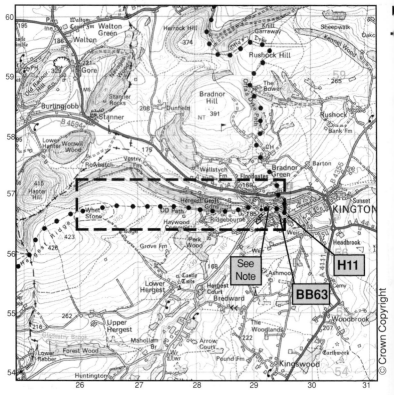

Kington (01544) (+1H,2BB,1C)
Note Dunfield House - next LMap.
Except H11/BB63, all accommodation
is located along Church St.

H10 - Swan Hotel
Tel. 230510
Jan-Dec (exc Xmas) Band 2
(1S,2D,1T,1F)
EM. Dogs. Lic'd. Pk'dL. Veg. Trans.
LTPk'g. Bags.

H11 - Burton Hotel
Tel. 230323 TB 4 Crown App
Jan-Dec (exc NY) Band 4
(1S,5D,4T,5F)(15PB)
Visa. M'Card. Amex. Diners.
EM. Dogs. Lic'd. Pk'dL. Veg. LTPk'g.
Bags.

IN(C)8 - Royal Oak Inn
Tel. 230484
Jan-Dec Band 2 (1S,1D,1T,1F)
EM. Lic'd. Pk'dL. Veg. Trans. LTPk'g.
Bags.

BB(C)60 - Cambridge Cottage
Tel. 231300
Jan-Nov Band 1 (1S,1F)
Dogs. Non-Smk'g. Pk'dL. Veg. Trans.
LTPk'g. Bags.

BB61 - The Benchmark
Tel. 230298
Jan-Dec (exc Xmas) Band 1
(1S,1D,1T)
Dogs. Non-Smk'g. Lic'd. Veg.

BB62 - Ardwyn
Tel. 231103
Jan-Dec Band 1 (1D,1T)
Dogs. Non-Smk'g. Pk'dL. Veg. Bags.

BB63 - Church House
Tel. 230534
Jan-Dec Band 2 (1D,1T)
Dogs. Pk'dL. Bags.

Campsite
Fleece Meadow (GR295564)
Tel. 230278 Apr-Oct

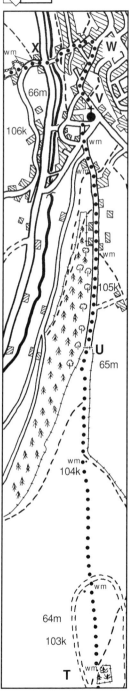

Hergest Ridge - Kington

Continuing from the stand of monkey-puzzle trees, cross the course of the former racetrack again and **continue** as you are funnelled towards a gate by a wood to your left and a field boundary to your right.

"U" - **Gateway onto Old Racetrack**. **Continue** down the road to emerge opposite, and cross to, the Church of St. Mary.

"V" - **Church of St. Mary**. **Continue through the grounds** of the Church to emerge onto Church Road. Continue **down Church Street** to the War Memorial on your left.

"W" - **War Memorial**. **Turn left** into Morris Square and pass the memorial on your right. At the end of the square **turn left again into Common Close.** Noting, but ignoring, the footpath to your right, continue along the Close **and at its end, turn right** to follow Crooked Well Lane to the bottom of the hill and a footbridge over a tributary of the River Arrow. *Grab the Children! There's even a barrier at the busy A44 to halt the rush of walkers eager to climb the hill and renew their acquaintanceship with the Offa's Dyke after all those miles of separation.*

"X" - **Footbridge**. **Cross** the brook, and the A44 beyond. **Follow the road opposite as it climbs the hill**. As the roads bends left, **turn right through a metal handgate** to cross a field to a gate immediately to the right of "Rhue Ville".

Kington (01544)
Banks - Barclays (ATM), Midland.
Taxis - No taxis
Buses -
M-Sa - Regular to Hereford.
Th - Shopper to Hay-on-Wye.
TuSa & schooldays - VLimited to New Radnor/
Llandrindod Wells.
TuFSa - VLimited to Leominster.
See Gladestry for schools service.
Sargeant Bros Depot in Kington (nr Campsite).

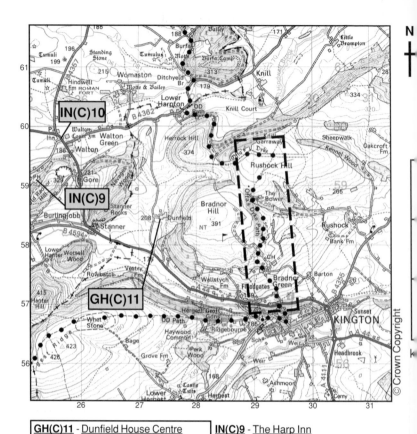

GH(C)11 - <u>Dunfield House Centre</u> Tel. 230563 Jan-Dec Band 1 (6T,20F) (3PB) EM. Non-Smk'g. Pk'dL. Veg. Trans. LTPk'g. Bags. *Set in beautiful Welsh border-country.* *Good home cooking, indoor heated* *swimming pool, recreation hall. Caters for* *individuals and groups up to a maximum* *of 100.*	**IN(C)9** - <u>The Harp Inn</u> Tel. 350655 Good Pub Guide Jan-Dec Band 2 (1S,2D,1T) EM. Dogs. Lic'd. Pk'dL. Veg. Trans. LTPk'g. Bags. **IN(C)10** - <u>The Crown Inn</u> Tel. 350663 Jan-Dec Band 2 (1S,1D,1T,2F) (5PB) EM. Dogs. Llc'd. Pk'dL. Veg. Trans. LTPk'g. Bags.

<u>Offa's Dyke on Rushock Hill.</u> The odd right-angled bend on Rushock Hill is one of the anomalies in the line of the Dyke. The route over the summit of Rushock Hill appears to be an obvious deviation from the best tactical route, although the Dyke either side has a clear enough view for such an apparent lapse to be inconsequential. Fox thought that it was a specific point agreed by treaty whilst others thought it was a case of construction gangs missing each other and having to make a last minute adjustment. Noble pointed to the possibility that the corner incorporated a "marking-out dyke" to point the line south-east over the Hereford Plain.

106

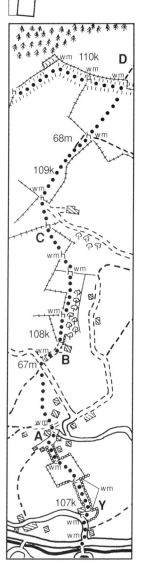

Rhue Ville - Rushock Hill

"Y" - **Rhue Ville**. **Through the gate** on the right of the house to take a green lane. **Continue** through a kissing gate and across a field to a second kissing gate. Pause to look back over Kington, before continuing along the twitchel beyond. **Emerging** through a third gate **onto a driveway**, **bear right** up the drive to a crossing track.

"A" - **Crossing track at Bradnor Green**. Cross and **bear left, up the hill** aiming to pass to the left of the property ahead. Continue to a National Trust sign warning of golfers. **Cross the fairway** of the golf course, over a road to a cattle-grid in the access road to Quarry House. *Take care, Local Rule 5 (suspended for male golfers) probably concerns the state of play if a ball hits a walker!*

"B" - **Access to Quarry House**. Ignore the OS map, and **take the access road**. **Bear left** to pass through a gate. **Bear left across a field to a stile (1st)** in the far right-hand corner. **Continue**, with a fence left and wood right, to a stile (2nd) in a crossing fence ahead. Straight away from the stile **to a stile (3rd)** in the fenceline to your left and **then bear right** to a stile (4th) at the junction of 3 fences.

"C" - **Stile at the junction of 3 fences**. With the buildings of The Bower over to your right, **continue**, contouring round the hill, **to a stile in the corner of the field**. **Straight away from the stile, up the hill** to intercept a fence coming from sharp right. Continue with the fence on your right, ignoring any suggestion on OS maps that you bear left away from it. The fence on your right, turns right but you continue, now bearing slightly left, to the Offa's Dyke ahead.

"D" - **Offa's Dyke on Rushock Hill**. At the Dyke, **turn left and follow the Dyke** to the corner by Fir Trees, where you turn left.

Kington. The name records the fact that it was claimed for King Edward the Confessor after a campaign to drive out the Welsh in the 11thC. Town became established in 13thC, which is when the Church of St.Mary was built. Note in the church the 15thC tomb of Thomas and Ellen Vaughan. As a girl she was famous for an incident at an archery tournament when she "missed" the target and put an arrow through the heart of her brother's murderer!

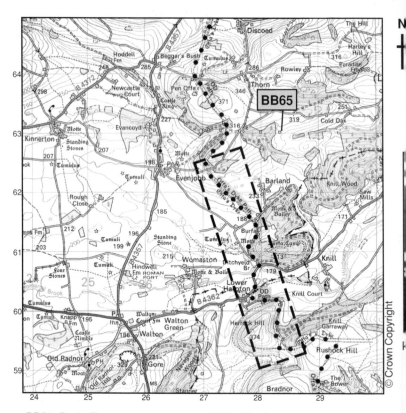

© Crown Copyright

BB64 - Bache Farm
Tel. (01544) 350680 TB 2 Crown
Jan-Dec (exc Xmas) Band 1 (2T)(1PB)
EM. Dogs. Non-Smk'g. Pk'dL. Trans.
LTPk'g. Bags.
Located at GR 226627 (1km west of
LMap)

BB65 - The Barn
Tel. (01547) 560402
Jan-Dec Band 2 (2D,1T)
EM. Dogs. Non-Smk'g. Pk'dL. Trans.
LTPk'g. Bags.
Lower Harpton - No facs
Evenjobb - PO only

Offa's Dyke on Herrock Hill. The Dyke rounds Herrock Hill before making
its steepest descent, of its entire length, down the northern flank to
cross the Hindwell Valley. Mr Noble noted that those working up and
round the hill from the North must have been unsighted from those coming
from the South and East; for there is a error in horizontal alignment that
necessitated a 6m vertical join on the side of the hill. The course of the
Dyke round Herrock Hill was seen as lending weight to the notion of a
defensive dyke. A simple boundary marker would have been more likely
to follow the route of the National Trail rather than enclose a hill of no
agricultural value.

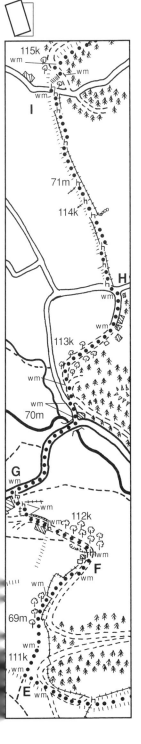

Rushock Hill - Evenjobb Hill

Having turned left on top of Rushock Hill, **follow the Dyke** as it gently descends to a stile in a crossing fence. Continue and **join a track** up from the left as the decent steepens. A track joins from sharp left and shortly after you **bear left to stay with the Dyke** until you reach the saddle mid-way between the two hills.

"E" - **Saddle between Herrock Hill and Rushock Hill**. Although a path appears to follow the Dyke round Herrock hill, the public right of way requires that you **turn right across the saddle and head North**. **Bear left to descend on a path** through the ferns. Pass through a gate and continue to descend. Join a track and pass the barns of "Herrock Cottage" to the gateway beyond.

"F" - **Gateway beyond Herrock Cottage Barns**. **Follow the track** as it bends left. As you cross a stile at a gateway ahead, look left to spot the Dyke descending to you. Continue past barns and a house. Just as a **Track splits off left into a field, turn right** through a gateway and bear left across the field to a stile in the far corner. Join a farm road to the B4326.

"G" - **B4326**. **Turn right** to follow the road. Cross the **Hindwell Brook** and **turn left** along a minor public road. **In 250m, turn right and then left to join a forestry track**. As the **Track bends right, continue on a green lane** eventually to pass, on your right, the medieval Burfa Farmhouse. Continue to a T-Junction with another minor road.

"H" - **T-junction**. **Turn left and in 50m, turn right**, over a stile and up **onto the Dyke** again. Parallel a fence along the Dyke, changing sides 4 times, finally to emerge at a minor public road. *The views to the West are excellent but don't forget to look back at Herrock Hill. From a distance it is much easier to make out the line of the Dyke.*

"I" - **Minor road over Evenjobb Hill**. **Turn left, then right**, over a stile and **Up** two flights of steps to emerge **onto a forestry track**. **Turn left** along the track and **in 10m turn right** to take a path through the coniferous trees.

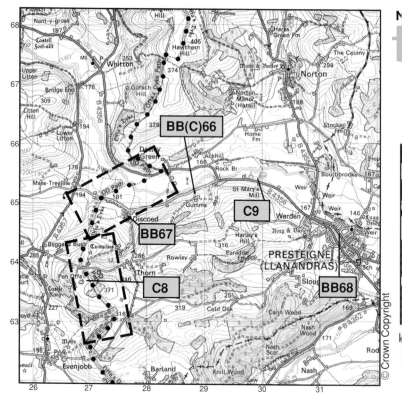

Discoed (01547) (+1BB)

No facs.

BB(C)66 - <u>Gumma Farm</u>

Tel. 560243 TB Listed

Apr-Oct Band 1 (1S,1D,1T)

EM. Dogs. Pk'dL. Veg. Trans. LTPk'g.
Bags.

BB67 - <u>Woodwinds</u>

Tel. 560302 TB Listed Comm

Jan-Nov Band 1 (1D,2T)(1PB)

EM. Dogs. Pk'dL. Veg. Trans. LTPk'g.
Bags.

C8 - <u>Penoffa Farm</u>

Tel. 560237

Jan-Dec Dogs. Toilet. Showers (Hot
water most of year!) No shop (it's a
farm!) but will try to get anything if
notified in advance.

Presteigne (01544) (+2H,2BB)

<u>Banks</u> - Lloyds, Midland.

<u>Taxis</u> - None

<u>Buses</u> -

M-F - VLimited to Knighton.

MWThFSa - VLimited to Leominster

TuThF & Schooldays - VLimited to
Knighton

BB68 - <u>The Cabin Restaurant</u>

Tel. 267068

Jan-Dec Band 1 (2T)

EM. Dogs. Lic'd. Pk'dL. Veg. Trans.

C9 - **<u>Rockbridge Park</u>**

Tel. 560300

Apr-Oct (30 pitches) Toilets. Showers.
Wash/Dry facs. Shop.

Evenjobb Hill - Dolley Green

Walking on a bed of pine needles, in the shade and scent of the trees ....

Continue along the Path through "Granner Wood" to emerge over a stile near the end of a steep cwm. The Path bears left to **join a track** at the head of the cwm. Pass an old quarry, on your right, to a corrugated iron barn.

"J" - **Corrugated Iron Barn**. **Bear right** before the barn, **up the steep bank** to a stile in a crossing fence. **Continue along the Dyke**, through the aptly-named "Hilltop Plantation", and descend along the Dyke to a stile with Pen Offa Farm over on your left. Continue on the Dyke, to emerge over a stile onto a minor public road.

"Pen Offa". *I recall once having to wait at the stile by Pen Offa. A large beef-bull had placed itself in front the stile and stubbornly refused to budge. Eventually the reason for the wait became clear. A calf and its mother slowly plodded up the field and together the three of them made their way over to the rest of the herd. It was quite touching and a reminder to always exercise caution when dealing with livestock. In case you can't remember the rule; beef-bull on its own - bad news, beef-bull and cows - OK, just don't make any advances to the cows; dairy-bull - bad news any time.*

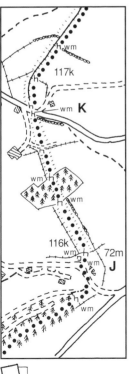

"K" - **Minor Road near "Pen Offa"**. **Straight across** the road and over a stile, then jink right and left **to put the Dyke on your left**. Continue with the Dyke, over 6 more stiles, until you emerge onto another minor public road.

"L" - **Minor Road**. **Turn right then shortly bear left to cross a stile** set at 45-degrees by a gateway. Straight away from the stile and, with ditch/hedge on your right, **continue to the River Lugg** where you walk along its bank for a short distance before crossing **over "Dolley Old Bridge"** (footbridge). Continue along the field edge, hedge right, to pass through a gateway and emerge onto the B4356 by Dolley Green.

"M" - **B4356**. **Continue**, along the road **for 200m and turn sharp left** to follow a lane up the hill. Pass through a gateway just before a coniferous plantation to your left ("N").

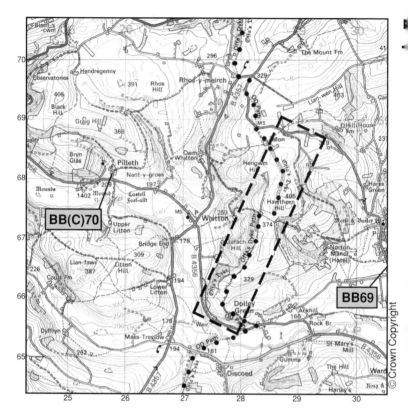

Norton (01544) (+1BB)
Telephone. PO/Shop
BB69 - Wellingtonia Cottage
Tel. 260255
Jan-Dec (exc Xmas/NY) Band 1
(1S,1D,1T)(1PB)
EM. Dogs. Pk'dL. Veg. Trans. LTPk'g.
Bags.

Whitton (01547)
No facs
BB(C)70 - Pilleth Court
Tel. 560272 TB 2 Crowns HComm
Jan-Dec (exc Xmas) Band 2
(1D,1T,1F)(1PB)
EM. Pk'dL. Veg. Trans. LTPk'g. Bags.

Presteigne.
Once the county town for Radnorshire, with the assize court held in the Shire Hall (now a museum). Although it has a Welsh name, "Llanandras", in appearance it is very English with many buildings having a distinct Georgian style. The Church of St.Andrew was originally Norman but much work was carried out on it in the 15th century. The 18th century Radnorshire Arms was a coaching inn but the building itself dates from circa 1600.

112

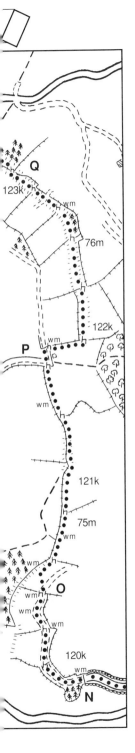

Dolley Green - Hengwm Hill

"N" - **Coniferous Plantation**. **Stay on the track** to pass the plantation on your left. With fence on your right, follow the track uphill, **over 3 stiles**.

"O" - **The 3rd Stile**. At the 3rd stile the fencing on your right ends and the track continues alone. **Over the stile and bear left to the fenceline** (and the line of the Dyke) over to your left and follow it **to cross 4 more stiles**. *Just before the 3rd stile, the Dyke bore off right aiming at the summit of Hawthorn Hill.* After the 4th stile, the fencing is on your right as you pass a ruined barn.

"P" - **Ruined Corrugated Iron Barn**. Pass the barn on your right to arrive at a gate across the path. **Turn right, over a stile** in the fence on your right and **after 250m, come to a stile** (1) in the fence on your left. **Turn left** and rejoin the Dyke *(discernible as a low mound)*. **Continue,** with a fence on your left to a stile (2). Then with a fence on your right, continue over a stile (3) **to pass a small stand of firs,** Over 2 more stiles (3 & 4) to the corner of a coniferous plantation.

"Q" - **Coniferous Plantation**. At the corner, jink right then left to **continue with the fence on your left**.

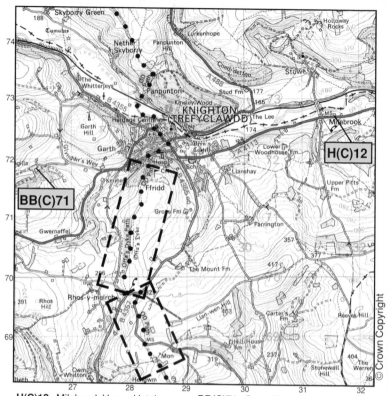

H(C)12 - Milebrook House Hotel
Tel. (01547) 528632 TB 3 Crown
HComm
Jan-Dec Band 5 (6D,4T)(10PB)
Switch. Visa. M'Card. Amex.
EM. Lic'd. Pk'dL. Veg. Trans. LTPk'g.
Bags.

BB(C)71 - Cwmgilla
Tel. (01547) 528387 TB 1 Crown
HComm
Easter-Nov Band 2 (1D,1T,1S)
Pk'dL. Trans. LTPk'g.

Knighton, or "Tref-y-Clawdd" (meaning Town on the Dyke), can trace its occupation as a settlement right back to the Stone Age. The remains of castles all along this stretch of the Teme Valley provide evidence of the strategic importance of a route giving access to the fertile lowlands to the East. Just to the northeast is the Iron-age fort of Caer Caradoc, reputedly the stronghold of the Celtic Prince Caractacus who resisted the Roman invasion. The Romans established the town of Branogen (Leintwardine) a little further down the valley and Offa's Dyke shielded the settlement from the Celtic strongholds to the west. The Normans built a castle or defensive position just to the east of the town, later replacing it with a stone castle, the remains of which are now hidden in the centre of the town.

Continued next page...

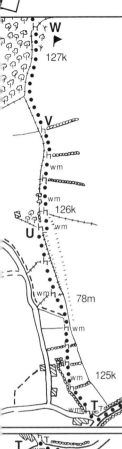

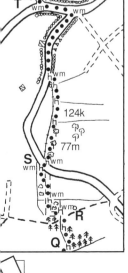

Hengwm Hill - Knighton Golf Cse.

Continuing on the edge of the plantation, cross a stile and pass a second plantation on your left. Note a monument to your right.

The monument was erected, by public subscription, to commemorate the life and work of Sir Richard Green Price 1st Baronet (b.1803 d.1887). He was the Member of Parliament for Radnor Borough (1862 -1869) and for the County of Radnor (1880 - 1885). He is credited with bringing the railway to Knighton, as well as to Presteigne and New Radnor.

"R" - **Monument**. After the second plantation, **turn left** to cross a stile. **Bear right** away from the stile, through dense gorse. Having braved the gorse, **bear right onto a track** to a stile in a crossing fence. The Path now bears left, through more gorse, into a stand of trees and **over a stile to emerge onto the B4355**. Cross the road to a stile and an "Offa's Dyke" stone.

The stone was erected in the 19th C. Whilst we don't actually know when the Dyke was constructed, AD757 would have been the first year of Offa's reign!

"S" - **"Offa's Dyke" Stone**. **Follow the Dyke** over 4 more stiles to rejoin the B4355. **Bear right along the road.** At the **Crossroads, turn left** to a telephone box along on your right.

"T" - **Telephone Box (& Postbox)**. **Pass the box and turn right** along a minor road. As the road bends left, **bear right over a stile (1) to continue along the Dyke**, which appears to abruptly end at a stile (2). Continue across a field to a stile (3) in a crossing hedge and over more stiles (4,5,6 & 7). **Turn right, over a stile (no.8) in the fence on your right**, to bear across the Dyke.

"U" - **Crossing the Dyke**. With the **Dyke now on your left, continue** over 4 more stiles to emerge onto Knighton Golf Course.

"V" - **Knighton Golf Course**. **Keep the fence on your left**, continue round the edge of the course. A wood appears on your left **and** you start to **descend** on an indistinct path. As the **Fence bears right, turn left over a stile and bear right to continue** in Great Frydd Wood ("W").

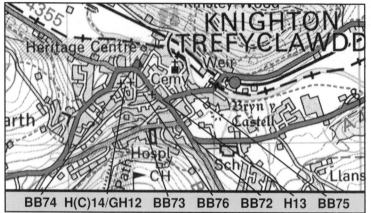

© Crown Copyright

| BB74 | H(C)14/GH12 | BB73 | BB76 | BB72 | H13 | BB75 |

Knighton (01547)

H13 - The Knighton Hotel
Tel. 520530 TB 4 Crown
Jan-Dec Band 4 (3S,7D,5T)(15PB)
All cards. EM. Dogs. Lic'd. Pk'dL. Veg.
Trans. LTPk'g. Bags.

H(C)14 - Plough Hotel
Tel. 528041
Jan-Dec Band 1/2 (1D,3T) (2PB)
EM. Dogs. Lic'd. Pk'dL. Veg. Trans.
Bags.

GH12 - The Fleece House
Tel. 520168 TB 2 Crown Comm
Jan-Dec Band 2/4 (6D)(2PB)
Lic'd. Pk'dL.

BB72 - Old Mansion House
Tel. 528248
Jan-Dec Band 1 (2D,1T,1F)
Pk'dL. Veg. LTPk'g.

BB73 - Larkey Lodge
Tel. 529011
Jan-Dec Band 1 (1S,1D,1T)
Non-Smk'g. Veg. Trans. LTPk'g. Bags.

BB74 - Wesley House
Tel. 520296
Apr-Oct Band 1 (1S,1D)
Non-Smk'g. Pk'dL. LTPk'g.

BB75 - Willow Cottage
Tel. 528060
Jan-Dec Band 1 (1S,1D,1T)
Dogs. Pk'dL. Trans. LTPk'g. Bags.

BB76 - The Lanterns
Tel. 528922
Jan-Dec Band 1 (2T)
EM. Dogs. Non-Smk'g. Pk'dL. Veg.
LTPk'g.

Campsite - See Panpunton Farm -
next LMap.
YHA
The YH in Knighton is closed! Contact
01222 222122 for details of nearest
alternative Hostel Accommodation.
LGNote. Nearest appears to be Clun
Mill, nr Craven Arms.

Facilities
Banks - Barclays (ATM), Midland
(ATM).
Laundrette (Church St.) - Does service
washes.
Taxis - Owen's - 528303. Knighton
Taxis - 528165 & 520274
Rail - See Section 2
Buses - M-Sa - Limited to Ludlow.
TuTh - VLimited to Craven Arms &
Newtown. Th - local villages shopper
(for market).

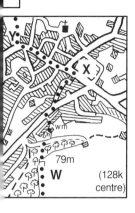

79m

W (128k centre)

Knighton

"W" - **Great Frydd Wood**. **Descend** through the wood to emerge **onto** the tarmac **drive to the Golf Club**.

Those going South must avoid being diverted onto another path when they reach the golf club drive. It's the steep one to the left, not the gentler path to the right.

Straight across to descend between fences and over a stile to emerge on the driveway of "Kedenide". **Turn right** to pass garages on your right **and then turn left** down "Frydd Terrace 31-42". Jink right and left **to cross the public road**. **Turn right and then bear left down Larkey Lane** to cross a car park and pass through the archway of the "Norton Arms" onto the A4113.

"X" - **A4113 (Norton Arms)**. **Turn left**, passing the clock tower on your left, **and follow the road**. Pass the former Primary School (and former Youth Hostel) to the Offa's Dyke Association's Centre ("Y").

Continued... Knighton has had a turbulent history and was wiped out by the Welsh in the 11th century. Later re-occupied, it was burnt down in the 13th century and again was attacked in the early 15th century by Owain Glyndwr. A market town since 1230, there is still a market every Thursday.

Offa's Dyke Centre. Alas, the former Primary School is crumbling and the Youth Hostel has already closed. The Offa's Dyke Association is clinging on but will have to vacate the building sooner or later. They have hopes of a new Centre in the grounds but need money to achieve their dream. The Association played a key role in establishing the National Trail and now that you have walked some of the Dyke, perhaps it has worked some of its magic on you. If the Centre's still there when you pass, why not call in and join the Association, better still, leave a donation; even better still, offer to build them a new centre (what do you mean - lottery winner's don't walk National Trails!).

There's another good reason for visiting the Centre (if it's there): it houses an exhibition about the Dyke and has an audio-visual presentation. You will recognise the hard work of Frank Noble MBE in the displays; don't forget the study of the Dyke is on-going and the findings of the Manchester University team have yet to feature much in the literature and exhibitions concerning the Dyke.

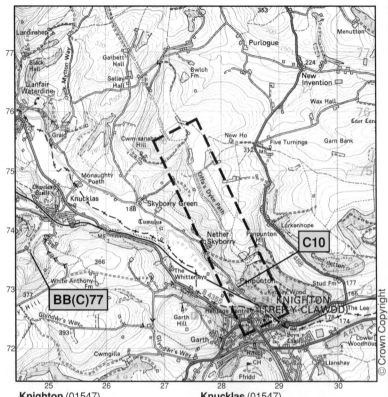

Knighton (01547)

C10 - <u>Panpunton Farm</u>
Tel. 528597
Jan-Dec (20 pitches) Toilets. Showers.
Dogs.

Knucklas (01547)

BB(C)77 - <u>Lower Dolwilkin Farm</u>
Tel. 528249
Easter-Sep Band 1 (2D/F)
EM. Dogs. Non-Smk'g. Pk'dL. Veg.
Trans. LTPk'g. Bags.

<u>*Offa's Dyke Commemorative Stone.*</u>

A section of Dyke runs through the Park near to the Offa's Dyke Centre. On 10 July 1971 it was the scene of the official opening of the Offa's Dyke Path National Trail. Lord Hunt of Llanfair Waterdine KG (famous for his successful expedition to Everest in 1953) was invited by the Chairman of the Countryside Commission to unveil a memorial plaque set in a 3-ton monolith that had been erected by volunteers to mark the occasion. He then led an inaugural walk over Panpunton.

<u>*Memorial Seat to Frank Noble MBE 1926-1980 (Point"A")*</u>

Note the seat erected in memory of Frank Noble. His contribution to our understanding of the Dyke is described in Section One. If Fox provided a base from which to expand our knowledge of the physical Dyke, Noble studied its impact on the surrounding communities and tried to place it in context. Above all, it was his determination that culminated in the creation of the Offa's Dyke Path.

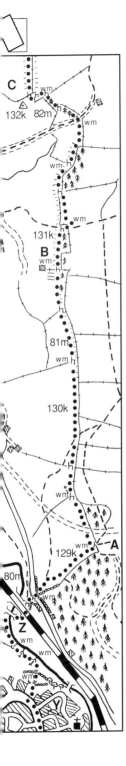

Knighton - Cwm Sanaham Hill

"Y" - **Offa's Dyke Centre** (Park with Children's Play Area). **Turn right down steps** to pass the (former) Centre on your right. **Bear left across the park** to a crossing line of trees. *You may wish to turn left and divert to visit the stone that commemorates the opening of the National Trail.*

Descend the bank via steps and cross to more steps in the opposite hedgeline. **Turn left to follow the riverbank** through 3 kissing gates to a footbridge.

"Z" - **Footbridge across River**. **Cross the river and turn left** to cross the railway (with care!). **Continue over a stile**, with the river on your left and a hedge on your right. The hedge turns right, **bear right to a stile**. Cross a minor public road to the left-hand of two gates opposite and **ascend the hill**, keeping the wood just on your right, to arrive at a crossing fenceline.

"A" - **Crossing Fenceline**. **Turn left in front of a stile** to join the Dyke. Over a crossing track and a stile, to pass on your left a memorial seat and stone. **With the fenceline on your right, continue** over 3 crossing fences. The fenceline bears off right and you continue to emerge over a 4th stile by some farm buildings over on your left.

"B" - **Farm buildings.** **Continue to a crossing track** where you **turn right** to cross the Dyke. Pass **through a gateway, turn sharp left to rejoin the Dyke** and follow it to a wood where you cross the fenceline to put the wood on your right. Continue to the **Head of a cwm** and a crossing track. Continue and **bear slightly right up through a shelterbelt of firs**, over a stile and up to a stile in a crossing fenceline. **Bear left to cross the fence a second time (!)** and continue towards the Triangulation Point on Cwm Sanaham Hill.

"C" - **Trig Point on Cwm Sanaham Hill** (serial no.S5645). **Before the trig point, turn right** over a stile in the fence on your right. Continue along the Dyke with a fence on your right.

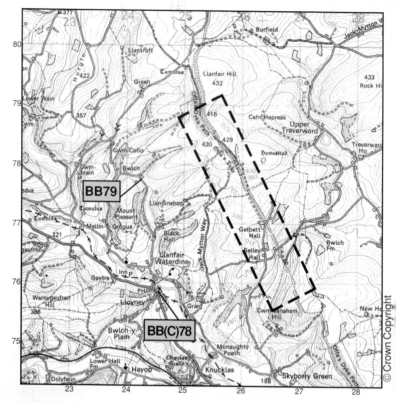

Knucklas
PH - Castle Inn. PO/Stores. Telephone
Lloyney (01547) (+1BB)
Telephone. PH - Lloyney Inn
BB(C)78 - The Mill
Tel. 528049
Jan-Dec (exc Xmas) Band 1
(1D,2T,1F)(4PB)
EM. Dogs. Non-Smk'g. Pk'dL. Veg.
Trans. LTPk'g. Bags.

BB79 - Cwm Cole
Tel.520357
Jan-Dec (exc Xmas/NY) Band 2
(2D,1T)
EM. Dogs. Pk'dL. Veg. Trans. LTPk'g.
Bags.

Offa's Dyke - Garbett Hall

The stretch of Dyke just North of Garbett Hall demonstrates the need for caution in drawing conclusions from the appearance of the Dyke today. Note the gap in the bank of the Dyke approximately level with the first crossing fence. The loose stones and the logs across the track are the clues. In heavy rain the water running off the hill is channelled by the Dyke and logs will have been put there to divert the water through the gap and down another valley. Just one example of later modification to the Dyke.

120

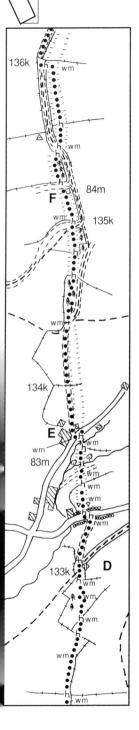

Cwm Sanaham Hill - Llanfair Hill

Continue from Cwm Sanaham Hill, over a crossing fence and as the **fence bends right, bear right** to a stile in a crossing fence. **Cut the corner of a field** to another stile **and descend steeply** to "Brynorgan" cottage.

"D" - **"Brynorgan Cottage"**. **Pass** through the sheep fold **immediately to the left of the cottage** and continue along <u>an</u> access track. **Minor public road, turn left and in 20m, turn right** over a stile **to climb** a steep bank **and rejoin the Dyke**. Follow the Dyke downhill to cross a track and enter a dingle. **Cross a footbridge and continue to another footbridge**, after which you emerge over a stile onto the road by Garbett Hall.

"E" - **Garbett Hall**. **Turn left along the road and then right into a gateway** to pass between the farmhouse and a barn. **Bear right to rejoin** the ditch of the Dyke or stay on the track. Follow **the Dyke uphill** through two gates. The Path continues on top of the Dyke, crossing 3 stiles to pass a lonely barn on your right.

"F" - **Lonely Barn**. **Continue** with the Dyke over a further stile and then cross a track to continue. Over on your left is a triangulation point which, at 430m, marks the highest point <u>on the Dyke</u>. Continue over a stile **until you are turned left in front of a crossing fence**. Now join the track that has been paralleling you on your left.

Tales of Offa. A manuscript in the monastery of St.Albans recorded that Offa was born lame, deaf and blind. Driven by Beornred into hiding, a miracle restored his powers and he slew Beornred thus taking the crown of Mercia.

Actually the story is a corruption of one relating to another Offa, a 4th century hero of the early Angli. On hearing that his father's kingdom was to be seized by the Saxons, Offa undertook to fight the Saxon King's son and his champion at the same time. The fight took place at Rendsburg on an island in the Eider and Offa killed both of them, thus winning a great kingdom as a result of his victory.

The story in the "Vitae duorum Offarum", somehow transferred events to England some four centuries later.

121

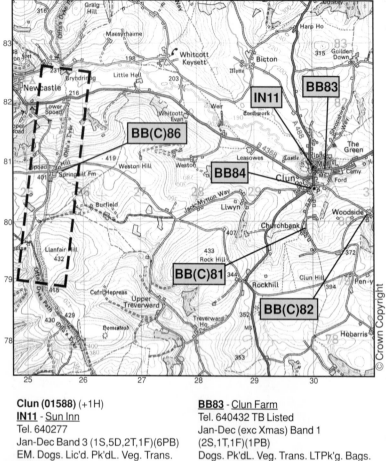

Clun (01588) (+1H)

IN11 - <u>Sun Inn</u>
Tel. 640277
Jan-Dec Band 3 (1S,5D,2T,1F)(6PB)
EM. Dogs. Lic'd. Pk'dL. Veg. Trans.
LTPk'g. Bags.

BB80 - <u>Hurst Mill Farm</u>
Tel. 640224
Jan-Dec Band 2 (1D,1T,1F)(1PB)
EM. Dogs. Pk'dL. Veg. Trans. LTPk'g.
Bags.
Not located - Grid Ref 317812

BB(C)81 - <u>Hill House Farm</u>
Tel. 640729/640325 TB Listed
Easter-Oct Band 4 (2D,1T)
Dogs. Pk'dL. Veg. LTPk'g. Bags.

BB(C)82 - <u>The Old Farmhouse</u>
Tel. 640695 TB Listed
Mar-Oct Band 1 (1D,1F)
EM. Dogs. Pk'dL. Veg. Trans. LTPk'g.
Bags.

BB83 - <u>Clun Farm</u>
Tel. 640432 TB Listed
Jan-Dec (exc Xmas) Band 1
(2S,1T,1F)(1PB)
Dogs. Pk'dL. Veg. Trans. LTPk'g. Bags.

BB84 - <u>Crown House</u>
Tel. 640780 TB 2 Crown
Jan-Dec (exc Xmas) Band 1
(1D,1T)(2PB)
Dogs. Non-Smk'g. Pk'dL. Veg. Trans.
LTPk'g. Bags.

BB(C)86 - <u>Springhill Farm</u>
Tel. 640337 TB Listed
Mar- ? Band 1 (1F,1D,1T)
Dogs. Pk'dL. Veg. Trans. LTPk'g. Bags.

YHA - <u>Clun Mill</u>
Tel. 640582
Apr7-Aug31(excW)
See Handbook for further details.

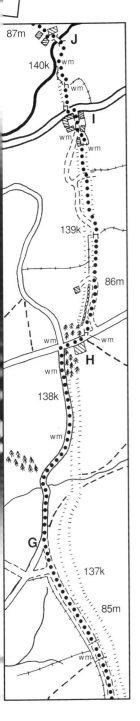

Llanfair Hill - Bryndrinog

Continue along the track and as it bends left to a minor road, continue ahead to join the road. **"G"** - **Minor Public Road**. **Continue to the crossroads**. **Turn right** to Springfield Farm.

"H" - **Springfield Farm**. **Pass** the farm on your right **and turn left**, over the stile or through the kissing gate. A track joins from sharp right and together you descend the hill. **The track bends left,** to go to "Scotland" (a house!), but you **continue with the fence on your left**. Over a stile to **Join the top of the Dyke** all the way to Lower Spoad Farm.

"I" - **Lower Spoad Farm**. Through a metal gate, and sludge, bearing left to join a track **through the farmyard.** Emerge onto the **B4368, turn left and in 20m, turn right** over a stile. Follow the bank of the Dyke to the corner of a fence where you cross a stile to continue with the fence on your left. **Adjacent to the river, bear right across a field and cross a footbridge** in front of the magnificent Bryndrinog Farmhouse "J".

Clun Facilities
No Banks. Shop sells Camping Gaz.
Buses -
M-Sa - VLimited to Ludlow & Bishops Castle
TuTh - VLimited to Knighton
Tu - Shopper - Ludlow-Clun-Newcastle-Newtown
WSa - Shopper to Shrewsbury (Sa starts Newcastle)
MTu - Shopper - Newcastle-Clun-Ludlow

Clun. The town grew up in the late 7th century although there is much evidence of major Neolithic settlement in the area. It later became part of an independent Marcher Lordship, The Barony of Clun, and a Motte & Bailey castle was built. This was replaced by the stone castle whose ruins you can see today. The castle was attacked in 1194 by Prince Rhys and burnt. It was later besieged by both Llewelyn the Great and Owain Glyndwr.
The "Hospital of the Holy and Undivided Trinity" was founded in 1614 by the Earl of Northampton as an almshouse "for 12 poor men" (now open to both sexes).

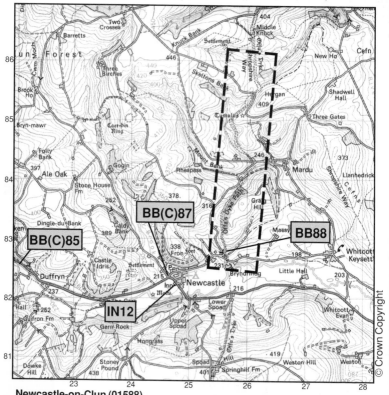

© Crown Copyright

Newcastle-on-Clun (01588)
(+1BB+1C) Telephone. PO/Shop
Buses - See Clun
IN12 - The Crown Inn
Tel. 640271
Jan-Dec Band 2 (1D,1T)(2PB)
EM. Dogs. Lic'd. Pk'dL. Veg. Trans.
LTPk'g.
BB(C)85 - Lawn Farm
Tel. 640303
Jan-Dec Band1 (2D,1F)
EM. Dogs. Pk'dL. Trans. Bags.

BB(C)87 - Newcastle Hall
Tel. 640350
Jan-Dec Band 2 (4rms)
EM. Dogs. Pk'dL. Veg. Trans. LTPk'g.
Bags.
BB88 - Quarry House
Tel. 640774 TB Listed
Jan-Dec Band 2 (2T)(2PB)
Non-Smk'g. PK'dL. Veg. LTPk'g. Bags.
Camping at "Ashgrove" nr Shop.

Church of St. John the Baptist - Mainstone. _A plain church with a magnificent Elizabethan oak ceiling, it was rebuilt in 1887. A board records the granting in perpetuity of the tithe to the Rector by "His sacred Majesty, Blessed Martyr, King Charles I, 4 December 1641, and goes on to list Parish benefactors whose generosity enabled the poor of the Parish to be given aid on various feast days during the Church Year._
Near the pulpit is a large stone that has a connection with Main-(Welsh= "stone")-stone as a trading post. Perhaps deals were struck "over the stone" or perhaps it weighed something being traded.

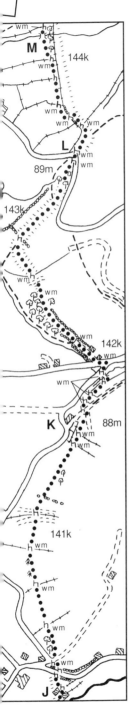

Bryndrinog - Hergan - Eaton Coppice

"J"- **Bryndrinog**. **Turn left** in front of the house and **bear right through the outbuildings.** **Turn left, over a stile** and bear left up the field to a stile. **Cross the road, over the stile opposite** and cross a field to another stile. **At a track jink right then left** to pass a water tap and **climb the hill** with the Dyke just to your left. **Follow the Dyke** over 3 stiles and just before the 4th, cross a track (noting how it has cut a section through the bank). Continue over the 4th and then 2 more stiles. Join a track coming in from sharp right to a crossing track with a stile in the hedge opposite.

"K" - **Stile by Bridge Farm**. Over the stile and **bear right** to cross 2 more stiles and then bear left over a stile in the hedge to your left. **Cross a footbridge** and up to a stile. At a **Minor public road. turn right** and at a **Road junction, turn left**. After 30m **bear right up a tarmac drive**. Pass a house on your right and continue through a gate and up a twitchel which becomes wood left and bank/bracken right. Continue across a small cwm and over a crossing fence. **Follow the Dyke** as it slowly bears right on its approach to Hergan Col. **At the road turn left and then right**, over a stile marked Hergan Col.

Hergan Col. The Dyke at Hergan Col has perplexed scholars. Fox thought that two separately constructed sections of Dyke met at this point; the one from the south being finished ahead of that from the North, thus causing the latter to divert off the best line to form a clumsy right-angle.

"L" - **Hergan Col**. Straight away from the stile and **bear left with the ditch of the Dyke**. Cross the Dyke as it bends left. **Turn left to cross a stile. Continue** with the Dyke on your left **until a stile, which you cross to put the Dyke on your right. Continue** over 3 crossing fencelines to a footbridge.

"M" - **Footbridge at Eaton's Coppice**. Cross and turn right to a stile. **Ascend the hill.**

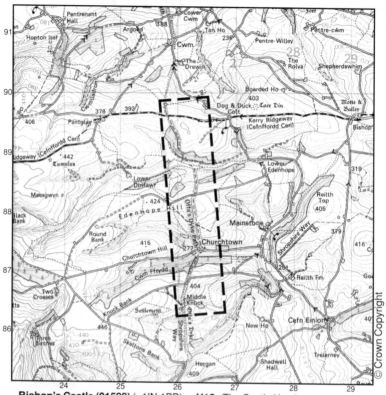

Bishop's Castle (01588) (+1IN,1BB)
Banks - Midland Bank, Barclays.
Taxi - Doug's Private Hire Tel. 638315
Buses - M-Sa - Ltd to Shrewsbury (Su
VLimited)
Shoppers - TuWSa-Shrewsbury/
MSa-Ludlow/ W-Telford & Wellington/
Tu-Newtown. Also see Clun & Knighton

H15 - Boar's Head Hotel
Tel. 638521 TB 3 Crown App
Jan-Dec Band 3 (1D,2T,1F)(4PB)
All cards. EM. Dogs. Lic'd. Pk'dL. Veg.
Trans. LTPk'g. Bags.
Traditional Coaching Inn with exposed
beams & log fire. Real ales, bar meals
& restaurant. En-suite accommodation.
Collect & Return transport available by
arrangement.

H16 - The Castle Hotel
Tel. 638403 TB 2 Crown Comm
Jan-Dec (exc Xmas) Band 2
(1S,3D,2T,1F)(2PB)
Switch. Visa. M'Card.
EM. Dogs. Lic'd. PK'dL. Veg. Trans.
LTPk'g. Bags.

GH13 - Old Brick Guest House
Tel. 638471 TB 2 Crown
Jan-Dec (exc Xmas/NY) Band 3
(2D,1T,1F)(4PB)
Visa. M'Card. EM. Dogs. Lic'd. Pk'dL.
Trans. LTPk'g. Bags.

BB90 - Old Time
Tel. 638467
Jan-Dec Band 2 (2D)(2PB)
Dogs. Pk'dL. Veg. Trans. LTPk'g. Bags.

Bishop's Castle - named after castle built by Bishops of Hereford 1085-
1100 against Welsh (no remains left). Once known as England's smallest
borough and one of the 18th century "Rotten Boroughs" (ie.
disproportionately small number of voters yet their own MP in Parliament).
Many fine 15th century buildings.

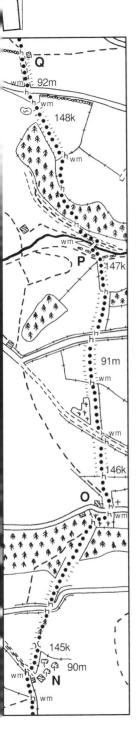

Middle Knuck - Nythbran

Continue up the hill to cross a stile in a crossing fence and **just past a barn on your right, turn right**, over a stile.

I wondered about the wisdom of calling a place a "Crisis Intervention Centre"; it's the sort of label that can be counterproductive, especially with young people. If the bulging car park was anything to go by, the staff-to-crisis ratio must be very high. The more I thought about it, the more depressed I got and then I felt a crisis coming on......

"N" - **Middle Knuck**. With the buildings of "Middle Knuck Crisis Intervention Centre" to your right, **walk straight away from the stile to rejoin the Dyke**, with its bank on your left. Cross over a small footbridge and put the Dyke on your right. Over a minor road (noting the "Wild Bedric's Way" waymark on the stile!). **Continue**, with the Dyke on your right, **to a coniferous plantation and a steep descent. Bear right over a stile** to cross a new plantation of young firs and emerge opposite the Church.

Fire. Please take great care not to start a fire. Especially in a dry summer, plantations such as this are a tinderbox waiting for a carelessly discarded cigarette or glass bottle.

"O" - **Mainstone Church**. Cross to a **Stile opposite, straight ahead**, ignoring the path bearing off left, and **up the bank** bearing slightly left. At a **Crossing track, turn left, through a gateway (with stile) and turn right to continue** along the Dyke. Cross a minor public road and descend with the Dyke to a footbridge over the river.

"P" - **River Unk**. **Cross the footbridge and turn left** to join a track. As the track meets the fence of a coniferous plantation, **continue, over a stile, up through the trees to the edge of the plantation. At a stile in the fence on your right, jink right then left to put the fence on your left**. Continue over a crossing fence. Follow the Dyke on your left until it abruptly ends *(see "Kerry Ridgeway" overleaf)* and you bear left cross a stile. At a **Minor public road, bear right** across the road to **take a drive down to "Nythbran"** "Q".

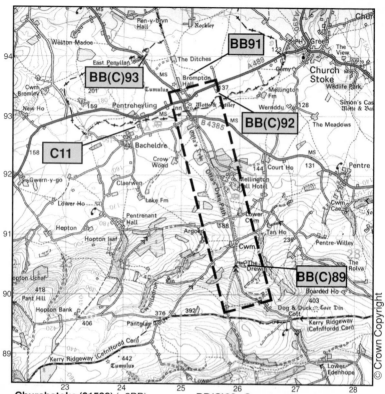

© Crown Copyright

Churchstoke (01588) (+2BB)
2xPH's (food).
<u>Buses</u> - Shoppers - W-Shrewsbury/
Tu-Newtown/ M-Montgomery
Schooldays - am - Montgomery-
Churchstoke-B'Castle (pm-return)

BB(C)89 - <u>Drewin Farm</u>
Tel. 620325 TB 3 Crown HComm
Apr-Oct Band 1/2 (2F/D)(1PB)
EM. Dogs. Non-Smk'g. Pk'dL. Veg.
Trans. LTPk'g. Bags.

BB91 - <u>Brompton Hall</u>
Tel. 620544
Feb-Dec (exc Xmas) Band 2/3
(2D,1T)(3PB)
EM. Dogs. Non-Smk'g. Pk'dL. Veg.
Trans. LTPk'g. Bags.
*Country House DB&B on the Dyke.
Also a perfect base for walkers
exploring the lovely unspoilt hills of
South Shropshire and the Welsh
Border Country.*

BB(C)92 - <u>Greystones</u>
Tel. 620393
Jan-Dec (exc Xmas) Band 1
(1D,1T,1F)(1PB)
EM. Dogs (not in house). Non-Smk'g.
Pk'dL. Veg. LTPk'g. Bags.

BB(C)93 - <u>Little Brompton Farm</u>
Tel. 668371 TB 3 Crown H Comm
Jan-Dec Band 1/2 (1S,1D,1T,1F)(4PB)
EM. Dogs. Non-Smk'g. Pk'dL. Veg.
Trans. LTPk'g. Bags.
*Charming 17th century farmhouse on
working farm. Traditional quality
furnishings. Excellent home cooking.
En-suite available. Central Heating.
Offa's Dyke runs through farm. Open
all year.*
LG Note - direct path signed off Dyke.

C11 - <u>Bacheldre Watermill Camping</u>
Tel.620489
Easter-Oct (16 pitches)
Toilets. Showers. Dogs.

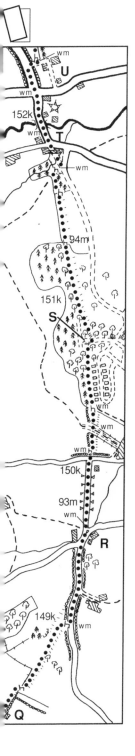

Nythbran - Brompton Hall

"Q" - **Nythbran. Straight ahead**, to pass the house on your right, and over a stile. **Continue**, hedge right, **to a stile in the fence on your right**. Jink right & left to continue with the Dyke until bearing right over a stile and down onto the road. **Continue down into Cwm.**

Grab the Children! It's a narrow lane with high hedges and no verges.

"R" - **Cwm.** Pass the Offa's Gallery on your right (an old Chapel) and **take the left fork ahead** down a sunken road. At a **T-junction, straight ahead** over a stile, immediately, **jinking right then left** to put the hedge on your left. **Continue** with the hedge/Dyke to enter the edge of a wood with the caravans of Mellington Hall CP on your right. A barrier forces you right and down to a crossing track.

"S" - **Crossing track Mellington Wood**. Cross the track and **continue** with wood left and park right. Leaving the park over a stile, continue to a **Small wood** where the **Path twists and turns before you turn right over a stile** and emerge onto a tarmac drive. **Turn left to** the gatehouse and the B4385.

"T" - **B4385. Continue** along the B4385 **to the crossroads** by the Blue Bell Inn. **Straight ahead**, on the Montgomery Road, and take the **first right turn** down the access to Brompton Hall.

Ignore any ideas about cutting the corner on a footpath. The Path goes down the drive.

"U" - **Brompton Hall. Just before** the buildings of Brompton Hall, **turn left over a stile** to follow the Dyke (not very distinct).

The Kerry Ridgeway. A major east-west drove road since the earliest times. Starting near Bishop's Castle and crossing the Clun Forest to end near Newtown. Because of its history, it was an obvious crossing place in the Dyke. The modern road has been realigned and much comment has been made about the "original" gap in the Dyke just South of the road. Proof of border controls and trade across the Dyke? Unfortunately, the gap may be a later levelling of the Dyke as excavation has revealed the ditch continuing across the gap.

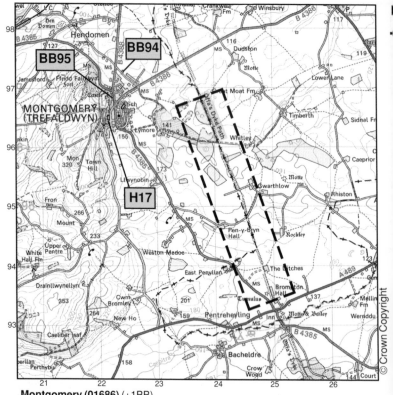

© Crown Copyright

Montgomery (01686) (+1BB)

<u>Banks</u> - Midland MThF1030-1500hrs.
NatWest MThF 1000-1500hrs.
<u>Buses</u> -
M-Sa Limited to Shrewsbury.
Shoppers -
M Welshpool. TuSa Newtown.
Schooldays - Bishop's Castle

H17 - <u>The Dragon Hotel</u>
Tel. 668359 TB 4 Crown Comm
Jan-Dec Band 5 (2S,9D,4T)(15PB)
Switch. Visa. M'Card. Amex.

Dogs. Lic'd. Pk'dL. Veg. Trans. LTPk'g.
Bags.

BB94 - <u>Beeches</u>
Tel. 668663
Jan-Dec Band 2 (1D,1T,1F)(3PB)
EM. Non-Smk'g. Veg. LTPk'g. Bags.

BB95 - <u>The Manor House</u>
Tel. 668736
Jan-Dec Band 1 (1D/T,1S,1F)(1PB)
Dogs. PK'dL. Veg. Trans. LTPk'g.
Bags.

Montgomery. Another town that grew up in a strategically important location; this time dominating a major route into the heart of Wales and overlooking a crossing point for the River Severn. Once a Borough, it was the County Town of Montgomeryshire.

The Iron Age hillfort of Ffridd Faldwyn is situated just to the NW of the town, whilst a Roman fort (believed to have been Lavobrinta) was placed nearer the Severn.

Following the Norman Conquest, Roger, Seigneur de Montgomery in Normandy, was granted lands here and built a motte and bailey castle to

(continued opposite)

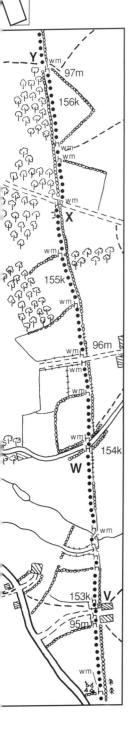

Brompton Hall - Lymore Park

Continuing from Brompton Hall, with the hedge/ Dyke on your right, over two stiles to cross the access track to "The Ditches".

"V" - **The Ditches**. With the farmhouse to your right, **continue** through a paddock. Once more in open fields with the hedge/Dyke on your right, pass the short-cut signs for Little Brompton Hall. **Cross a footbridge** over a stream and then **turn right over a second footbridge and then left** to

The stream marks the Welsh/English Border and you are walking along it until point "Y".

continue with the Dyke/hedge right. Emerge over a stile onto a minor public road.

"W" - **Public Road to Pen-y-Brn Hall**. **Continue** with the hedge/Dyke on your right for 4 fields. Just after passing a fenced off spring on your left, emerge onto a track leading to Gwarthlow Farm (right).

"X" - **Gwarthlow Farm Track**. **Turn right, over a cattle grid and then left**. **Continue** with the **Dyke** and BoardyHall Wood **on your left**. **After 3 fields** and the end of a wood on your left, cross a stile to **put the hedgeline on your right**.

.... defend them. This first castle was built at Hendomen, just north of the town, and although it was well situated, the castle was sacked by the Welsh in 1095. Another castle was built on the same site but was replaced in circa 1230AD by the present stone castle which is built on an outcrop of rock. A town grew up around the castle and a Charter granted by the King enabled the town to be enclosed and to hold fairs and a market.

The castle withstood a number of attacks by the Welsh although the town was sacked in the 15th century by Owain Glyndwr. During the Civil War the castle was held initially for the King but it was quickly surrendered without bloodshed to the Parliamentarians. The Royalists attempted to regain the castle but were decisively routed in a bloody battle. In 1649, the year of the King's execution, Parliament ordered the castle's demolition. Continued overleaf....

131

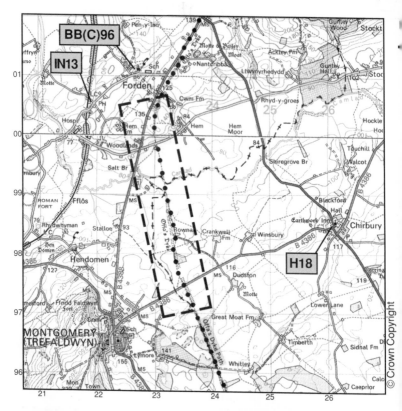

Chirbury (01938) (+1BB)
PO/Stores (ec SaSu)
H18 - The Herbert Arms Hotel
Tel. 561216
Jan-Dec (exc Xmas/NY) Band 1
(1S,1D,2T)
EM. Lic'd. Pk'dL. Veg. Trans. LTPk'g.

Forden (01938) (+1BB)
IN13 - Railway Inn
Tel.580237 TB 2 Crown
Jan-Dec (exc Xmas) Band 1/2
(2D,3T)(2PB)
EM. Dogs. Lic'd. Pk'dL. Veg. LTPk'g.
Bags.
BB(C)96 - Church House
Tel. 580353
Jan-Dec (exc Xmas/NY) Band 1
(1D,1T,1F)
EM(only if booked). Pk'dL. Trans.
LTPk'g. Bags.

Montgomery continued....
The Church of St. Nicholas was built at the same time as the town
although the tower had to be rebuilt in the early 19th century. It is
particularly noted for being the last resting place of two individuals, who
it might be said were at the opposite ends of the social spectrum. Inside
the church is the magnificent 16th century canopied tomb of Richard
Herbert of Montgomery Castle. Outside, and originally in unconsecrated
ground, lies the "Robbers Grave".

Continued overleaf...

132

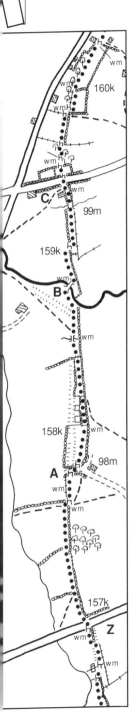

Lymore Park - Forden

Having put the hedge on your right at the end of the wood, continue to a stile in a crossing fence and bear right onto the bank of the Dyke. Over a stile by some sheep pens and on to the B4386.

Montgomery Castle is a fine sight from the Dyke and the B4386 is probably the best place to turn off into the town.

"Z" - **B4386**. **Straight across** and through a gateway. **Continue** with a hedge on your right **along 3 fields** until a stile in the hedge on your right. **Turn right across the Dyke and then left** up onto the bank of the Dyke.

The Path lies along the Dyke but it is so overgrown and obstructed that you will be forced down onto the field edge.

Continue to a stile in a crossing hedge. **Emerge onto a track,** by some sheds, and **turn right** 50m towards "Rownal" farmhouse.

"A" - **Rownal**. Just **before the house, turn left over a stile**. With the Dyke 50m away to your left, follow the hedge on your right to a gate leading into a twitchel. **Continue along the twitchel** to pass some ruined houses and emerge **into a large field**. Continue, with the hedge on your right, **to the river Camlad** and a large footbridge.

"B" - **Footbridge over Camlad**. **Cross and turn left**. Halfway along the field, jink **right and left over a stile** to follow a track to Pound House which you pass on your left.

"C" - **Pound House**. **Continue** across the minor public road and over 3 stiles. After the 3rd stile, bear right to gain a path **up the steep bank**. At the top, cross a stile into the corner of a field. **Continue with hedge on your right** until a stile in a crossing fence. Over the stile and **Turn right** over a second stile **to cross the Dyke**. **Turn left and continue**, with at first a fence on your left and later a hedge, until you emerge, over a stile in a crossing hedge, into a small triangular field.

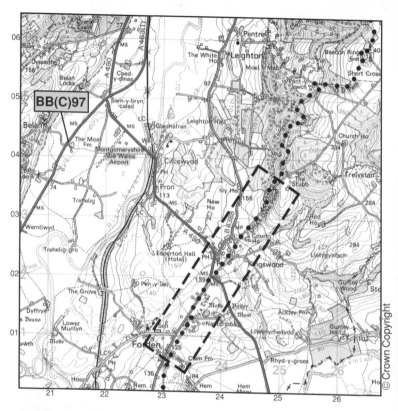

BB(C)97 - Moat Farm
Tel. (01938) 553179 TB 2 Crown HComm
Apr-Oct Band 2 (2D,1T)(3PB)
EM. Pk'dL. Veg. Trans. LTPk'g. Bags.

The Robbers Grave (continued). In 1821 William Jones appeared before magistrates accused by his employer, Thomas Pugh, of assault and robbery. He was alleged to have stolen a watch and five pence. Two witnesses testified that, in company with Pugh, they had apprehended Jones and found the watch and money on him. Jones was later tried and convicted of the offences and sentenced to death. Jones protested his innocence on the scaffold and prayed that God would not allow grass to grow on his grave as a sign of his innocence. As he was executed, the skies darkened and there was a furious thunderstorm. Nothing grew on the grave until a rose bush was planted on it in the early part of this century!

Forden - Greenwood Lodge

Continue across the small triangular field to cross a stile and emerge onto a minor road leading to Cwm Farm.

"D" - **Minor road leading to Cwm Farm**. **Straight across** and over a stile (1) to follow the field edge with the hedge on your left. Cross a stile (2) to follow the Dyke over the next field and over a stile (3) in a crossing hedge. **After the 3rd stile, bear left to rejoin the low bank of the Dyke to a hidden stile** in a corner of the field. **Turn left** to join the B4388.

"E" - **B4388**. **Turn right** along the B4388 to the junction with the A490.

"F" - **A490**. **Turn right** along the A490. **Turn left** to cross a stile immediately **in front of the first house** on the left. Continue over 2 more stiles (only 1 is drawn on the map) **to emerge into a field**. **Continue** with hedge left over 4 more stiles. After the 4th, jink left to continue and soon put the hedge back on your left. Cross a further stile (with string!) to pass hen coops and finally over another stile with string, to emerge onto a minor road.

"G" - **Minor Road**. **Turn left for 20m then bear right down a driveway**, continuing along a twitchel before emerging once more in fields. Continue with hedge left for two fields until bearing left to emerge on the **Corner of a minor road** and **turn right** to follow the road. **In 800m, a track bears off left** to a cattle-grid **and** stile. The track **immediately forks**. **Take the right fork** to pass the Lodge ("H") on your right.

"H" - **Greenwood Lodge**. **Continue** past sheds, along a forest track.

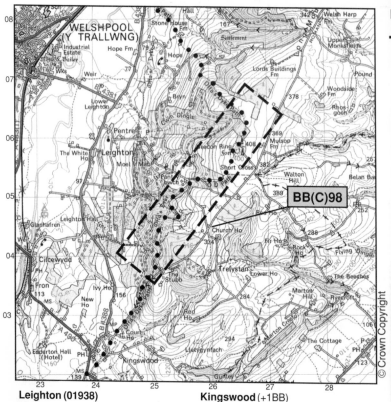

Leighton (01938)
No facs
BB(C)98 - Chapel House
Tel.580476
Mar-Oct Band 1 (2D,1F)
EM. Non-Smk'g. Pk'dL. Veg. Trans.
LTPk'g. Bags.

Kingswood (+1BB)
Buses - See Welshpool
Telephone
PH - The Cock Hotel (not B&B)

Leighton Park. Bought in 1849 by a Victorian banker, John Naylor, who had a mansion built in the Gothic style and who planted the "monkey puzzle" trees (you will see them by the Path) and a Redwood grove, which is now in the care of Royal Forestry Society.

He was a man of vision whose building programme included farms and even his own gas works; the latter fed the house, the church and some of the farm buildings. He built a funicular railway to transport guano and bone-meal to storage tanks on Moel-y-Mab. There the liquid manure and piped down to the fields where it provided irrigation and fertiliser.

Water from the hills above the estate was carefully channelled into holding pools, two of which you pass on the Path. Water was even pumped up from the River Severn. It was then piped to turbines to provide power to machinery at the farm. Alas, the elaborate equipment was requisitioned for scrap in World War I and nothing remains of it.

136

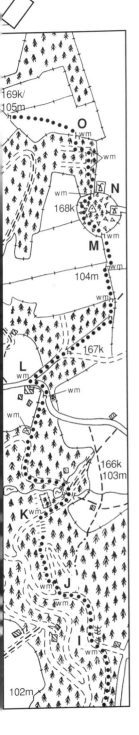

Greenwood Lodge - Beacon Ring.

Continuing away from Greenwood Lodge along a minor forest track, a major forest road joins from sharp right.

"I" - **Major forest road**. **Continue**, passing occasional monkey puzzle trees right. The track starts to descend and as a track comes up from the left, another track bears up right.

"J" - **Track bears up right**. **Bear right** up the track. After **100m turn left** on an indistinct path, **10m turn right** to parallel the track and rejoin the Dyke. Continue on a path to **descend 40 "steps"** to emerge on a forest track.

"K" - **Forest track by enclosure**. **Turn right along the track** to immediately pass, on your left, a high wire-mesh fence protected by a low electric fence. Soon cross a bridge then a second bridge as another track goes off right. *Offa's Pool, the holding pool for water used by the Leighton Estate, is down to your left as you cross the bridges.*

Continue along the track **to a pond on your right**. **Bear right to pass it on your left**. Continue with a fence left to emerge onto a **Minor public road** where you **turn left** to follow the road to "Pant-y-bwch".

"L" - **"Pant-y-bwch"**. Just before the buildings, **turn sharp right up a "No through road"**. **Road forks,** but you **continue** over a stile and **up the field edge** with a forestry plantation on your left. **At the top, turn left** to cross the top of the plantation and continue up to Beacon Ring, first with the fence on your right and then on your left.

"M" - **Beacon Ring**. **Turn LEFT** in front of the plantation that now crowns the top of Beacon Ring. Follow the earthworks of the fort **round to** a radio tower.

"N" - **Radio Tower**. **Immediately before** the fence of the radio installation, **turn left over a stile**. Straight away from the stile, first on the edge of the wood and then just inside on a green track. **The track bends left, in 100m, bear right to a stile** on the edge of the plantation ("O").

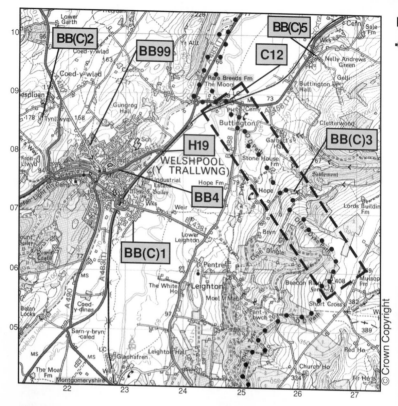

Welshpool (01938)(+4BB)

Banks - Midland(ATM), Barclays(ATM),
NatWest(ATM), Lloyds(ATM), TSB.
Outdoor Shop - W Alexander Ltd
(Broad St opp Boots the Chemist)
Taxis - Doug's 553970, Mount 554976,
Steve's - 304904, Stonebridge - 555119
Buses - See next LMap

H19 - Royal Oak Hotel
Tel. 552217 TB 4Crown HComm
Jan-Dec Band 5+ (24rms)(24PB)
All cards. EM. Dogs. Lic'd. Pk'dL. Veg.

BB99 - Tresi-Aur
Tel.552430 TB 2 Crowns
Jan-Nov Band 1 (1S,1T,1D/F)(1PB)
Non-Smk'g. Pk'dL. Veg. Trans. LTPk'g.
Bags.

BB(C)1 - Severn Farm
Tel.553098 TB 1 Crown
Jan-Dec (exc Xmas/NY) Band 1
(1S,2D,2T,2F). EM. Dogs. Pk'dL. Veg.
Trans. LTPk'g. Bags.

BB(C)2 - Tynllwyn Farm
Tel.553175 & 553054 TB 1 Crown
Jan-Dec Band 1 (2D,2T,2F)(Single - no
extra) EM. Dogs. Lic'd. Pk'dL. Veg.
Trans. LTPk'g. Bags.

BB(C)3 - Buttington View
Tel.552295
Mar-Oct Band 1 (1S,1D,1T)
EM. Dogs. Non-Smk'g. Pk'dL. Veg.
Trans. LTPk'g. Bags.

BB4 - Hafren
Tel.554112 & (0831) 183152
Jan-Dec Band 1 (1D,1F,1S/T)
Dogs. Pk'dL. Veg. Trans. Bags.

BB(C)5 - 1 Plas Cefn
Tel. 570225 Jan-Dec Band 1
(1S,1D,1F) EM. Dogs. Pk'dL. Veg.
Trans. LTPk'g. Bags.

C12 - Bridge End
Tel. 552249
Apr-Oct (5 pitches)
Toilets. Showers. Dogs. Shop

138

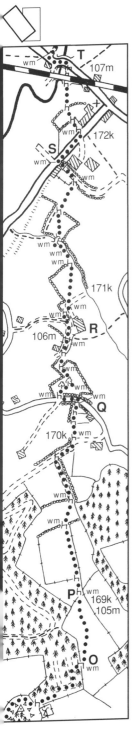

Beacon Ring - Buttington Bridge

"O" - **Stile on Edge of Plantation**. Ignore waymark, **bear left** across field to round the head of Cwm Dingle on the left **and then increase the bear left** to head for stile in far corner of field.

"P" - **Stile beyond Cwm Dingle**. **Bear right, along the edge of the field**, over a stile in a fence and down to a stile in the bottom right corner. **Bear right** away from the stile **to descend steeply to** another stile at the end of **a green track**. Down to the **Bottom of the field** to **turn right along a green lane**. **In 200m the lane bends right, continue over a stile** to cross 2 more stiles with "Buttington View" signed over on your right. Emerge over a further stile onto a minor public road.

"Q" - **Minor Public Road**. **Turn left and in 150m turn right** over a stile in the hedge on your right. **Bear right across the field** to the far end of a line of trees, **turn left towards** the outer corner of a hedge. Pass it on your left, to **a stile in the corner. Bear right** along a narrow field **to a stile by a house** over to your left. **Continue down the access track** to pass Stonehouse Farm.

"R" - **Stonehouse Farm**. **The track bends left** as it passes the farm, **continue to a stile in the hedge over to your right**. Turn left along a track and as the track bends right, **continue to a stile in the furthest corner of the field**. Straight away from the stile with a ditch on your right. **In 150m, turn right** over a concrete footbridge and a stile. **Bear left to cross the field** to a stile in the far corner. Straight away towards factory units ahead. Cross a stile onto a **Green lane** and **turn left.** Pass along the drive of a house to emerge onto the B4388.

"S" - **B4388**. **Turn right** to follow the B4388. **In 200m turn left to cross a stile** before the first house. Cross 3 fields to the railway and continue to the A458 and Buttington Bridge. *You can join the canal at Buttington Wharf (and follow it to Llanymynech if you wish).*

"T" - **Buttington Bridge**. **Turn left to cross the bridge** and **take the first track right**. Pass between a house (left) and sheds (right) to pick up a path alongside the River Severn.

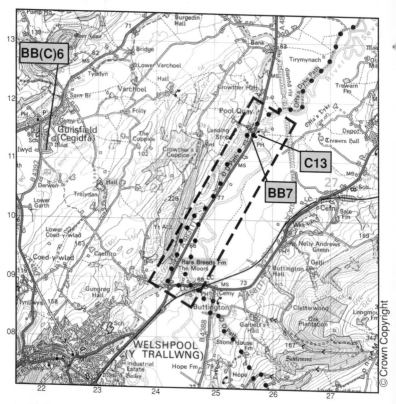

Welshpool

Buses -
M-Sa Limited to Oswestry (via Llanymynech)
M-Sa Regular to Newtown & Shrewsbury (Su VLimited)
See Montgomery.
Daily coach to/from London

Guilsfield (01938)

BB(C)6 - Lower Trelydan Farmhouse
Tel. 553105 TB 3 Crown HComm
Jan-Dec Band 2 (2D,1T)(3PB)
EM. Lic'd. Pk'dL. Veg. Trans. LTPk'g. Bags.

Buttington (+1C)
Telephone. PH - Green Dragon (food)

Pool Quay (01938) (+1IN)
PH - Powis Arms

BB7 - Severn View
Tel. 590464
Jan-Dec Band 1 (1D,1T,1D/T)(1PB)
EM. Dogs. Non-Smk'g. Pk'dL. Veg.
Trans. LTPk'g. Bags.

C13 - Little Bank
Tel. 590505
Easter-Oct (5pitches)
Toilets. Showers. Wash/Dry facs.
Dogs.

Welshpool. Founded in the 13th century, it developed as a market town (the Severn was navigable up to Buttington). It was originally known as Poole, from a word that described flooded creeks and land continuously under water, but in later times drainage schemes enabled the land to be reclaimed for agricultural use. There is a "Powisland" museum & Montgomery Canal Centre (Closed W)
See "Powis Castle" & "Offa's Dyke & The River Severn"

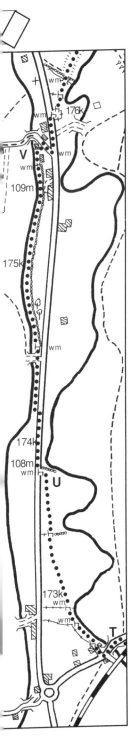

Buttington Bridge - Pool Quay

Continuing away from Buttington Bridge on the path by the River Severn, cross 2 stiles and pick up a low flood defence bank. **Continue across fields until the river and the A483 meet.**

"U" - **A483**. Turn left over a stile, cross the A483 and **turn right** alongside it. In **250m bear left to join the canal towpath**. Follow the canal to the lock at Pool Quay.

"V" - **Pool Quay**. Just before the lock, **bear right** down to the road **and turn sharp right to the A483. Turn left** alongside the A483 **and just past** the buildings of **a farm, turn right** across the road **to a stile. Bear left** to immediately cross a second stile and cross two fields **to join the flood defence bank by the river**.

Offa's Dyke & The River Severn

Having crossed the River Camlad, the Dyke heads straight up Long Mountain to a height of 300m before descending to the River Severn. In following this route it initially places higher ground to its West (blocking a clear view) and takes a much more difficult line than would be necessary had it simply aimed straight for Buttington. The reason for this choice of route has perplexed scholars and even prompted Fox to dig one of his rare excavations. It has been suggested that the Dyke's engineers wanted to make it especially impressive before descending to an ancient and major crossing of the river at Buttington.

The route of the Dyke between Buttington and Trederwen isn't certain and the small isolated piece of "dyke" identified on the OS maps near Trewern Hall may not be Offa's Dyke after all. This is one stretch where Fox thought that no dyke was necessary because the river and floodplain offered a sufficient barrier. Noble wasn't convinced and wasn't prepared to accept that a Dyke that followed cliffs above a much more formidable river barrier, the Wye in the South, would simply peter out at this point. He was to have investigated further when he undertook his study of the Dyke beyond the Severn. Alas, he died before he could complete his work.

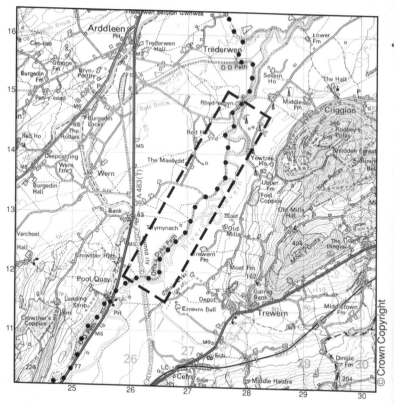

Powis Castle.

A stronghold from the earliest times, which might explain why the adjacent stretch of Offa's Dyke on the other side of the River Severn was placed so high up Long Mountain. The castle can be seen from the Path (just to the SW of Welshpool), its red stone standing out amongst the trees and terraced gardens.

The present building was begun circa 1200 but most the work was carried out in the last quarter of that century following the renunciation by Owain ap Gruffydd ap Gwenwynwyn of his royal title as Prince of Powys. In return for paying homage to Edward I he was created Baron de la Pole (Poole). The castle was essentially Norman in design, featuring a keep with an inner bailey and enclosed by a large curtain wall. It was surrounded on three sides by a moat.

Baron de la Pole's daughter, Hawys, inherited the estate following his death in 1309. She was forced to defend her inheritance in 1312 when her right of succession was challenged and the castle was besieged. Such was her valour that she became known as "y Gadarn" ("the Hardy") and her succession was recognised by Royal Charter.

Continued opposite

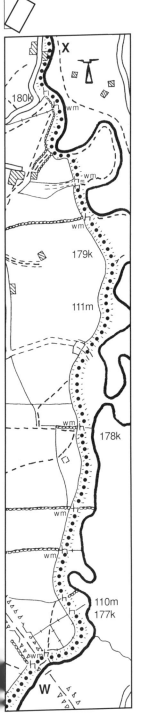

Pool Quay - Rhyd-esgyn

Continue to the line of an old railway.

"W" - **Old Railway Line**. Cross the line of the former railway and **continue along the flood defence bank** to pass, on the other side of the river, the masts of Criggion Radio Station. A road joins from the left to paralell the Path to the houses at "Upper House".

"X" - **Upper House**. **Stay on the bank** to pass the houses immediately on your left.

Powis Castle Continued....

The castle was again besieged in the first years of the 15th century following the Welsh uprising under Owain Glyndwr and the English citizens of Welshpool were massacred.

Powis Castle passed to Sir Edward Herbert in 1587. He made extensive improvements to the castle before he died in 1595. His successor, Sir William Herbert, was created Lord Powis by Charles I and the castle was in Royalist hands at the start of the Civil War. However, the Parliamentarians, under Sir Thomas Myddelton, took the castle in a surprise night attack having blown up the outer gates. The castle was not returned to the family until the restoration of Charles II. Major additions were made to the castle in the latter part of the 17th century but political misfortune and large debts saw a general decline in the fortunes of the Herberts.

The marriage in 1784, between Lord Powis's daughter and Edward Clive (eldest son of Clive of India), led to a union of the Clive and Powis estates in 1801. New money was introduced into the estate and much needed repairs were carried out, during which the gardens were improved. The Herbert name continued when Edward Clive, who had inherited the estate, changed his name to Herbert as a condition of the inheritance.

The castle was bequeathed to the National trust in 1952 on the death of George Herbert, Fourth Earl of Powis, whose wife had died in 1929 and whose two sons had died in the World Wars. Open (1995) 1Apr-Jun (exc MTu), Jul-Aug (excM), Sep- 29 Oct (excMTu). Hours 1200-1700 (Gardens 1100-1800). Information (01938) 554336.

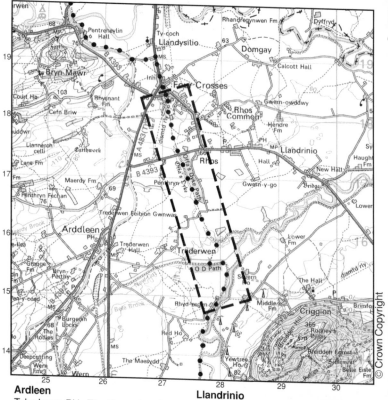

Ardleen
Telephone. PH - The Horseshoe (food)

Llandrinio
"P" at Grid Ref 280175 is PO/Happy
Shopper (Telephone opposite)
Grid Ref 275179 is Shop & Newsagent
(open Su am!)

The Brieddens.

*Whether you stayed on the Path or opted for the canal towpath to Four
Crosses, the dominant feature is the Briedden Hills, large outcrops of
hard igneous rock. Enjoy the view from the southwest for the northern
end is scarred by a large quarry. Note the precipitous road that snakes
its way down from the quarry; not a place to have brakes fail!*

*On top of the 365m (1200ft) summit of Briedden Hill stands a monument
to Admiral Rodney. Erected by local subscription in 1781 in memory of
his victory in the French Wars. There are remains of an Iron Age fort
and this is one of the places where Caractacus was said to have mustered
his forces against the Romans.*

*Another feature is the masts of the Criggion radio station. A masterpiece
of aerial engineering, it is interesting to compare the early steel girder
masts with the later and more economic guyed masts. Whether the
quarrying of the rock is affecting the performance of the apparatus is
something we are unlikely to learn!*

Rhyd-esgyn - Four Crosses

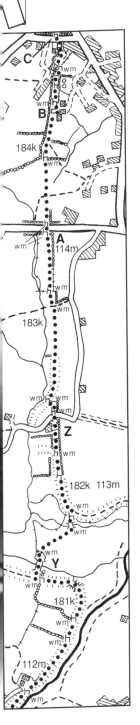

Continuing on from Upper House, **stay on the flood defence bank**. The bank turns left and you cross a triple sluicegate. At the next stile, turn right to the "Derwas Bridge".

"Y" - **"Derwas Bridge"**. **Cross the bridge** and through the gate ahead, now **bear right to cross the field to a plank footbridge and a stile**. Up onto the **Flood defence bank** and **turn left**. Follow the bank, over a stile, until the **Bank bends left** and you **continue** over a stile and along a twitchel to emerge onto a minor public road by "The Nea".

"Z" - **Minor Public Road by "The Nea"**. **Turn right for 20m** then **turn left** to cross a stile. **Straight away from the stile** with hedge right to a waymark and **then bear left** to a stile in the corner of the field. **Turn right and rejoin the bank** as it meanders parallel to a ditch left. Continue, crossing a footpath and rejoin the low mound **of Offa's Dyke** to the B4393.

Quite where the flood defence bank becomes Offa's Dyke is a difficult one to answer. The flood defence you joined beyond Derwas Bridge was probably built on the line of the Dyke. The Dyke was traced heading down to Buttington but although odd traces of Dyke are believed to have been identified opposite Pool Quay on the East side of the Severn, it is likely that the whole area was a flood plain at the time the Dyke was constructed.

"A" - **B4393**. Cross and **continue** along the low bank of the Dyke to a stile in a crossing hedge. Continue with hedge left to the buildings of Gornel Farm.

"B" - **Gornel Farm**. **The Path continues with hedge left** but an inconvenient silage clamp forces you into the slurry of the farmyard until you can rejoin the Path. **Pass an old sewage works on your right and then turn left, over a stile**, descend steps to **cross in front of a dairy building and** turn right to **take the access road** out of the yard to the public road "C".

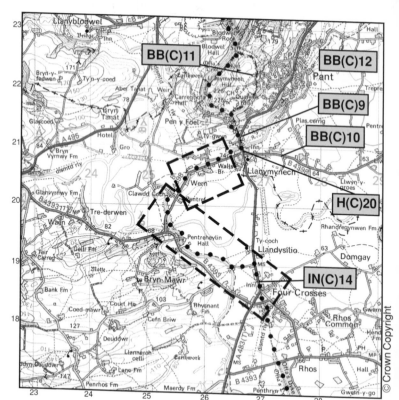

Facilities - see next LMap
Four Crosses (01691) (+1BB)
IN(C)14 - Golden Lion
Tel. 830295 TB 2 Crown
Jan-Dec Band 2 (2T,2F) EM. Dogs.
Lic'd. Pk'dL. Trans. LTPk'g. Bags.
BB8 - Haimwood
Tel.830764
Jan-Dec Band 1 (1D,1T,1F)
EM. Pk'dL. Trans. LTPk'g. Bags.
Grid Ref 318162 (5km off route)
Llanymynech (01691)(+1BB)
H(C)20 - Lion Hotel
Tel. 830234 TB Listed
Jan-Dec(exc Xmas) Band 2
(3S,2D,4T,1F)(5PB)
EM. Dogs. Lic'd. Pk'dL. Veg. LTPk'g.
BB(C)9 - Cae Bryn
Tel. 830655 TB 2 Crown HComm
Mar-Dec(exc Xmas) Band 1/2
(2S,1D,1T,1F)(1PB)
Dogs. Pk'dL. Veg. LTPk'g. Bags

BB(C)10 - Hospitality
Tel. 830427 TB Listed
Mar-Jan Band 1 (1S,1D,1T)
EM. Dogs. Pk'dL. Veg. Trans. LTPk'g.
Bags.
*Interesting house on Welsh Border -
Excellent accommodation - High
standard of catering - 4-day transport
package for walkers of Offa's Dyke to
save carrying packs (ring for details).*

BB(C)11 - Three Firs
Tel. 831375 TB Listed
Jan-Dec Band 1 (1S,1d,2F)(1PB)
EM. Dogs. Pk'dL. Veg. Trans. LTPk'g.
Bags.
BB(C)12 - Cliffe Point
Tel. 830356
May-Oct Band1 (2S,1D/T)(2PB)
Dogs. Non-Smk'g. Pk'dL. Trans.
LTPk'g. Bags.

146

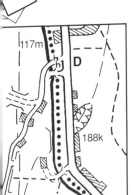

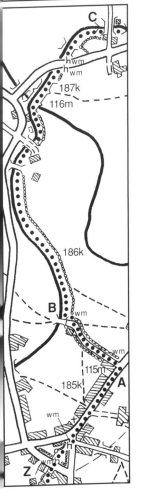

Four Crosses - Walls Bridge

"Z" - **Public Road outside Dairy entrance**. Cross to a stile opposite. **Continue** away from the stile to cross the field **to a stile in the far corner.** Emerging onto a **Minor road, turn left then turn right along the A483. Pass** the Golden Lion Hotel and just beyond **"Bryn Offa", turn left on a minor road**.

"A" - **Road to "Pont-y-Person"**. Follow the road to its end and continue to join the canal.

"B" - **Shropshire Union Canal**. **Turn right** and follow the canal towpath to the locks at Carreghofa.

Swans. I had read about swans on this stretch of canal but wasn't prepared to meet a pair, together with their two cygnets, blocking the towpath. Gentle encouragement to allow me to pass was met by much hissing and I had to resort to sharing my lunchtime biscuits with them. They didn't touch the biscuits, but as tribute had been paid, they obviously felt honour was satisfied and decided to go for a swim. I've never been mugged by swans before but there must be a first time for everything!

"C" - **Carreghofa Lock**. Continue along the towpath to the now redundant "Walls Bridge, just beyond which a minor road blocks the canal.

The Canal. The lock is a good spot for a break and there is an information board about the canal. The lock marked the meeting of the former Montgomeryshire Canal (1794) with the Llanymynech branch of the Ellesmere Canal, hence the tollhouse by the lock pool. As water flowed from the Ellesmere Canal, a bone of contention between the two canal companies, the Montgomeryshire Canal was compelled to provide a water supply from the River Tanat and this can be seen coming in just before the bridge over the canal. However, in 1845 the two companies merged into the Shropshire Union Canal and the arguments about water became academic.

"D" - **Walls Bridge**. Continue across the road and rejoin the canal towpath to Llanymynech.

147

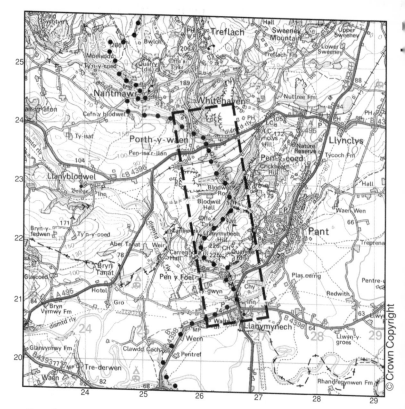

Four Crosses - Facilities
(Point Z on previous Routefinding Map)
- Left to PH - "Four Crosses" (food)
and a Spar Shop (groceries).

Llanymynech - Facilities
Telephone. Public Toilets. Shop & PO
(M-Su 0800-1800hrs) (PO ec WSaSu).
Buses - M-Sa Frequent to Oswestry,
Limited to Welshpool.
TuSa Shopper to Shrewsbury.

Llanymynech

Rich in minerals, the limestone hills above Llanymynech have been mined for centuries. The Romans mined silver and copper and at various times there has been copper, zinc and lead mining.
Llanymynech was a village engaged in the small-scale quarrying of limestone. It was carted by packhorse to barges (called trows) before being sent on the Rivers Vyrnwy and Severn to limekilns. There it was burnt to produce the quicklime used in iron furnaces. The arrival of the Ellesmere canal in 1795 transformed the village; incline planes and tramways were constructed to bring the limestone down to two canal basins where barges were loaded with the broken stone (the limestone was transported to kilns elsewhere due to the hazards involved in the transport of caustic quicklime).

continued next LMap

148

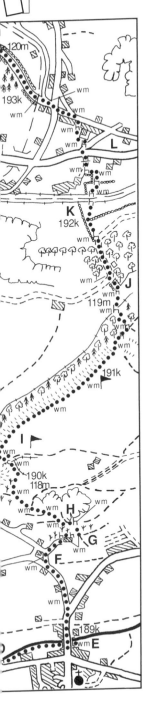

Llanymynech - Porth-y-waen

Continue along the towpath from Walls Bridge and **under a bridge. Turn right, up steps** to the A483.

"E" - **A483**. **Turn right** and as the road bears right go **straight ahead on a minor road**. The **Road forks**, take the **right fork** to a crossroads.

"F" - **Crossroads at Pen y Foel**. **Bear right**, as the lane ends at a house, **continue over a stile** to pass it immediately on your right. Over another stile to a crossing path.

"G" - **Crossing Path**. **Turn left to climb** the hill to a "T-junction" with another path.

"H" - **T-junction with Path**. **Turn left**, to cross a stile and **immediately bear left** at a fork. **Keep bearing right at forks** but do not turn right up into the quarries. The object is to contour the hill, climbing gently. The Path enters scrubwood and bears left to a "Wildlife Trust" sign. Through the gate onto the Golf Course. *The Path never crosses the fairway!*

"I" - **Golf Course**. **Bear left**, behind the "Tee". The **Path turns right to follow the edge** of **the course for 900m**, with the Dyke on your left, **before bearing left** to leave the Course. Cross a stile and continue to a **Major crossing path. Turn left and descend steeply** on a meandering path **to** emerge at a stile at **the edge of the wood. Bear right** to a stile in a crossing hedge and bear left to a wood.

"J" - **Jones Coppice**. **Continue onto a track**, bearing right. Pass a woodman's "chalet" on your right. **As the track bears right, continue ahead over a stile** and along a field edge. Through a crossing hedge, bear right to a mineral railway/

"K" - **Mineral Railway**. **Cross and bear right to a stile**/ footbridge. **Straight ahead and turn left to a stile. Turn right** along a track to the A495.

"L" - **A495**. **Cross, bearing left** to a joining road and **continue over a stile.** Continue across a field to the corner of a small coppice and **turn right to a stile hidden in the corner**. **Up to the road and turn left. Take a left fork**, then straight over a crossroads and continue to Cefn Lane Farm "M".

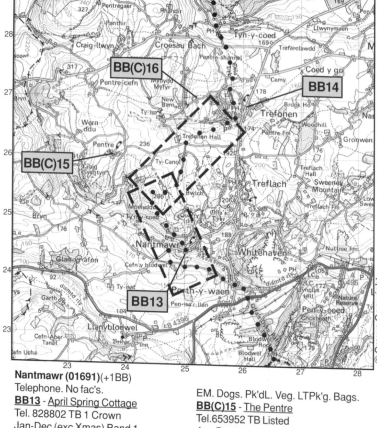

Nantmawr (01691)(+1BB)
Telephone. No fac's.
BB13 - April Spring Cottage
Tel. 828802 TB 1 Crown
Jan-Dec (exc Xmas) Band 1
(1D,1T)(2PB) EM. Non-smk'g. Pk'dL.
Trans. LTPk'g. Bags.
Trefonen (01691)
Telephone. PH - Effel Inn (food)
PH - Barley Mow (food).
Stores - M-Su(ecSu)0800-2000hrs.
BB14 - Plas Offa
Tel.653440
Jan-Nov (excNY) Band 1 (2D,1T)

EM. Dogs. Pk'dL. Veg. LTPk'g. Bags.
BB(C)15 - The Pentre
Tel.653952 TB Listed
Jan-Dec (exc Xmas) Band 1
(2rms)(1PB)
EM. Dogs. Pk'dL. Veg. Trans. LTPk'g.
Bags.
BB(C)16 - Under Hill Farm
Tel.653687
Mar-Oct Band 1 (2rms)(2PB)
EM. Dogs. Non-Smk'g. Pk'dL. Veg.
Trans. LTPk'g.

Continued from previous LMap.. *The arrival of the railways in the second half of the 19th century began a slow inexorable decline in the canals. More efficient kilns shifted the emphasis away from Llanymynech and by 1914 the quarries had ceased operation. The canal lasted a little longer but by 1921 the canal company had sold its fleet of barges. By 1932 the canal was in poor condition and barely navigable. The coup-de-grace came in 1936 when a breach in the canal near Welsh Frankton left it isolated and in 1944 navigation was abandoned.*

Cefn Lane Farm - Trefonen

"M" - **"Cefn Lane Farm"**. **Continue** along Cefn Lane to Cefn Farm

"N" - **Cefn Farm**. **Opposite** the farm, **turn right**, over a stile, and follow a field edge **down to a wood**. Bear left to a stile **and descend** through the wood to a minor road.

"O" - **T-junction at Minor Road**. **Turn right**, along the road, to a telephone box by April Spring Cottage.

"P" - **April Spring Cottage**. **Just before** the cottage, **turn left up a twitchel** and over a stile. **Bear left to a stile** in a crossing hedge. **Turn right**, up the field, to steps and a stile in a crossing hedge. Emerge onto a **Minor road** and **turn left**. At a fork, bear right to Sycamore Cottage.

"Q" - **"Sycamore Cottage"**. **Turn right** up steps **to a stile** and "Jones Rough" (a wood). Bear left, **up through the wood to a stile and across a field** to join a path. **Turn right, over a stile** in the fence right, **and up a field** with fence left. Bear left with the fence, a track (signed as a mountain bike course) joins from sharp right.

"R" - **Track joins (mountain bikes!)**. **Continue** past a house on your left. **As the** fence on your left, bears left, **the track heads for a gate. Bear right** up the hill to the flagpole at the summit.

"S" - **Summit of Moelydd Uchaf**. **Execute a 3/4-turn right from your approach** to head along the summit. **Bear left down to join the track** and follow it as it turns left to a farm.

"T" - **Farm**. **Just** before the track passes through the gate **in front of the farm**, **bear right to a hedgeline and** follow it down to **a stile** in a crossing fence. **Turn left, along a track** (becomes tarmaced) to "Ty-Canol Farm" where you turn right to take its access road down to a minor road.

"U" - **Minor Road**. **Turn left and shortly turn right over a stile** in the hedge. **Bear right** away from the stile **to cross a field** to a stile. Now with a hedge on your right, continue over a stream to another stile. Continue with, at first, hedge left to a gate leading **to a short lane** "V".

151

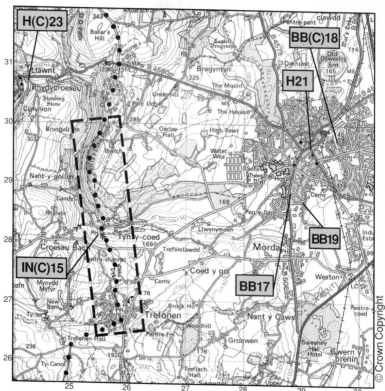

IN(C)15 - <u>The Old Mill Inn</u>
Tel.(01691) 657058 TB 1 Crown
Jan-Dec Band 1 (1S,1D,2T)
Visa. M'Card. EM. Lic'd. Veg. LTPk'g.

Rhydycroseau (01691)
Telephone. PO/Stores
 (Open (!) W 0900-1230 & 1330-1700,
Th 0900-1300)
H(C)23 - <u>Pen y Dyffryn Hall Hotel</u>
Tel. 653700 TB 3 Crown HComm
Jan-Dec Band 4+ (1S,3D,3T,1F)(8PB)
Switch. Visa. M'Card. Amex.
EM. Dogs. Lic'd. Pk'dL. Veg. Trans.
LTPk'g. Bags.

Oswestry (01691)(+2BB)
See next L Map for Facilities
BB17 - <u>The Hawthorns</u>
Tel.657678 TB 2 Crown HComm
Jan-Dec Band 2 (1D,1T)(2PB)
Non-Smk'g. Veg. LTPk'g.

BB(C)18 - <u>Elgar House</u>
Tel. 661323 (0585 171112) TB 2 Crown
HComm Jan-Dec (exc Xmas/NY)
 Band 1 (3D/F)(3PB) EM. Lic'd. Pk'dL.
Veg. Trans. LTPk'g. Bags.
BB19 - <u>Montrose</u>
Tel. 652063 TB Listed
Jan-Dec Band 1 (2T)
Non-Smk'g. Pk'dL. Veg. Trans. LTPk'g.
Bags.

H21 - <u>Bear Hotel</u>
Tel. 652093 TB 3 Crown Comm
Jan-Dec (exc Xmas/NY) Band 2
(3S,4D,2T,1F)(5PB)
Switch. Visa. M'Card. Amex. EM.
Dogs. Lic'd. Pk'dL. Veg. Trans. LTPk'g.
Bags.
*Warm family welcome and excellent
home cooking whether bar food or a-la-
carte menu. Try our comfortable town
centre hotel.*

Trefonen - Oswestry Old Racecourse Wood

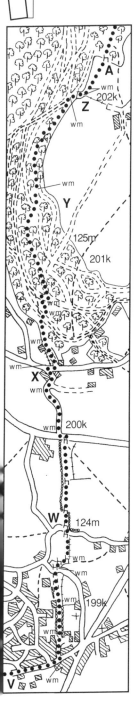

"V" - <u>**Short Lane**</u>. **Continue**, down "Bellen Road", **and turn left along** "Malthouse Lane. The **Lane forks, go straight ahead** along a twitchel then a drive. Continue to a **Minor road** (first). **Straight across,** into a rough parking ground and **bear right** over a stile (of railway sleepers!). Continue along a field edge to a stile in a crossing fence. **Turn left in front the Dyke**. With the Dyke on your right, continue to a second minor road.

"W" - <u>**Second crossing road**</u>. **Turn left** and in 20m **turn right, over a stile**. **Follow the** field edge with a hedge/**Dyke on your right**. When the **Hedge steps out** left, cross a **stile ahead onto the bank of the Dyke** to eventually emerge onto a **Third crossing road. Turn left and then turn right down a road** to the Mill Inn.

"X" - <u>**Old Mill Inn**</u>. Pass the Inn to a **road junction** and **turn right** to cross over a river. **Turn sharp left along a track** with ranch fence left. At a house on your left, **bear right up a twitchel.** Enter a wood and **Cross a forestry road to take a path ahead** up through the trees. In 75m the **Path emerges onto a forest road. Turn right and in circa 50m turn sharp left on a broad path**. The Dyke is on your right. Continue along the narrowing Path to a resting place hewn out of the rock.

Tracks in the wood are shown as depicted on the 1:25,000 OS map. Many of the "tracks" are now only paths and some of them are indistinct.

"Y" - <u>**Rock Resting place**</u>. **Continue** as a path joins from the right. The **Path bears right.**

"Z" - <u>**Path bears right**</u>. Ignore paths ahead, **bear right** with the Path to pass **through a gateway** and cross the line of the Dyke. **Turn left to put a wall on your left and follow the Dyke** as it emerges from the wood. Continue to a stile in a crossing wall and more woodland.

"A" - <u>**Stile in crossing wall**</u>. **Continue** through the wood, on a broad path, to a stile at the far edge.

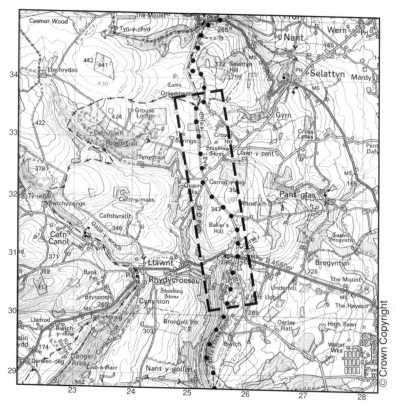

Oswestry Facilities (01691)

<u>Banks</u> - Barclays (ATM), Midland(ATM) NatWest (ATM), Lloyds (ATM), TSB (ATM).

<u>Outdoor Shop</u> - Famous Army Stores (next to PO)

<u>Taxis</u> -
A-B 657721, Berwyn Cars 652000, Border 656149, Burgess 652080, G&H 656565. Oswestry Taxis 658658. For Chirk area - see Chirk B&B's.

<u>Buses</u> -
Going South - see Llanymynech & Welshpool.
M-Sa - Frequent to Wrexham (Su Limited), VFrequent to Chirk (Rail) (Su Limited).
M-Su - Limited to Llangollen (link via Chirk or Acrefair),
M-Sa - Frequent to Shrewsbury (Rail)

Oswestry.

The remains of an Iron Age Fort dating from circa 550BC indicate settlement long before the Romans . Like Hay-on-Wye, its one of those towns that kept getting in the way; King John burnt it in 1215, Llewellyn in 1233. Owain Glyndwr sacked the town in 1400 and there were three accidental but disastrous fires in the 16th century, which is when the plague struck.

Continued opposite

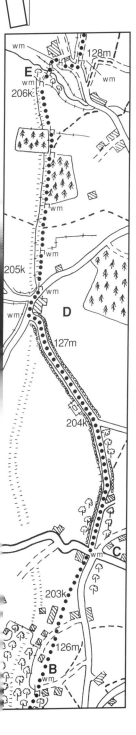

Racecourse Wood - Selattyn Hill

Emerge from the wood, over a stile, and **bear slightly left** to pass a sculpture!

"B" - **Horse Sculpture**. **Continue** along a broad green swathe with houses left and scrub right. A road comes in to paralell you on the right and you arrive at a crossroads with the B4580.

There is a fine stretch of Dyke across Bakers Hill but there is no right of way along it! The Path follows the road until you can rejoin the Dyke at Carreg-y-big. Just before rejoining the Dyke, turn left across it to gain a better view. Although the fence along the top of the bank is modern, it highlights the fact that the Dyke would have been topped by a palisade making it a formidable obstacle.

"C" - **B4580** . **Continue** across the B4580 **on a minor road**. As the Dyke comes in from the left, the road descends to a T-junction by "Carreg-y-big".

"D" - **"Carreg-y-big"**. **Turn right** to pass the farm buildings on your right and turn left to **cross a "mileage" stile on your left**. Continue with the bank of the Dyke on your left until you descend to cross a footbridge over a stream.

"E" - **Footbridge over stream**. Up the other bank of the stream and then **bear gently right to cross a stile by a cattle grid. Follow the track** away from the grid for a few metres **then turn sharp left** to take a track up Selattyn Hill.

Oswestry continued... *Oswestry was the scene of a battle in AD642 during which Penda slew Oswald of Northumbria (see Section One). King Oswald's Well was said to have been fed by a spring which sprang up to mark the spot where an eagle dropped one of Oswald's limbs after the battle. Penda didn't just kill him, he chopped him up to make sure!*

Much of the town is 19th century but you can still see the Old Grammar School (now a Tourist Information Centre) dated from 1407, the 14th century Fighting Cocks Inn and the early 17th century Llwyd Mansion. The Norman Oswestry Castle was demolished by the Parliamentarians after the Civil War and little now remains.

155

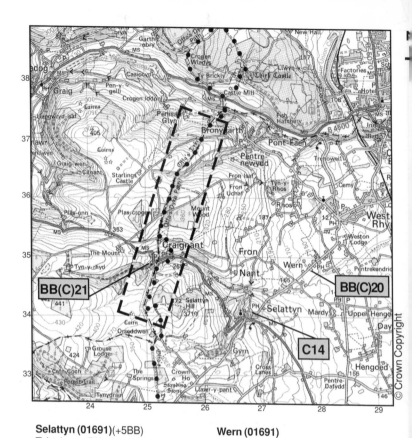

Selattyn (01691)(+5BB)
Telephone. PH - Cross Keys
C14 - <u>The Cross Keys Inn</u>
Tel. 650247
Jan-Dec (4 pitches- pub garden)
Toilet.
Craignant (01691)
No fac's.
BB(C)21 - <u>Craignant Lodge</u>
Tel. 718229
Jan-Dec Band 1 (1D,1T,1F)
EM. Pk'dL. LTPk'g. Bags.

Wern (01691)
PH - The Butchers Arms (food)
BB(C)20 - <u>Spring Cottage</u>
Tel. 650293
Jan-Dec Band 1 (1S,1D,1T)
Non-Smk'g. Pk'dL. Trans. LTPk'g.
Bags.

Selattyn Hill - Bronygarth

Continue along the track to pass a ruined house, through two gateways, and bear left to the corner of a wood.

"F" - **Corner of Wood**. **Turn left to cross a stile**. Straight away from the stile and as you **cross the brow of the field, turn right** to the outer corner of a hedge. With the hedge on your right, continue over a stile and **along a green lane**. **Join a drive** at "Woodside" to follow it to the public road at Craignant.

At the road you may decide to take a short diversion (left) to a picnic site and to view a 19thC "Offa's Dyke" sign set high up on a stone buttress. Don't forget to look north to see the Dyke crossing the valley floor.

"G" - **Craignant**. **Turn right** along the road **and take the first sharp left turn**. Descend **along a road which turns sharp right** to pass an old lime kiln and then bends to end at a house left. **Continue along a twitchel.** At a **Minor public road turn left** and opposite a house on the left, **turn right to cross a stile** and rejoin the Dyke.

"H" - **Dyke**. Keep **on the Dyke, or keep it on your left**, crossing a road and a track before descending to cross a footbridge.

"I" - **Footbridge over a stream**. **Continue**, up the bank to cross a road and once more **stay on the dyke or keep it on your left**. Cross a green lane and descend over stiles set in a number of electric fences. Pass a cottage on your left "J".

157

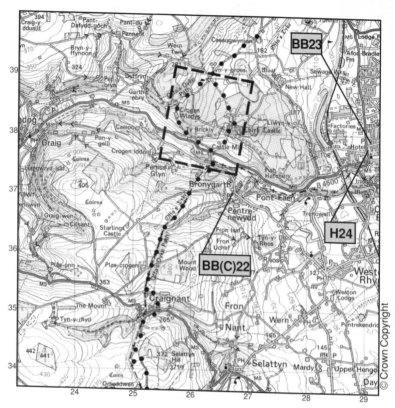

Bronygarth (01691)
No fac's

BB(C)22 - Old School Bronygarth
Tel 772546
Jan-Dec (exc Xmas) Band 1 (1S,2T)
Dogs. Non-Smk'g. Pk'dL. Veg. Trans.
LTPk'g. Bags.
(Camping - Toilet. Shower. Wash/Dry facs)

Chirk (01691) (+1IN,1H)
Bank - Midland (ATM)
Shops, Co-op Shop (0800-2000)
Taxis - Geoff's 774132

Chirk Castle.

Chirk was one of a chain of castles built in the late 13th century to hold the lands won by Edward I. It was begun in 1295 and was a very strong castle due to its "drum" towers and 15-foot thick walls (the mullion windows were later additions).

It was built by Roger Mortimer, Lord of Chirk, and later passed to the Earls of Arundel, to the Lancastrians, the Beauforts and the Yorkists. By the end of the Wars of the Roses it was held by Sir William Stanley.

Buses - See Oswestry.
M-Sa - Limited to Glyn Ceirog.
Rail - See Section Two.
H24 - The Hand Hotel
Tel.773472 TB 3 Crown HComm
Jan-Dec Band 4/5 (14rms)(14PB)
Switch. Visa. M'Card.
EM. Dogs. Lic'd. Pk'dL. Veg. LTPk'g.
BB23 - Pedlar Corner
Tel.772903
Jan-Dec (exc Xmas) Band 1 (2T)
Pk'dL. Veg. Trans. Bags.

Continued next LMap..

158

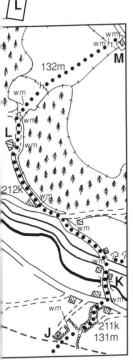

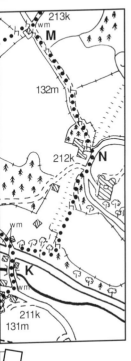

Bronygarth - Tyn-y-groes

(from the bottom of the upper map)

Pass the cottage on your left ("J") to cross a stile in the corner of the field and continue down a twitchel to the public road. Cross the road to turn left down to the river and to a T-junction with the B4500.

Between 1April - 30 September there is a permissive path through the grounds of Chirk Castle. Well worth a visit and the alternative route stays with the Dyke!

Official All-Year Route.

"K" - **B4500**. **Cross** the road **and bear left up a minor road**. The road forks, **bear right to** Crogen Wladys Farm.

"L" - **Crogen Wladys Farm**. Follow the road **through the farm and continue along a track** up into woods. As the **Track levels and bends left, turn right** to cross a stile and walk up the field between Warren Wood and Mars Wood. Cross a stile in a crossing fence and descend to the road at "Tyn-y-groes" "M".

Summer Route.

"K" - **B4500**. **Cross** the road **and bear right through a stone gateway**. Follow the path as it bears left away from the road. Just past a storm damaged oak on your left, the **Dyke** and another path **crosses**, Do not turn left up the other path, but continue for a few metres more. **The Path** now **bears left steeply up through the trees** to a stile in a crossing fence. With the Dyke on your left, **continue up a field**, over a stile **and join a stone track** through the trees to emerge before the Castle. The track joins a **Tarmac road, turn left** to follow the road. The road forks at a GR postbox.

You can still see the line of the Dyke which was levelled to form a cart track. From the air the Dyke can be seen continuing through the lake and it is sometimes exposed when the water level is low.

"N" - **GR Postbox**. **Bear left** towards the stables **and almost immediately bear right**, over a stile, **to follow a track**. Crossing further stiles, the track emerges at "Tyn-y-groes""M".

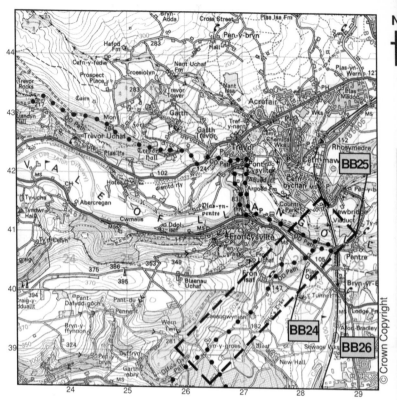

BB24 - Plas Offa Farm
Tel.(01691) 773760
Jan-Dec Band 1 (2D,2T/F)(4PB)
EM. Dogs (outside accommodation).
Pk'dL. Veg. LTPk'g.
Pentre (01691)
BB25 - Sun Cottage
Tel. 774542

Jan-Dec (exc Xmas) Band 1 (1S,2F)
EM. Dogs. Non-Smk'g. Pk'dL. Veg.
Trans. LTPk'g. Bags.
BB26 - Pentre Cottage
Tel. 774265
Jan-Nov Band 1 (1D,1T,1F)
Dogs. Pk'dL. Veg. LTPk'g. Bags.

Chirk Castle continued.. *It was administered by the Tudors until being
granted to the Earl of Leicester in 1495. In 1595 it was purchased by Sir
Thomas Myddelton. The second Sir Thomas Myddelton was the
distinguished Civil War commander on the Parliamentarian side. During
his absence, Chirk was seized by Royalists and he had the unenviable
task of assaulting his own home. His halfhearted attempts cost him the
lives of many of his men! Eventually the Royalists were bribed to leave.
Sir Thomas later changed sides and the whole business started again.
Chirk remained in the Myddelton family until it was transferred to the
State in 1978, and then to the National Trust in 1981.
(Open 1200-1700hrs (Gardens 1100-1800) Apr-Jun & Sep (exc MSa),
Jul-Aug (exc Sa), Oct (SaSu only)) Info Tel. (01691) 777701*

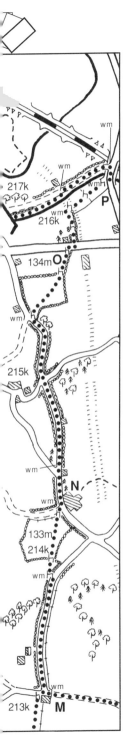

Tyn-y-groes - Shropshire Union Canal

"M" - **Tyn-y-groes**. **Follow the road NE** past "The Kennels". Just past a small wood on the left, the **Road bears right** and on the bend, **continue over two stiles**. Aiming to the left of the farm buildings ahead, emerge over a stile onto a minor road.

"N" - **Minor Road at Caeugwynion Farm**. **Turn left to follow the road**. **Opposite a track** joining from the left, **turn right over a stile** in the hedge on your right. **Cross** an earthwork (not the Dyke) **to a stile in the far corner** of the field. Now **follow a field edge to** a stile by **the A5.**

Grab the Children! The stile is straight onto the A5!

"O" - **A5**. Cross and **turn right, then left down a drive**. **Continue** along a twitchel into a field. With the Dyke on your right, continue for 100m **until turning right over a stile**.

Sadly, this is where you say goodbye to Offa's Dyke. Just a border marker or just a barrier to control trade and stop rustling? It didn't take much imagination for me to see that it looks like a defensive dyke. It took the tactical route in preference to the easiest line and it didn't compromise when crossing difficult ground. It certainly didn't leave me in any doubt as to what it was!

Cross the middle of two fields to **emerge by a bridge** over the canal. **Turn left** and cross the canal.

"P" - **Shropshire Union Canal**. Turn left down to the canal and **follow the towpath** to the aqueduct (see note below).

*To avoid a clumsy mismatch in the orientation of the next section of maps, I have omitted the short section of canal which takes you to the aqueduct. You may want to **keep children under close control** when crossing and I can think of better places to be in high winds or very icy conditions. Fortunately there is an alternative route. Just before the canal bends right to the aqueduct, cross the canal and follow the road down (!) to the river. Shortly after crossing the bridge and turning right, turn left up (!) a waymarked path to join the Llangollen branch of the canal.*

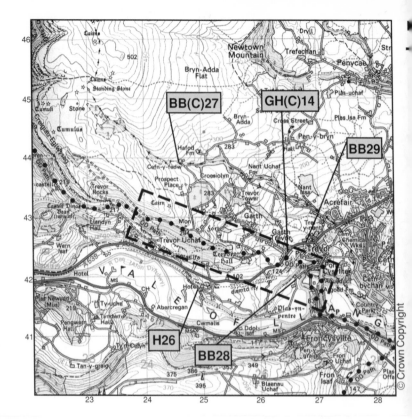

© Crown Copyright

ERRATUM

Page 162 - Trevor. Turn right not left to Australia Arms Public House
See "STOP PRESS" page 224 for last minute changes.

H26 - Bryn Howell Hotel
Tel. 860331 TB 4 Crown HComm
Jan-Dec (exc Xmas) Band 5++
36rms (36PB)
Switch. Visa. M'Card.Amex.
EM. Dogs. Lic'd. Pk'dL. Veg. LTPk'g.
Bags.

GH(C)14 - Oaklands Guest House
Tel. 820152 TB 1 Crown
Jan-Dec (exc Xmas/NY) Band 1
(4S,2D,2T,1F)
Veg.

Mar-Oct Band 1 (2D,2T,2F)(6PB)
Dogs. Non-Smk'g. Pk'dL. Veg. LTPk'g.
*Attractive Country House set in own
grounds overlooking river. 200yds off
Offa's Dyke path. Spacious quality
accommodation. Bar and Restaurant
meals 400yds. Very peaceful location.*

BB29 - The Old School
Tel. 820412
Jan-Dec (exc Xmas/NY) Band 1
(2S,2D,2T)(1PB)
EM. Dogs. Pk'dL. LTPk'g.

Pont Cysyllte Aqueduct - Panorama Walk

"Q" - **Aqueduct**. Immediately **after crossing** the aqueduct, **turn sharp right to pass underneath** it and emerge on the road. **Turn right** and follow the road **to cross** over **the Llangollen Branch of the canal. Turn left to follow the towpath**, shortly using a footbridge to cross back over the canal. The "official Path" joins from the left.

Aqueduct. Built 1795 by Thomas Telford. 1000ft (300m) long and 120ft (36m) high.

"R" - **Official Path rejoins**. **Continue** along the towpath to a footbridge where you **Cross the canal again**. From the stile, **bear left across a field to pass under an old railway embankment. Turn right then left to the A539.**

"S" - **A539 at Trevor**. **Turn left** alongside the road **and take the first minor road right**. The road bends right in front of the entrance to Trevor Hall.

"T" - **Entrance to Trevor Hall**. Continue **down the drive to the Hall** (signposted "To the Church"). **In 75m** the wall on your left turns left and you **bear right up a path into the wood** (not the track). **The Path** emerges at the edge of the wood but soon **re-enters the wood over a stile**. Ignore a path off right, **bear slightly left and down.** With a moss covered wall on your left, the Path continues through the wood. **As the footpath bears left and starts to descend, bear slightly right to emerge in a firebreak**. The Path follows the firebreak, crossing under a power line. **Bear right up into the trees** and emerge over a stile onto a minor road. Turn left along the road towards a monument.

The Monument is dedicated to I D Hooson 1880 - 1948, a Bard Eisteddfod. The monument offers good views over Llangollen and towards Castle Dinas Bran.

"U" - **Monument**. **Continue along the road** to follow the "Panorama Walk".

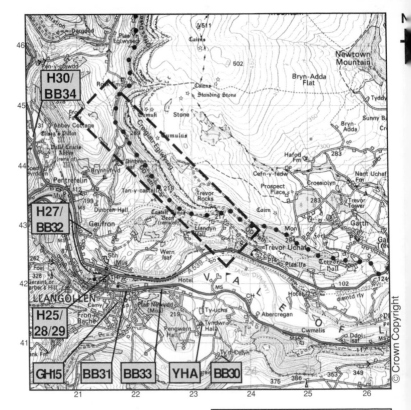

© Crown Copyright

Llangollen (01978) (+5H,13BB)
NB. Accommodation can be difficult to obtain during Eisteddfod week (in July).
<u>Banks</u> - Barclays(ATM, Midland(ATM), NatWest(ATM).
Launderette. Camping equipment.
<u>Taxis</u> - Llangollen Taxis 861018
<u>Buses</u> - M-Sa Frequent to Wrexham, Regular to Chester (Su Limited).
M-Sa - Regular to Bala (Su VLimited)
See Chirk for Southbound buses.
H25 - <u>The Hand Hotel</u>
Tel. 860303 TB 4 Crown
Jan-Dec Band 5+(58rms)(58PB)
All cards. Dogs. Lic'd. Pk'dL. Veg.
LTPk'g.
H27 - <u>Bryn Derwen Hotel</u>
Tel. 860583 TB 3 Crown Comm
Jan-Dec Band 3 (4S,5D,5T,2F)(16PB)
All cards. EM. Dogs. Lic'd. Pk'dL. Veg.
Trans. LTPk'g.

H28 - <u>Gales of Llangollen</u>
Tel. 860089 TB 3 Crown HComm
Jan-Dec (exc Xmas/NY) Band 3
(10D,4T,1F)(15PB)
All cards. EM. Lic'd. Veg. Trans.
LTPk'g. Bags.
Wine List of Year Award 1993. Great food at reasonable prices. Entries in GFG, GHC, Michelin and Routier.

H29 - <u>Bridge End Hotel.</u>
Tel. 860634
Jan-Dec Band 1/2 (4D,4T,1F)(5PB)
Visa. M'Card. Amex.
EM. Dogs. Lic'd. Pk'dL. Veg. Trans.
LTPk'g.

Panorama Walk

Unfortunately, the next 5km's are along a road. However, the views across the Vale of Llangollen are superb and the Castle of Dinas Bran offers a rewarding diversion. Fortunately, the verges are wide so you don't have to walk on the road itself.

"V" - **Dinbren-uchaf Farm**. Over a cattle grid and continue along the road. In 750m you pass Bryn Cottage and in a further 200m the road bears left to Rock Farm "W".

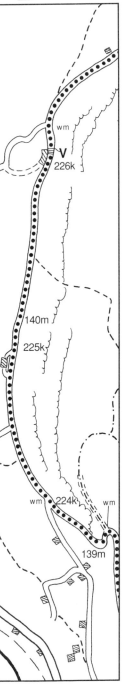

H30 - <u>Abbey Grange Hotel</u>
Tel. 860753 TB 3 Crown
Jan-Dec Band 2 (3D,3T,2F)(8PB)
Visa. M'Card. Amex.
EM. Dogs. Lic'd. Pk'dL. Veg. Trans. LTPk'g. Bags.
Excellent base for walkers. All rooms en-suite. Central Heating. Log fires. Food and drink served all day. Idyllic setting. A warm and friendly welcome.

GH15 - <u>Hillcrest Guest House</u>
Tel. 860208 TB 3 Crown
Jan-Dec Band 2 (3D,2T,2F)(7PB)
EM. Non-Smk'g. Lic'd. Pk'dL. Veg. LTPk'g. Bags.
BB30 - <u>Tyn Celyn Farmhouse</u>
Tel. 861117 TB 3 Crown
Jan-Dec (exc Xmas) Band 2 (1D,1T,1F)(3PB)
Non-Smk'g. Veg. Trans. Bags.
BB31 - <u>Oakmere</u>
Tel. 861126 TB 2 Crown HComm
Jan-Dec Band 2 (2D,2T,2F)(6PB)
Non-smk'g. Pk'dL. Veg. Trans. LTPkg.
BB32 - <u>Dinbren House</u>
Tel. 860593 TB 2 Crown
Jan-Dec Band 1 (2D,2T,2F)(2PB)
Dogs. Pk'dL. Veg. Trans. LTPk'g. Bags.
BB33 - <u>The Hollies</u>
Tel. 869037 TB Listed
Jan-Dec Band 1 (1D,2T)
Non-Smk'g. Pk'dL. Veg. Trans. LTPk'g. Bags.
BB34 - <u>Hendy Isa</u>
Tel. 861232 TB 2 Crown
Jan-Dec Band 1 (4F)(4PB)
Non-Smk'g. Lic'd. Pk'dL. Veg. Trans. LTPk'g.
YHA - <u>Llangollen</u>
Tel. 860330
Open - Apr-Oct (No camping)
Large Hostel. Gets busy with groups especially in school holidays!

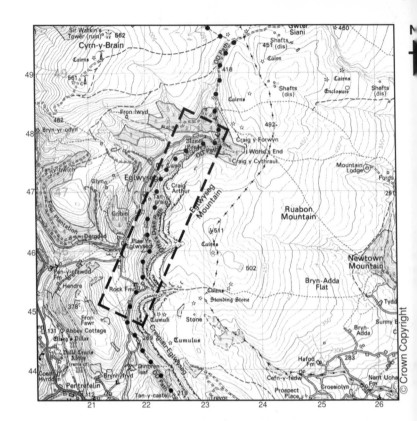

Llangollen.

Situated in the beautiful valley of the River Dee (Afon Dyfrdwy), Llangollen may seem an obvious place at which to break your journey but do heed the warning about accommodation being difficult to find during the Eisteddfod which is held in July (dates vary!). In fact there's some event or other going on from May to November (there's usually a good reason for a place having so many B&B's!).

There has been an Eisteddfod here for at least 200 years but it wasn't until the last century that it became established as a National event, and since the Second World War it has become an International Music Festival. To say it is a festival of music and dancing (mostly country and folk) is really an understatement; culturally, it's much more important than that.

There are a number of places to visit in and around Llangollen and there's more about them in the pages that follow. In the town itself there is Plas Newydd, the home of the Ladies of Llangollen; just to the North lies the ruins of Valle Crucis Abbey, with the Pillar of Eliseg nearby, and to the Northeast is Castle Dinas Bran.

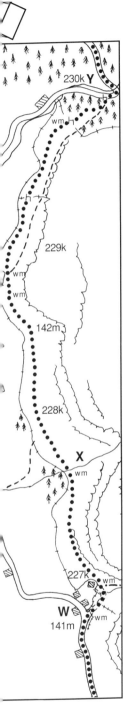

Rock Farm - World's End

"W" - **Rock Farm**. **As the road bears left** down to Rock Farm, **bear right through a gate,** along a track. **Follow the track as it bends left to** cross a stream and then, as it bears left to the cottage of **Bryn Goleu, continue on a path ahead, passing the cottage on your left**. Continue along the Path, over scree, to the small coniferous wood above Plas Yn Eglwyseg.

The Path contours the edge of the valley just above cultivated land and below the cliffs of Eglwyseg Mountain. It crosses scree slopes but they should not present a problem to the average walker. The Path is indistinct in places so in very poor visibility you might decide to follow the road.

"X" - **Small coniferous wood**. The Path passes immediately above the wood, crossing a stream. **Continue, paralleling above the field boundary** on your left, over two more scree slopes. An otherwise clear path can become rather indistinct in places, just maintain your heading and it soon becomes obvious again. **In 1km**, just as you lose a wood down to your left, a field boundary on your left does a left turn, there is a fork in the path and you **take the left fork**. Cross a high stile and soon you will see the 17th century manor house of Plas Uchaf down to your left. The Path enters a forest and descends to the road at World's End "Y".

You might be tempted to take the right fork along a public footpath which rejoins the official Path at World's End. I haven't walked it, but I understand that the descent from Craig yr Adar (above the Manor House) can be difficult.

167

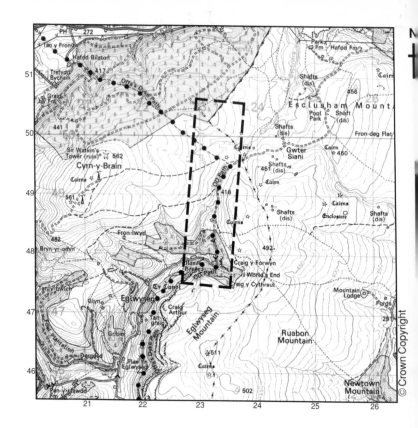

Plas Newydd & The Ladies of Llangollen.

In the late 1770's, Lady Eleanor Charlotte Butler and her companion, Miss Sarah Ponsonby, left Waterford in Ireland to escape the constraints of Irish country life. They settled in Llangollen and set about creating a garden and improving the house, "Plas Newydd", that they had rented. Their eccentric lifestyle and dress, together with a preference for short haircuts, made them the talk of society. Known for their hospitality and good company, they were visited by many leading people of that time, Sheridan, Browning, Tennyson, Sir Walter Scott, Wordsworth, Burke, and even the Duke of Wellington.

The "Ladies of Llangollen" as they were known, lived at Plas Newydd for over 50 years. Lady Eleanor died in 1829 aged 90 and Miss Ponsonby died in 1831 aged 76.

The black and white "magpie"-styled house is full of intricate oak carvings and stained glass, whilst the 12 acres of gardens are a haven of peace and tranquillity. It is owned by the local authority and is open to the public between May and September (Information Tel.(01978) 861314).

World's End - Llandegla Forest

Alas, another stretch of road but this time it's for less than 2km. In summer this is a popular picnic spot and a stream of cars using the narrow and steep road can be wearing. There is a forest trail to a car park that you pass at the edge of the forest, but it's not as direct as the road.

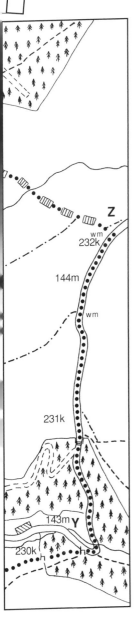

"Y" - **World's End**. **Turn right to follow the road**, paddling through the stream that crosses at a hairpin bend. Pass the stile to the forest trail and continue along the road, eventually emerging from the forest over a cattle grid.

If visibility is poor you will have to stay alert, for there is no distinct feature to mark the point at which the path across the moor comes in to the road. The only clue next to the road itself is an earth hump placed to deter parking. If visibility is reasonable the path is all too obvious. There is a waymark on the left and a notice about the Cyrn-y-Brain SSSI; but the biggest giveaway is the almost continuous boardwalk stretching out across the moor!

"Z" - **Path across the moor**. **Turn left** and soon pick up a boardwalk that goes almost to the stile on the edge of the forest.

The Pillar of Eliseg.

Erected by his grandson, the pillar commemorates Eliseg, who ruled the ancient kingdom of Powys in the mid-eighth century. The inscription on the pillar records how he united the inheritance of Powys from the power of the English and made a "sword-land by fire". The pillar is believed to have stood at around 20ft high but now only 8ft remains. Fortunately, someone recorded the inscription in 1696.

The boundary of Powys from circa 600-850AD is said to have extended from Mold down to the R.Wye at Glasbury! As Dr Hill points out, "whilst we are warned about the facile naming and delimitation of the early medieval kingdoms, it would seem there is a striking correlation between the continuous central section of Offa's Dyke and the possible boundary between Mercia and Powys".

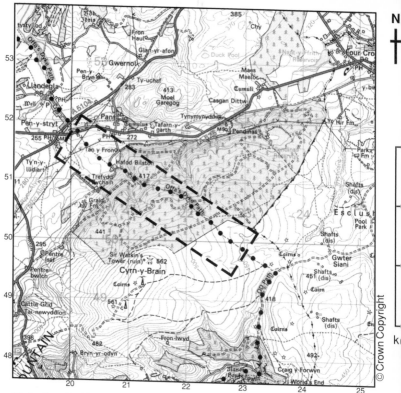

Valle Crucis Abbey.

The Abbey at Valle Crucis was founded in 1201AD by Madog ap Gruffudd, ruler of northern Powys. A Cistercian community (see Tintern Abbey) of "White Monks", it built up considerable estates in the area. By the mid 13th century it derived much of its wealth from wool production. The Abbey suffered a disastrous fire in the mid 13th century following which much of the Abbey's church was rebuilt. The fortunes of the Abbey declined after Edward I's Welsh campaign in the late 13th century, but it had recovered by the 15th century and prospered until its dissolution in 1537.

The Abbey is now in the hands of CADW. CADW's normal opening times - Summer (late March to late October) daily 0930-1830hrs and Winter (late October to late March) M-Sa 0930-1600hrs & Su 1100-1600hrs. (Information Tel. (01978) 860326).

Castle (Castell) Dinas Bran.

Built in the 13th century (possibly by Madog ap Gruffudd (see above)) on the site of an earlier Iron Age hillfort which had long been a stronghold of the Welsh princes. The castle fell into decay after Edward's campaign at the end of the 13th century and played no part in Owain Glyndwr's uprising.

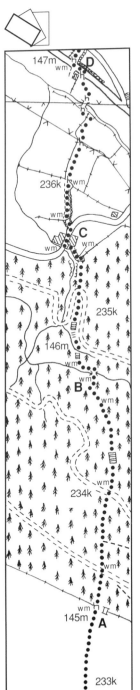

Llandegla Forest - Llandegla

The descent through Llandegla forest used to test your navigational skills but the waymarks and boardwalks now provide ample clues to the Path.

"A" - **Stile at the edge of the forest**. **Straight ahead** from the stile. **Cross two forest roads**, over some boardwalk eventually **Emerging in a cleared area.**

"B" - **Cleared area**. Bear right to **cross a plank footbridge** over a stream. **Turn left and then turn right to resume your heading**. Cross over a crossing path and **Descend a series of boardwalks and steps**. Paralleling a forest track on your left, emerge onto the track at a bend, straight across and **Descend by a ravine to a gate at the edge of the forest. Turn left** down to the houses at Hafod Bilston where you turn left to emerge through a gate on to the road (note the wording in the ironwork).

"C" - **Hafod Bilston**. **Turn right** along the road and, **once clear of the buildings, bear left down a track to a gate**. **Bear right** away from the gate and follow a green lane with the hedge on your right. **Over a stile** to put a fence on your left, **continue to the river** where you **Turn left** through a gateway **and then right over a footbridge**. **Bear left** away from the river to a stile in the far corner of a field and emerge onto the A525.

"D" - **A525**. **Turn left** along the A525 **for a few metres before turning right to** cross the road and **a stile** and go up a path to emerge between houses on a **Minor road. Turn left**, over a crossroads, and follow the road into Llandegla Village. Head for the Church "E".

Llandegla - See over for Facilities & Accommodation
Buses -
MFSa - Shopper - Wrexham-Llandegla-Ruthin
MSa - Shopper Corwen-Llandegla-Wrexham
Schoolbus to Wrexham.

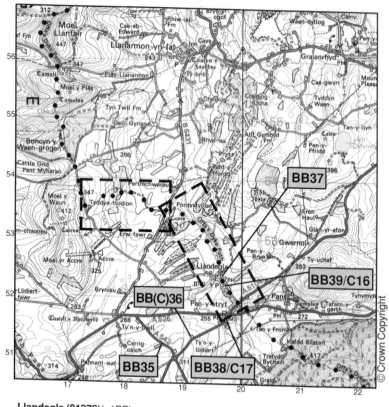

Llandegla (01978)(+1BB)
Telephones (opp PO & A5104)
PO (0830(Su0930)-1800hrs,
lunch 1230-1400hrs, ec WSaSu).
Stores & Off-licence (0800-1730hrs &
1900-2100hrs, lunch 1300-1400hrs,
ec WSa(open in evening),
Su 0900-1230hrs
Knock if it's urgent when closed).
BB35 - Saith Daran Farm
Tel. 790685 TB 2 Crowns
Mar-Nov Band2 (1D,1T)(2PB)
Pk'dL. Trans. LTPk'g. Bags.
BB(C)36 - Tyn y Llidiart
Tel. 790236
Jan-Dec Band 1 (1D/F)(1PB)
Dogs. Pk'dL. Veg. Trans. LTPk'g. Bags
BB37 - The Hand
Tel. 790337
Jan-Dec Band 1 (1S,2D,1F)
EM. Non-Smk'g. Lic'd. Pk'dL. Veg.
LTPk'g. Bags.

BB38 - Raven Farm
Tel. 790224
Mid-Apr - Mid-Sep Band 1
(1S,3D,1T,1F)(1PB)
Non-Smk'g. Pk'dL. Veg. Bags.
BB39 - 2 The Village
Tel. 790266
Apr-Oct Band 1 (1F)(1PB)
Pk'dL. Veg. Trans. LTPk'g. Bags.
C16 - Memorial Hall Field
C/O BB39
Jan-Dec Toilets. Shower. Dogs.
C17 - Llyn Rhys Farm
Tel. 790627
Mid-May - Oct (30 pitches)
Toilets. Showers. Dogs.
Pant
PH - The Plough (B&B?)
Pen-y-stryt
PH - Crown Inn (food)
NB The PH at Llandegla is closed.

172

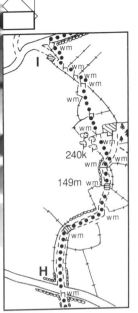

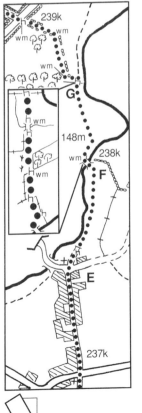

Llandegla

The Path from Llandegla to the B5431 is not shown clearly on the OS maps, some of the hedgelines have disappeared and, just to make life difficult, the route has changed to adapt to some new fences: I suggest you keep the guide handy! Remember, "continue" means - maintain your heading.

"E" - **Llandegla Church**. Pass the Church on your left **down a green lane**. **Over a stile**, **continue**, with the river on your left, to the end of the field and a footbridge.

"F" - **Footbridge over river**. **Cross and bear right** away from the footbridge. **Bear left in front of a fence** (with an inviting stile). **As the fence** (now on your right) **steps out in front of you, cross a stile to put it on your left**. **Continue to** the corner of a field by **a wood and cross a high stile. Continue,** with a fence and the wood on your right. The fence turns right, away from you, as you continue, now picking up a fence on your left. **Cross a stiled footbridge over a stream and continue**, across a gap between two fields, **to a stile in a crossing fence**.

"G" - **Stile in crossing fence**. Over the stile, **turn left, for 25m to cross through a crossing hedgeline, and then turn right.** With an intermittent hedge right, **Continue to an old crossing hedgeline and turn left to follow it towards an outcrop of rock** where you **Continue along an ancient sunken lane** to a stile and the B5431 (a very minor road).

"H" - **B5431**. **Straight across** to take a track to "Chweleiriog". **Follow the track across two cattle-grids and through a gateway**. The track bears right and becomes tarmaced. Leave the track to **Bear left across a field to a stile** situated in a crossing fence (level with and between the farm right and a wood left). Straight away to another stile in a crossing fence and **Continue to a third stile** in the far corner of the field. **Turn left**, over two more stiles, heading for the buildings of Tyddyn-liodion.

"I" - **Tyddyn-liodion**. Jink right and left to **pass the buildings over on your left**. Over a stile in a crossing hedge **to emerge onto a minor road where you turn right**.

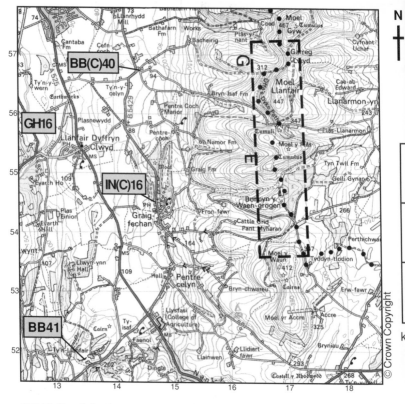

GH16 - <u>Eyarth Station</u>
Tel. (01824) 703643 TB 3 Crown
HComm
Jan-Dec Band 2 (2D,2T,2F)(6PB)
Visa. M'Card. EM. Dogs. Non-Smk'g.
Pk'dL. Veg. Trans. LTPk'g. Bags.
BB(C)40 - <u>Gorffwysfa</u>
Tel. (01824) 702432 TB 3 crown
Jan-Dec Band 1 (1D,1T,1F)(3PB)
EM. Dogs. Non-Smk'g. Pk'dL. Veg.
Trans. LTPk'g. Bags.
BB41 - <u>Ty Brith</u>
Tel. (01978) 790279 TB 2 Crown H
Comm
Jan-Dec Band 2 (1D)(1PB)
Non-Smk'g. Trans. LTPk'g.

Graigfechan
Telephone.
<u>Buses</u> - M-Sa Denbigh - Waen -
Llanbedr DC - Ruthin - Graigfechan.
Bus service at least 3 times daily ea
way linking villages near the B5429 with
Ruthin & Denbigh (extra services on
the Denbigh- Ruthin part) (Funded by
Clwyd County Council (post Apr 96?))
IN(C)16 - <u>Three Pigeons Inn</u>
Tel. (01824) 703178
Jan-Dec Band 1 (2D,1T)
EM. Lic'd. Pk'dL. Veg. LTPk'g.
Showers & Drying facs for
Backpackers
Llanarmon - yn - Ial
Telephone. Shop/PO
PH - The Raven Inn (B&B)
<u>Buses</u> - M-Sa Limited service Ruthin -
Llanarmon-yn-Ial - Mold
MThSa - VLimited to Wrexham

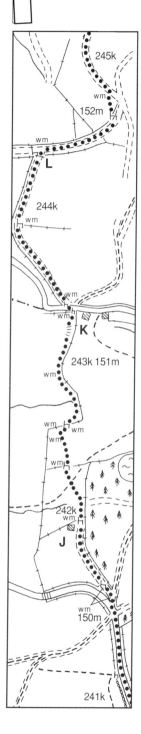

Clwydian Hills (Moel Llanfair)

Continue along the minor road from Tyddyn-liodion. **As the road bends left, continue along a track** that forks in front of a plantation. **Take the left fork** up to the radio mast.

"J" - <u>Radio Mast</u>. **Pass the mast** on your left, over a stile in a crossing fence and bear left **down to a stile. At the crest of the hill ahead, bear right to a stile**. Bear right to follow the fence, now on your right. **Stay with the fence** as it bears right and descends **to a minor road** by the buildings of Ty'n-y-mynydd.

"K" - <u>Tyn-y-mynydd</u>. **Turn left** along the road and **then turn right to cross a stile. Bear left away on a track** that skirts Moel Llanfair to a T-junction with another track.

"L" - <u>T-junction with track</u>. **Turn right** and take the track to the col between Moel Llanfair and Moel Gyw. **Just before the col**, **turn left** to cross a stile **and cut the corner** over to join a track skirting Moel Gyw.

Ruthin.

A town that retains its medieval street plan and has many interesting and historic buildings. St.Peter's Church (1310AD) has a very fine carved and panelled roof donated by Henry VII. It has 14thC cloisters and nearby is Christ's Hospital, a 16thC almshouse. Nant Clwyd House (private) is one of Wales' finest Elizabethan townhouses and the Manor Courthouse is a half-timbered house built at the beginning of the 15thC. A number of the town's Inns are particularly fine buildings with unusual features.

Ruthin Castle (now a Hotel) was built in the late 13thC during Edward I's campaigns but largely demolished in the 17thC.

Altogether a charming town and if it is sometimes a little overshadowed by neighbouring Denbigh, my preference is certainly for Ruthin which has much to commend a visit.

175

YHA - Maeshafn
Tel. Cardiff (01222) 237817.
Open Mid-Apr - Jun (FSa only). Jul-Aug. Sep (FSa only)
5km off Path. GR SJ 208606
Llanbedr DC (01824) (+1IN,1BB)
H32 - Clwyd Gate Motel
Tel. 704444 TB 3 Crowns HComm
Jan-Dec Band 3 (11rms)(11PB)
Visa. M'Card. EM. Dogs. Lic'd. Pk'dL.
Veg. Trans. LTPk'g. Bags.
BB42 - Bwlch Uchaf
Tel. 780229 Jan-Dec Band 1 (1D.1T)
Dogs. Pk'dL. Veg. LTPk'g.
BB43 - Fron Deg
Tel. 702931Apr-Oct Band 1 (1S,1D)
Pk'dL. Trans. LTPk'g. Bags.
BB(C)44 - Ffynnon Berth
Tel. 780298
Apr-Oct Band 1 (1S,1D,1T,1F)(1PB)
EM. Dogs. Pk'dL. Veg. Trans. LTPk'g.
Bags.

Ruthin (01824) - Facilities & more
B&B's on next LMap.
H33 - Manor House Hotel
Tel. 704830 TB 3 Crown HComm
Jan-Dec Band 3 (2S,5D,2T)(9PB)
Visa. M'Card. EM. Dogs. Lic'd. Pk'dL.
Veg. Trans. LTPk'g.
H31 - The Coach House Hotel
Tel. 704223 TB 3 Crown
Jan-Dec Band 2 (1S,5D,1T)(7PB)
Switch. Visa. M'Card. EM. Lic'd. Pk'dL.
Veg. Trans. LTPk'g.

IN17 - Ye Olde Anchor Inn
Tel. 702813 TB 3 Crown HComm
Jan-Dec Band 2 (1S,6D,7T)(14PB)
Switch. Visa. M'Card.
EM.Dogs. Lic'd. Pk'dL. Veg. Trans.
LTPk'g. Bags.
Family run 17th century Inn decorated
to the highest standard. AA Two
Rosettes for our cuisine, "Just taste
that home-baked bread"

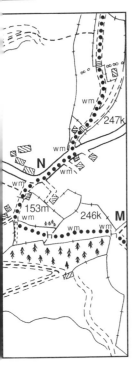

Clwydian Hills (Moel Eithinen)

Continue along the track that skirts Moel Gyw, to the tip of a coniferous plantation on your left.

"M" - **Coniferous Plantation**. **Cross a stile** in a crossing fence **and bear left**. Pass just to the left of the first summit and then over the next. **Cross a stile** situated in a crossing fence between the forest left and a small plantation to the right. **Bear gently right** across a field to the far right corner and **Turn right along a track to the A494** and the Clwyd Gate Motel.

"N" - **A494 Clwyd Gate Motel**. **Turn right along the A494** for 300m **and then** cross to **bear left up a track**. Bear right in front of a house and **Continue on the track**, over a cattle grid. The track forks, take the left fork, cross another cattle grid. **As the track bears right through a gateway, bear left to a stile** by a gate ahead. **Continue on a green track** to pass along the edge of a small plantation. Continue along a field edge (wall right), passing Moel Eithinen Farm down on your right.

"O" - **Moel Eithinen Farm**. **Continue** above the farm **and at the end of the field turn left**. Pass a small plantation on your right **and cross a stile**. Now with fence left, **Continue** along a field edge **until turned right by a crossing fence to a stile** by the tip of a coniferous forest on your right.

The Path used to go over Foel Fenlli but concern over the erosion that was being caused to the hillfort has resulted in it being rerouted. Strange as it may seem, the forest on your right is not shown on the 1:25,000 OS and is barely noticeable on the 1:50,000 OS map. Yet the trees are mature! Perhaps someone has found a super-fast growing conifer? The fencelines do not match the 1:25,000 and the line of the rerouted Offa's Dyke Path on the 1:50,000 is not correct. Stick with the guide!

"P" - **Bwlch Crug-glas Forest**. **Cross the stile and descend to, and cross, two stiles. Straight away from them to climb halfway up the hill until turned left to contour the hill.** The Path eventually joins the outer defensive ditch of the hillfort.

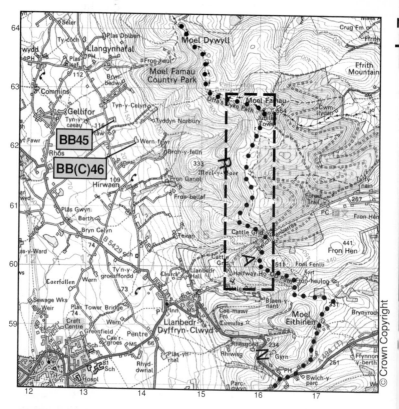

Ruthin cont'd (01824)
H36 - Castle Hotel
Tel. 702479 TB 3 Crown
Jan-Dec Band 2 (20rms)(20PB)
Visa. M'Card.Amex. Diners.
EM. Dogs. Lic'd. Pk'dL. Veg. Trans.
LTPk'g. Bags.

C18 - Minffordd
Tel. 707169
Apr-Oct (15 pitches)
Dogs. Trans! Bags. Shower. Breakfast!

Ruthin Facilities (01824)
Banks - Midland(ATM), Barclays,
NatWest.
Camping Shop - Army & Navy Stores.
Taxis - BJ Taxis - 702765

Ruthin Buses (+Llanbedr DC)
M-Sa Frequent to Rhyl via Denbigh-
St.Asaph-Rhuddlan
M-Sa Limited to Mold (via Llanbedr DC,
Clwyd Gate & Llanferres)
M-Sa Limited to Corwen
See page 174 for local bus on B5429.

Llangynhafal (01824)(+2BB)
PH - The Golden Lion (food)
Buses - see page 174.
BB45 - Esgairlygain
Tel. 704047 TB 3 Crown
Apr-Nov Band 1 (1D,1T,1F)(3PB)
EM. Dogs. Non-Smk'g. Pk'dL. Veg.
Trans. LTPk'g. Bags.
BB(C)46 - Wern Fawr
Tel. 703165 TB 2 Crown
Jan-Dec Band 2 (1D,1T)(2PB)
Non-smk'g. Pk'dL. Trans. LTPk'g.
Bags.

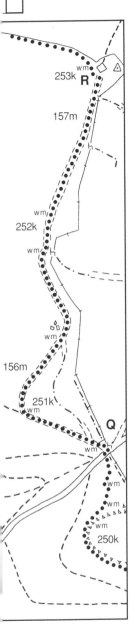

Clwydian Hills (Moel Famau)

Welcome to the Moel Famau Country Park where walkers are welcome but you <u>will</u> stick to the Path. There are railings, steps, more waymarks per kilometre than anywhere else on the route, and "traps" to catch those that stray off the designated Path!

Continue round the outer defence of the hillfort until the Path bears off left (North-East) to descend to the road and the Moel Famau Car Park.

"Q" - **Moel Famau Car Park**. **Take the track to the summit.**

Moel Famau & The Jubilee Tower

At 554m (1818ft) Moel Famau (trans. "Mother Mountain") is the highest of the Clwydians. The Jubilee Tower was built in 1810 to celebrate the 50th year of George III's reign. It wasn't completed and what was built collapsed! In 1970, as a European Conservation Year project, funds were obtained to smarten it up and put toposcopes on the remaining stump.

What a shame there wasn't enough money to remove it altogether. Instead it has become a tourist attraction, complete with motorway to the top. All that's missing is a cafe or ice-cream parlour.

However, the views on a clear day are exceptional but you may find yourself jostling with all manner of tourists and school parties. I once heard a teacher brief his group of primary school children for the descent to the bus; "Nobody goes faster than me. If you run and break you leg, don't come running to me!" With that the children swarmed off the hill leaving the remnants of their packed lunch bags blowing gracefully around the tower. As a result of so many people feeding the sheep the animals now demand food with menaces and I do mean nose-to-nose confrontation!

"R" - **Jubilee Tower**. **Head away** from the tower **with a wall on your right**.

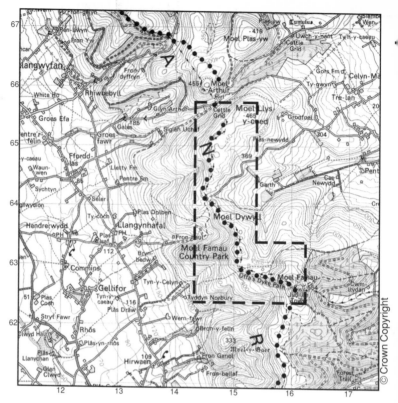

Denbigh (Dinbych).

Denbigh (the name means "fortified place") was a stronghold of the Welsh until Edward I's conquest when Llewelyn the Last's lands were granted to Henry de Lacy, Earl of Lincoln and the first Lord of Denbigh. He started building a castle in 1282 and a fortified town grew up around it. The town was granted a Borough Charter in 1290. The Welsh captured the town in a brief uprising in 1294. However their success was short-lived and when the town was recaptured work was put in hand to further improve the town's fortifications.

Owain Glyndwr attacked and burnt the town in 1402, and following a second devastation in the Wars of the Roses (1468), the town was moved to its present site.

Denbigh prospered as a market town and in Elizabeth I's reign it was held by Robert Dudley, Earl of Leicester, until his death in 1588. It continued to prosper and in the Civil War was held by the Royalists. The castle was surrendered to the Parliamentarians and became redundant. The castle is now in the hands of CADW. See page 170 for CADW opening times (Denbigh Castle Info (01745) 813979).

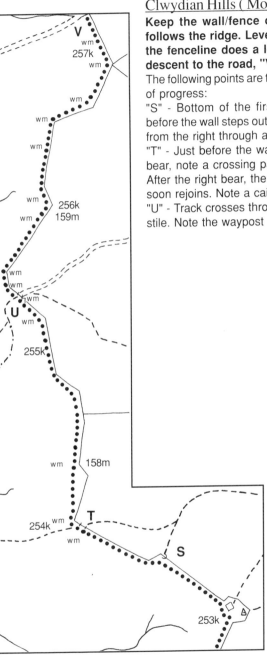

Clwydian Hills (Moel Dywyll)

Keep the wall/fence on your right as it follows the ridge. Level with Moel Arthur, the fenceline does a left turn for a steep descent to the road, "V".

The following points are to help you keep track of progress:

"S" - Bottom of the first stepped descent, before the wall steps out left, note a path joins from the right through a kissing gate.

"T" - Just before the wall/fence does a right bear, note a crossing path with a gate right. After the right bear, the wall bears away but soon rejoins. Note a cairn left.

"U" - Track crosses through a gate, next to a stile. Note the waypost with distances.

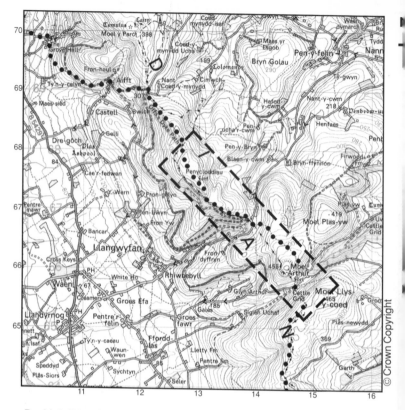

Denbigh (01745) (+2H,1IN)

<u>Banks</u> - NatWest(ATM), Midland(ATM), Barclays(ATM)

<u>Taxis</u> - Peter's 812476. Evans 812052.

<u>Buses</u> -
M-Sa Frequent to Rhyl (Su Regular)
M-Sa Regular to Mold (via Bodfari)
M-Sa Limited to Holywell (via Bodfari)

GH17 - <u>Cayo Guest House</u>
Tel.812686 TB 3 Crown
Jan-Dec (exc Xmas/NY) Band 1
(1S,2D,3T)(4PB)
Visa. M'Card. Amex. Diners.
EM. Dogs. Lic'd. PK'dL. Trans. LTPk'g.

Llangwyfan
It's a Hospital! Nearest PH at roundabout by Waen B5429 - Kimmel Arms (food)

Llandyrnog (+1BB)
Telephone. PO/Stores.
PH's - The Golden Lion (food) & The White Horse Inn (food).

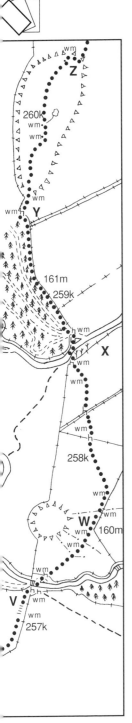

Clwydians (Moel Arthur) -
Penycloddiau Fort

The Path descends to a minor road where you bear right over a stile and cross the road to a parking area.

"V" - **Moel Arthur Carpark**. Cross the stile to your right on the other side of the parking area. The **Path bears right before climbing** to pass to the East of the hillfort on Moel Arthur. At the top of the climb a fence joins from the right and together you cross a green track linking Moel Arthur and Moel Plas-yw.

"W" - **Moel Arthur - crossing track**. **Continue and** just as you start to lose height, **bear left away from the fence to descend** on a well-defined path to a stile in a crossing fence. Cross to a further stile in a double fence and descend steeply to a stile. **Turn right to follow the minor road for 100m** before bearing left to a parking area.

"X" - **Forest parking area**. Just beyond gates into the forest, **turn left through a hand-gate and take the right-hand track for only 30m before bearing up right on a path** between the edge of the forest and a fence on your right. Continue with the fence to a stile at the top of the hill where you turn right to the hillfort of Penycloddiau.

The Path used to go westwards around the rampart of the fort, but it now passes through the centre of the fort.

"Y" - **Penycloddiau Hillfort**. Straight away from the stile to **follow a broad path through the centre of the fort**. A path crosses from the left but you continue to a cairn which marks the highest point of the fort, "Z".

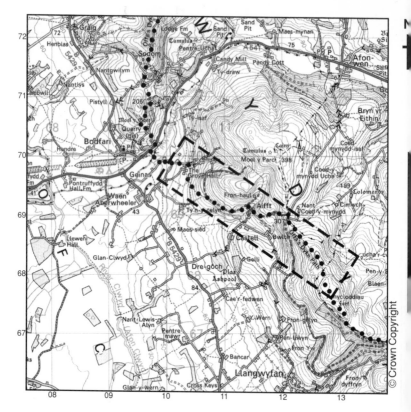

Langton's Guides - Your help is requested

You are on the last lap of your coast to coast walk. Soon you will see the sea and thoughts will turn to getting home. Before it is too late and you consign this guide to your bookshelf; I'd like you to consider how well it has served you on your journey and how future Langton's Guides can be improved. In this guide; the inclusion of a few photographs, the cumulative distances (in km's and miles), the OS grid on the location maps etc, were all introduced as a result of feedback from the users of our previous guides. In the next guide, we hope to develop the expedition planning maps and will be looking at introducing some colour.

One special plea. The waymarks north of Bodfari seem to disappear at a rate that is frankly ridiculous. Walkers couldn't be taking them for souvenirs, could they?

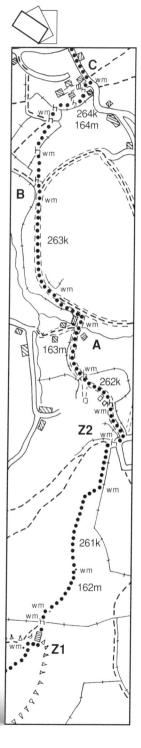

Penycloddiau - Bodfari

"Z1" - **Cairn**. **Continue**, dropping down into a ditch and then up onto a **Defensive bank** where you **turn right and in only a few metres turn left** down an artificial "rock slide". Straight away to a **Memorial stile** in a crossing fence. Straight away from the stile but after only 30m, **bear right with the Path to follow the ridge**. The Path bears right down to follow a field boundary to a stile in a corner with a crossing fence. Turn right to cross the stile onto the access road for Nant Coed-y-mynydd.

"Z2" - **Access road to Nant Coed-y-mynydd**. **Turn left then immediately bear left down a rough track**. Follow the track as it descends, through gates and past barns, to pass the farm buildings of "Ty Newydd" (west of Aifft).

"A" - **Ty Newydd Farm**. **Continue on the track** past the farm and **across a stream**. **Bear left onto a green path and then rejoin the track for 600m** as it contours the hill. **As the track bears right, bear left on a path to descend** away from the track. A path (not marked) and fence join from the left.

"B" - **Fence joins**. **Continue** with the fence on your left **to a corner** with a crossing fence, **where you jink left and then right over a stile** (1) **to continue ahead** across a field. Cross a stile (2) in a fence joining from sharp left and turn right to continue across 2 more stiles (3 & 4). After the second stile (4), turn right to follow the field edge across a further stile (5) before bearing left to emerge over a last stile onto the access road for Grove Hall Farm.

"C" - **Grove Hall Farm access road**. **Turn right and at the public road, turn left.**

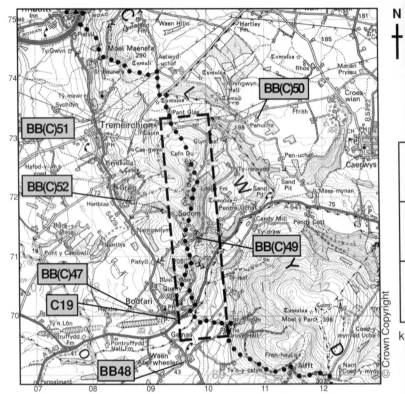

Bodfari (01745) (+1BB)
PH's - Dinorben Arms (food)
PO/Stores M-Sa (ec ThSa)
<u>Buses</u> - See Denbigh
BB(C)47 - <u>Ty'n y Ffordd Isa</u>
Tel. 710273
Jan-Dec Band 1 (1S,1T)
Dogs. Non-smk'g. Trans. LTPk'g.
BB48 - <u>Bryn Clwyd</u>
Tel. 710357 Mar-Oct Band 1
(1S,1D,1T) Non-Smk'g. Pk'dL. Veg.
Trans. LTPk'g. Bags.

BB(C)49 - <u>Fron Haul</u>
Tel. 710301 TB 2 Crown Comm
Jan-Dec Band 1 (1D,1T,1F)(1PB)
EM. Dogs. Pk'dL. Veg. Trans. LTPk'g.
Bags.
Discover an oasis of calm and taste at
Fron Haul, 200yds off the Offa's Dyke
Path. Good wholesome cooking from
home grown produce. A guaranteed
taste of Wales.

<u>**C19**</u> - <u>Station House Caravan Park</u>
Tel. 710372
Apr-Oct (6 tent pitches)
Toilets. Showers. Dogs.
Caerwys (01352)
BB(C)50 - <u>Plas Penucha</u>
Tel. 720210 TB 3 Crown HComm
Jan-Dec Band 2 (2D,2T) (2PB)
EM. Dogs. Non-Smk'g. Pk'dL. Veg.
Trans. LTPk'g. Bags.
Tremeirchion (01745)
PH - The Brynhyfryd Inn
BB(C)51 - <u>Ffynnon Beuno</u>
Tel. 710475
Feb-Dec (exc Xmas) Band 1
(1D,1T,1S)(1PB)
Dogs. Pk'dL. Veg. Trans. LTPk'g.
BB(C)52 - <u>Pen y Graig</u>
Tel. 710253
Jan-Dec Band 1 (3D) (3PB)
EM. Dogs. Pk'dL. Veg. Trans. LTPk'g.
Bags.

186

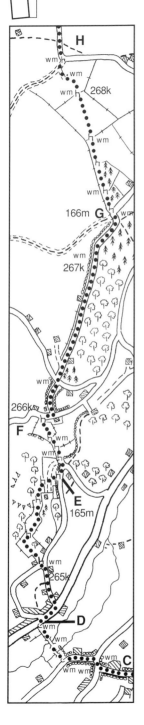

Bodfari - Tremeirchion

Continue along the minor road from Grove Hall ("C") **to a T-junction. Turn right and in 50m turn left** along another minor road. **As the road bends left, turn right through a kissing gate.** Cross a stream and then the River Wheeler to the A541.

"D" - **A541 Trunk Road**. **Turn right and opposite the Downing Arms public house, turn left up a very steep minor road. At a T-junction bear left to a stile opposite. Ascend the hill and** just before a crossing fence, **bear right to a stile** in the top right-hand corner. **Straight away from the stile**, with a fence on your right, towards some firs. **Bear left and continue to a stile**. Over the stile into woodland and continue. **Bear right down to a fence. Parallel the fence** and track beyond, for 20m **until you turn right to cross a stile. Bear left down to a stile** and emerge once more onto the road.

"E" - **Minor Road**. **Turn left and at a hairpin bend go straight ahead** on a track. The track bends left in front of a field entrance**, continue over a stile** and with a field boundary on your left, continue over 2 more stiles. Cross the centre of a field to a stile and a minor public road.

"F" - **Minor Public Road**. **Turn right and in 50m turn left to take a minor road** for just over a kilometre. On the way you pass deciduous and then coniferous forest. The road bends left and in 50m bends right.

"G" - **Road bends left then right**. **On the right bend, continue ahead over a stile (1)** to pass a young coniferous plantation on your right. Continue over two stiles (2&3) to emerge into a field. Continue with fence left to a crossing fence and Stile (4) where you bear right away from the stile to cross the centre of the field. At stile (5) head straight away from the stile and down the field bearing slightly left (see below) to join a track. Down to a stile where you emerge onto a minor road at a bend.

If you are doing the Offa's Dyke Path by night do **look out for the sudden drop into a spring!**

"H" - **Minor Road**. **Continue ahead**, along the road.

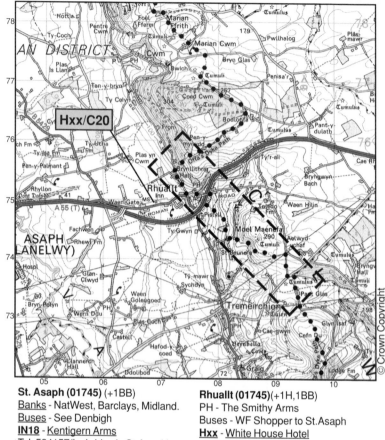

Hxx/C20

© Crown Copyright

St. Asaph (01745) (+1BB)
Banks - NatWest, Barclays, Midland.
Buses - See Denbigh
IN18 - Kentigern Arms
Tel. 584157(by bridge in St.Asaph)
Jan-Dec Band 2 (Single 3) (4F)
EM. Lic'd. Pk'dL. Veg. LTPk'g.
BB(C)53 - Pen-y-Bryn Farm
Tel. 583213 TB 1 Crown
Jan-Dec Band 1 (1S,1D,1T)(1PB)
Visa. Dogs. Non-smk'g. Veg. Trans.
LTPk'g. Bags. (1km W of St. Asaph
GR025744)

Rhuallt (01745)(+1H,1BB)
PH - The Smithy Arms
Buses - WF Shopper to St.Asaph
Hxx - White House Hotel
Tel. 582155
Jan-Dec (exc Xmas) Band 1/2
(1S,5D,1T)(3PB)
Visa, M'Card, Diners.
EM. Lic'd. Pk'dL. Veg. Trans.
C20 - White House Caravan Park
Tel. 582155
Jan-Dec (8 tent pitches) Toilets.
Showers. Wash/Dry facs. Dogs.

St. Asaph.

Its Welsh name "Llanelwy" is derived from the Elwy, by which river and the River Clwyd it stands. Asaph, to whom the cathedral (one of the smallest in Great Britain) is dedicated, was bishop here during the Celtic period (6th century). The early cathedral, built of wood, was burnt by the English in 1247 and 1282. That built by Bishop Anian in the 13th century was mostly destroyed by Owain Glyndwr in 1402. Bishop Redman's building (circa 1480) was finally completed in 1770.

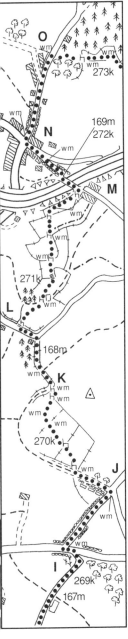

Tremeirchion - Rhuallt

Continue along the road until it bends left in front of a wood to arrive at a T-junction with the road to Tremeirchion.

"I" - **T-junction with Tremeirchion Road**. **Turn left and in 50m turn right** along a minor road. In 400m a road joins from the right.

"J" - **Road joins from the right**. **At the junction turn left down a track**. After only one field, **200m turn right over a stile** next to a field entrance. **Bear left away from the stile** to cross to a stile in a fence. Bear slightly right to a waymark on an old field boundary and start to descend on a path through gorse. Cross two stiles in quick succession to emerge onto a bridleway between fences.

"K" - **Bridleway between fences**. **Turn right, follow the bridleway** as it bends left and continue to where it joins a Minor road on a bend. **Turn left down the minor road. After only 200m look out for steps** on your right leading up to a stile (easily missed!).

"L" - **Stile at top of steps**. **Straight away from the stile** aiming left of a barn at the end of some coniferous trees ahead. **Cross the belt of trees and aim across the next field at the outer corner of a line of trees. Descend steps** and straight ahead to a stile opposite. **Continue** over two stiles to the fence bordering the **A55 dual carriageway. Turn right** at the fence to a stile by houses and a footbridge.

"M" - **Footbridge over A55 Dual Carriageway**. **Cross** the footbridge and **continue straight down** to a crossroads in the village.

"N" - **Crossroads by Smithy Arms Public House**. **Turn right** at the crossroads and **follow a minor public road for 500m** to the buildings (right) of Brynllithrig Hall.

"O" - **Brynllithrig Hall**. Pass the buildings and **just as a wall on your left ends, turn right, ascend steeply** up a path through the edge of a deciduous wood. At a stile on the edge of the wood, **continue up a field** to a crossing fence with **Coniferous forest** beyond. **Turn right**.

189

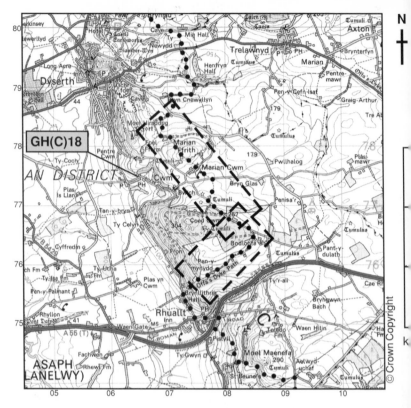

Cwm (01745)
PH - The Blue Lion (& Restaurant - for that special last lap celebration?)
Telephone at crossroads.

<u>GH(C)18</u> - <u>Two Hoots Guesthouse</u>
Tel.570226 TB Listed
Jan-Nov Band 1 (2T)(1PB)
EM. Dogs. Pk'dL. Veg. Trans. LTPk'g.
Bags.

Offa and Rhuddlan

Tradition has it that Offa died at Rhuddlan in 796AD although, as mentioned in Section One, this is almost certainly an error. The 10th century "Annales Cambriae" recorded a number of events involving Offa including:

> *778   Devastation of South Britons by Offa*

> *784   Devastation of Britain by Offa in the summer.*

> *796   Offa King of the Mercians and Maredudd King of the Demetians die, <u>and</u> the Battle of Rhuddlan.*

Other early histories confirm the events and dates also without suggesting that Offa died at Rhuddlan. Dr Hill is convinced that the death of Offa <u>at</u> Rhuddlan is a distortion in much later and less reliable histories.

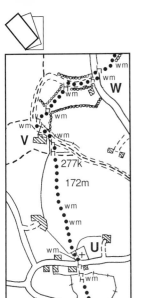

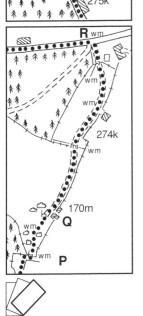

Rhuallt - Bryn Cnewyllyn

Having turned right in front of the forest fence, continue for 20m to a stile at the corner of the forest.

"P" - **Stile at Forest Corner**. **Turn left** and follow a path through gorse bushes to a redundant stile.

"Q" - **Redundant stile by Pen-y-mynydd farmhouse**. **Bear right to join a track** which you follow all the way to a minor public road.

"R" - **Minor Public Road**. **Turn left** and follow the road for just under 1km to the end of the forest on your left.

"S" - **Forest ends**. **Just after the forest on your left ends, turn right to cross a stile**. Follow the field edge with fence right until turned left at a corner. Within 20m turn right at a second corner and bear left across the field to a stile opposite and a minor road.

"T" - **Second Minor Public Road**. **Turn left and in a few metres turn right to cross a stile. Bear left** away from the stile to head for a clump of trees. Cross stile to continue up a twitchel and emerge opposite the chapel at Marian Cwm.

"U" - **Chapel at Marian Cwm**. **Turn left and then right to take a track besides the graveyard**. Through a gate, continue **Over the hill** to a stile to the right of farm buildings. Continue across a small field to emerge over a second stile **onto a green lane. Turn left** to pass the buildings immediately on your left.

The waymarks over Marian Ffrith Hill tend to pull you off your heading. Once over the summit, bear slightly right as you descend. Keep clear of a new tipping operation!

"V" - **Farm Buildings**. **Continue** through a gate and **along the track. After 100m turn right to cross a stile**. Straight away from the stile to cross a field to a second stile. Bear left to keep the hedge on your left and **continue to a stile and the track again. Turn right** along the track to a minor public road.

"W" - **Minor Road by "Morwylfa"**. **Turn left and in a few metres turn right to cross a stile. Aim for a waypost set in the very end of a hedge** (the hedge would have come up to the stile but it has obviously been grubbed up).

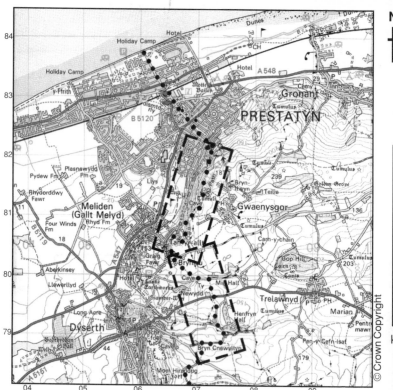

Offa's Dyke - The Northern Section

For some three centuries historians have attempted to locate the missing section of Offa's Dyke from Llanfynydd (near Treuddyn) to the sea, a distance of some 35km (22 miles). Discontinuous sections of earthwork (spread over a total distance of only 6km (3.75 miles)) ending at Trelawnyd (GR 090795) were taken to be part of Offa's Dyke and Fox added a further fragment at Gop Hill just to the NW. Excavation has shown these sections to be of different construction to Offa's Dyke and no evidence has been found of any earthwork in between the sections, let alone on any postulated line to join the known Dyke.

Even if one were to accept the hypothesis that the Dyke ran to Prestatyn, Dr Hill points out that it would follow no natural or historical frontier nor any known division of agricultural, linguistic or topographical origin. The missing northern section has all the appearance of an attempt to rationalise the line of a Dyke that has always been known as "the Dyke that ran from sea to sea".

The author is grateful to Dr David Hill and Mrs Margaret Worthington for the generous access they have allowed me to their notes. References to their work in this guide can only be a brief and very crude summary. Unfortunately, any such summary is bound to appear conclusive and it is important to note that their research continues.

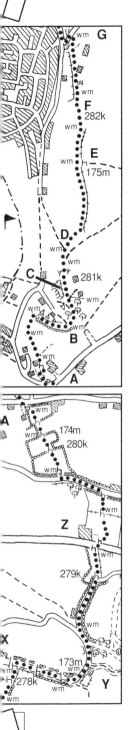

Bryn Cnewyllyn - Prestatyn.

"W" - continued. **Continue** over stiles to emerge onto a green lane.

"X" - <u>Green Lane by Bryn Cnewyllyn</u>. **Turn right and follow the lane** to the old watermill.

"Y" - <u>Marian Mill</u>. **Continue, pass a fish farm, bear right at a fork** in the road. As the **Road bends right, continue ahead** across stiles to emerge at the A5151.

"Z" - <u>A5151</u>. **Bear right across to a stile** and detour round a silage clamp **to cross two fields to a minor road. Turn left and in 200m turn right up steps** to a stile. Cross the field under power lines to a stile. **Continue over** 4 more **stiles until emerging onto** the drive of "Clarence House" and **a minor road.**

The objective on the next section is to skirt a quarry but don't get diverted down left. Then follow the edge of the scarp, don't get diverted inland and don't descend before passing Point "E".

"A" - <u>Minor Road</u>. **Turn left**, then **fork right** down a road, then **right again through a kissing gate**. Bear right in front of a bungalow to cross a stile. Fork left to emerge onto an open area. **At a quarry edge turn right** through a kissing gate and descend slightly to the top of the rear of the quarry.

"B" - <u>Quarry</u>. Continue **above and round the end of the quarry**. Ignore paths descending left. Fork left at a split in the path. A fence comes up on your left.

"C" - <u>Fence up from left</u>. **Continue** with the fence on your left. The fence turns away, **pass a public footpath off right**. The path forks.

"D" - <u>Path Forks Down Left, Up right</u>. **Bear right to climb** steeply up the hill until turned left in front of a fence at the top. Continue with the fence on your right.

"E" - <u>Public Footpath off right</u>. **Continue,** the Path soon leaves the fence to **descend steeply** to join a chain link fence.

"F" - <u>Chain Link fence</u>. **Continue** with the fence on your left. Soon after the fence turns left away from the path, emerge onto a **Minor road "G"** and **turn left.**

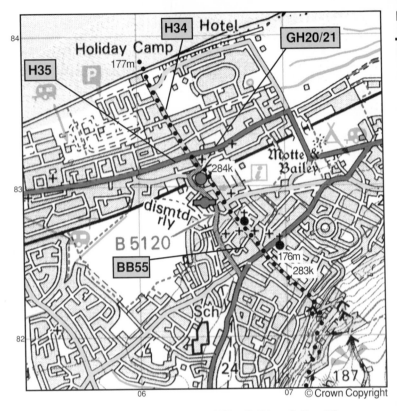

© Crown Copyright

Prestatyn (01745)
Banks - TSB(ATM), Barclays(ATM),
Bank of Scotland(ATM),
NatWest(ATM), Midland(ATM).
Taxis - G Cabs 888522,
Home & Away 888333/852541
Buses - See Section One!
Frequent buses Rhyl-Prestatyn-
Chester (more in summer!)
H34 - Traeth Ganol Hotel
Tel. 853594 TB 3 Crown HComm
Jan-Dec Band 2 (1S,1D,1T,6F)(9PB)
Visa. M'Card. EM. Lic'd. Veg.
H35 - Hawarden House Hotel
Tel. 854226 TB Listed
Jan-Dec Band 1 (1S,5D,2F)(2PB)
EM. Pk'dL. Trans. LTPk'g. Bags.
GH20 - Roughsedge House
Tel. 887359 TB 2 Crown Comm
Jan-Dec Band 1 (2S,4D,2T,2F)(3PB)
Visa. M'Card. Amex. Diners.
EM. Lic'd. Pk'dL. Veg. LTPk'g.

GH21 - St.Edward's Guest House
Tel. 853994 TB Listed
Jan-Dec (exc Xmas/NY) Band 1
(1S,2D,1T,1F)
EM. Dogs. Pk'dL. Veg. LTPk'g.

BB55 - Bryngele
Tel. 886514
Jan-Dec (exc Xmas) Band 1 (1D,1T)
Non-Smk'g. Pk'L. Veg. LTPk'g.
A warm welcome awaits you at our
small friendly guesthouse. Convenient
for all amenities. Very highly
recommended.

Prestatyn

Having emerged onto the road, turn left. The road bends right at a hairpin bend where Bishopswood Road joins from sharp left. It then bends left (Mount Ida Road joins from the right at the bend. You are now on Ffordlas Road. **Straight ahead to the sea!**

Note the Offa's Dyke Information Board on the right at the junction with Gronant Road (A547).

The last couple of kilometres to the sea seems a very odd way to finish a National Trail. At the end of what is in my opinion one of the most delightful long distance footpaths, the raucous bustle of Prestatyn, complete with holidaymakers in kiss-me-quick hats, seemed completely at odds with the peace and tranquillity to be found on the Path. The Offa's Tavern (thankfully, a suggestion of a book to be signed in the bar was not accepted!), the Offa's Dyke benches by the road, the Offa's Dyke Centre, the Offa's Dyke Commemorative Stone etc etc; it all just seems so inappropriate.

As you gaze out over the sea or retrace your journey on the display in the Offa's Dyke Centre, you can be justifiably proud of your achievement. One thing is for sure, few of the holidaymakers around you will have done what you have done or even attempted it. Isn't it great that people take their pleasure in such diverse ways, otherwise that peace and tranquillity on the Path wouldn't be there!

Have a safe journey home and don't forget to write and let us know what you thought of the guide.

Section Four
Getting the most from your Langton's Guide

To get the most from this guidebook you need to know the basis on which it was compiled and the criteria used in the various entries. A little time spent studying the following paragraphs could save a tiresome mistake on the walk.

Maps & Directions

Routefinding Maps. The 1:21,000 (approximate) routefinding maps are based on both 1:50,000 and 1:25,000 OS maps, supplemented by our own survey. Whilst the scale for distance along the route and between designated points is normally maintained, the scale of the features themselves are distorted in the interests of clarity and to highlight features useful for navigation. In rare instances a section of path may have to be omitted to fit the map on the page. Care has been taken not to omit any important detail where this "cut" has been necessary. Cumulative distances, as shown on the maps, have been measured in kilometres on 1:25,000 OS maps and overall they are +/- 0.5km.

Route Description. The directions are especially precise to see you through each "designated point" (which is also indicated on the routefinding map). Where the direction and the map appear to conflict with each other, it is normally due to the orientation of a stile or footbridge that has necessitated a "turn" or "bear" not apparent on the map. Directions from stiles assume that you have your back to the stile.

In addition, some terms are defined:

- "turn" indicates a near 90-degree turn (especially "sharp turn" which means over 90-degrees).
- "bear" indicates a near 45-degree change of direction.
- "gently" implies a slow and gradual change.
- "continue" is very specific and means maintain your general heading.
- "straight ahead" means just that.
- "on your left/right" is more positive than
- "to your left/right" indicating anything off-centre.
- "over ...." suggests that something is at a distance

EG. <u>**"M"**</u> - <u>**Stone Cross crossroads**</u> **Cross** the minor road and take the tarmac road **straight ahead** passing the stone cross on your left. Continue to a level-crossing.

The Directions that appear in **bold** typeface enable you to skip through the directions but rely on you to take the obvious route with only major changes given. If you read the name of the designated point and just the **bold** directions, using capital letters as punctuation, you will see a flow to the directions; eg. **"Gas Pumping Station". .....turn left .....First right turn......"B4235"** (equates to: At the gas pumping station turn left. Take the first right turn. There are now no major changes in direction until you come to the next designated point, the B4235).

Twitchel. A useful expression meaning a path between close hedges.

Stiles. There are reported to be over 650 stiles along the Offa's Dyke Path. To avoid the monotonous repetition of "cross the stile"; if you are directed to a stile or footbridge, **assume that you are to cross it unless directed otherwise!**

Location Maps. The location maps are a monochrome copy of the 1:50,000 OS Landranger series. The original scale is reduced to cover a larger area and to meet an OS copyright requirement. They enable you to place the routefinding maps in context with the surrounding area. They also serve to "locate" B&B's and other facilities. There is a degree of overlap between maps, so if something is covered by an inset box on one map, have a look at the preceding and subsequent maps to see if the feature is revealed on another map.

Map Orientation. Whilst North is always at the top of the Location maps, the orientation of the routefinding maps depends on the direction of the Path. However the area covered by the routefinding map is outlined on the location map by a dashed-line box and the "designated point identifying letters" provide the clue as to whether you are to read the routefinding maps up or down the page. A further aid to orientation is the small graphic located at the top or bottom of the routefinding maps. The underlying vertical box represents the routefinding map on the right-hand page whilst the overlying **bold** box is rotated to show the orientation of the routefinding map on the location map shown on the left-hand page.

Footpath Information. The public footpaths shown on the OS maps were compiled from definitive maps dated as follows: OS Sheet 162 (Chepstow to Monmouth) - February 1993, 161 (Monmouth to Hay) - September 1993, 148 (Hay to Knighton) - June 1991, 137 (Knighton to Montgomery) - August 1994,

126 (Montgomery to Chirk) - February 1993, 117 (Chirk to Llandegla) - June 1992, 116 (Llandegla to Prestatyn) - December 1992.

Facilities Information

The information shown in the inset boxes was compiled from surveys carried out in late 1995.

Accommodation.

Always check details and prices when booking or accepting accommodation. Note that Langton's Guides does not charge for a standard entry in the guide and has no vested interest in promoting any of the services featured. Boxed entries are paid for by the establishment concerned and the descriptive text is their's not our's.

Note the following with regard to accommodation and campsite/bunkhouse entries:

Location of Facilities. We try to show accommodation as close as we can to its actual location. Nevertheless, as we sometimes have to rely on OS grid references given by the proprietor, it is prudent to double-check the exact location when telephoning establishments.

Gradings/Awards. In some of the entries we give Tourist Board gradings; see advertisement for further details.

Open Period. The month in which an establishment opens or closes is shown to the **nearest whole month**. If you plan to use somewhere in the opening/closing month, check the actual date with the establishment concerned.

Evening Meal. Unless it is an Hotel, ask about evening meals when booking, don't leave it until you arrive!

Dogs. Please check ahead when booking accommodation if you plan to walk accompanied by a canine friend.

Baggage Transfer. The seasoned backpacker will no doubt recoil in horror at the very idea of having his pack taken on to his next night stop. If you do decide to take advantage of the offer of a baggage transfer, double-check that the transfer arrangements are satisfactory. Just because your host says he will have your pack taken over, do not assume that the next B&B will have someone there to receive it! The last thing you want to happen is to arrive at the next B&B only to find no trace of your pack and a host who has arrived home at the same time! Note that some B&B's use a local taxi to transfer bags so it is a good idea to check the situation before you book in.

Transport. A number of proprietors have generously indicated a willingness to offer a lift to their B&B guests. The offer is always accompanied by, "if convenient", so if you ask for a lift at a meal-time when the proprietor may be busy, do not be surprised if the answer is No!

There's no "nod & a wink" or "make it worth his while". If money does come into it make sure you know where you stand insurance-wise. Acting as a paid taxi is not covered by normal car insurance.

Backpackers. A (C) after the H, I, GH or BB on the map indicates that the establishment is prepared to consider letting backpackers camp in their grounds. This is a generous offer, but does not mean they are a campsite nor that any facilities are available and it only covers backpackers arriving on foot. If there are more than three or four of you, ring first! Please be as unobtrusive as possible and remember that a polite approach often leads to the use of a shower and sometimes even a meal. My experience of such camping locations is that the people offering the pitch for the night do so out of the kindness of their hearts and at a minimal cost to you. Please ensure that you give them no reason to regret their generosity.

Additional Accommodation.

At the time of going to press, this Langton's Guide contained the most comprehensive accommodation listing of any guide. During our facilities survey we drove hundreds of miles along roads adjacent to the Path, in our quest to identify hotels, guesthouses, inns, B&B's, and campsites on or close to the Offa's Dyke Path. Nevertheless, we would be the first to admit that no list gets even close to showing 100% of the accommodation available.

The difficulty is that some proprietors do not wish to be on any walkers' list (even if the entry is free!). Others simply didn't accept our offer of an entry.

In the unlikely event that you are unable to find a bed or pitch using the list in this guide, there is another way in which the

Langton's Guide can help you. After the name of a village or town in the facilities information box, you will see a figure in brackets (+). That is the number of unlisted establishments believed to exist in that local vicinity.

Most village shops and public houses know the B&B's in their locality and most B&B's can suggest someone else if they are full. Do not forget that almost all tourist information offices have a list of B&B's in their locality although, unlike the English Tourist Board, the Welsh Tourist Board appear only to list accommodation that is registered with them (see Section 5).

Selecting Accommodation

Those who are baffled by the wide choice of accommodation listed in the guide might appreciate some advice on selecting somewhere to stay.

There is no clear distinction between an hotel and a guesthouse nor is there between a guesthouse and a bed & breakfast. Some B&B's offer a standard of accommodation and service that would shame some hotels, and some establishments charge prices that bear no relationship to what they actually provide. Our experience tells us that it is not any one detail in the description that indicates whether a place is likely to be good value or not, it is the combination of details.

It may seem obvious, but generally speaking, you get what you pay for! A B&B charging Band 1 prices is likely to be a far better bet than a hotel charging Band 1 prices. A Band 4 Guest House is either overcharging or feels that it has something extra to offer; so how to tell which is which? Look for some independent quality rating; not just the number of TB Crown's but one of the quality assessments that are additional to the basic Crown. Incidentally, just because an establishment does not have TB gradings, it does not necessarily mean that it is substandard. The establishment has to pay for the basic grading and is charged extra for the quality assessment (see page 223). If it has a grade and a quality assessment that is positive, if it has not, that is not necessarily negative.

A simple B&B would not be expected to offer "en-suite" facilities (ie. PB = private bathroom/shower) but if a hotel/guesthouse has none, it could indicate a lack of modernisation. The sort of welcome you may expect can often be anticipated by the "additional" services offered by the establishment. Of course, not all B&B's are able to offer transport and parking etc, but a proprietor who is prepared to collect you from the Path (and drop you off the next morning), let you leave a car, and arrange transfer of your bags; is walker-friendly by any definition. Even if you are not camping, a willingness to let a backpacker camp on the property is another good sign.

The price banding is based on the mid-season price of B&B per person (two sharing a room) inc VAT. Single occupancy of a double/twin room will often attract a surcharge; hence an additional and higher band may be shown where we know of such a surcharge.

Section Five
Additional Information

Update

The accommodation database is fully updated annually (in February/March) and the appropriate authorities are contacted for information on the Path. As far as we are able, checks are made to ensure that the other facilities information in the guide is current. Alterations to the Guide are reflected in an annual "Update".

If you are using this guide after 1996, you can obtain a free copy of the Update by simply completing and returning the enclosed registration card.

Tourist Information

Tourist Information Centres are an invaluable source of information on a local area (normally open 1000 - 1730hrs). Larger centres operate a book-a-bed ahead service and even the smaller centres have B&B lists (although it seems that in Wales, they only list B&B's registered with the Tourist Board). The following centres are on or near the Path (* denotes April - September opening only):

Chepstow -	Bridge Street, Chepstow, NP6 5EY (01291 623772)
Monmouth* -	Shire Hall, Agincourt Square, Monmouth. NP5 3DY (01600 713899)
Abergavenny* -	Swan Meadow, Monmouth Road, Abergavenny. NP7 5HH (01873 857588)
Hay-on-Wye -	Craft Centre, Oxford Road, Hay-on-Wye HR3 5DG (01497 820144)
Kington* -	2 Mill Street, Kington.
Knighton -	Offa's Dyke Centre, The Old School, West Street, Knighton, LD7 1EW (01547 528753)
Welshpool -	Flash Leisure Centre, Salop Road, Welshpool, SY21 7DH (01938 552043)
Oswestry -	Mile End Services, Oswestry SY11 1AH (01691 662488)
Oswestry -	The Old Grammar School, Oswestry SY11 2TE (01691 662753)

Llangollen -	Town Hall, Castle Street, Llangollen LL20 5PD (01978 860828)
Ruthin -	Craft Centre, Park Road, Ruthin LL15 1BB (01824 703992)
Prestatyn* -	Scala Cinema, High Street, Prestatyn LL19 9LH (01745 889092)

Additional Reading

"Offa's Dyke Reviewed" by Frank Noble (SBN 0 86054 210 6). Sold by the Offa's Dyke Association (ODA). Edited extracts from his thesis; very hard reading and probably best left to those with an academic interest in the Dyke.

"The ODA Book of Offa's Dyke Path" by Frank Noble (SBN 0 9507227 0 7). Sold by ODA. First published 1969 (revised Reprint 1975). Now very dated and a descriptive narrative rather than a walker's guide. Nevertheless, it was the first guide to the Path and no Dyke devotee's bookcase can be considered complete without it.

"A Guide to the Offa's Dyke Path" by Christopher John Wright (ISBN 0 09 469140 1) Constable. First published 1975, second edition 1986. Lots of background and history (15 pages on Chepstow alone!). However, the otherwise excellent routefinding maps and the photographs, are now looking dated. Don't be misled by the wording on the cover of the 1995 reprint, that it is now reissued in a new third edition, that seems to refer to a 1989 reprint with corrections.

"Through Welsh Border Country" by Mark Richards (ISBN 0 904110 53 2) Thornhill Press. Published 1976. Wainwright-style guide with pen and ink drawings.

National Trail Guide (two volumes) (ISBN 1 85410 295 8 & 322 9). First published 1989. Revised editions published 1994/95. Full colour, with 1:25,000 OS Pathfinder mapping. Lots of photographs and circular walks (almost a book's worth on their own!).

Welsh Placenames

aber - estuary, mouth of river
afon, afan - river
allt - hill, wooded hill, cliff
bach, bychan, fach - little, small
blaen - head of vale, point
bro - lowland, vale
bryn - hill
bwlch - pass, gap
cae - field
caer - fort
cefn - ridge, back
celyn - holy
coch - red
coed - trees, wood
cwm - valley
dyffryn - vale
ddu - black
dwr - water
eglwys - church
ffynnon - spring
gelli - woods
glyn - valley
hafod - summer dwelling
hendre - winter dwelling
heol - road, street
hyfryd - beautiful, pleasant
Llan - enclosure, church
llwyd - grey
llwyn - grove
llyn - lake
maen - stone
mawr, fawr - big, great
mynydd - mountain
nant - stream
newydd - new
pandy - mill
pant - hollow

plas - place, hall
pont - bridge
pwll - pool
rhiw - hill
rhyd - ford
teg - fair (as in beauty)
tir - land
tref - home, town
twr - tower
ty - house
y, yr - the
yn - in, at
ynys - island
ystrad - vale

Accommodation

Accommodation (including that which permits backpackers to camp in the grounds) is listed below in alphabetical order, with the name of the proprietor. Refer to the location maps for names and details of establishments in a particular area.

1 Plas Cefn
Heldre Lane
Buttington
Welshpool   Powys
SY21 8SX
(01938) 570225
M Broxton

2 The Village
Llandegla
Nr WREXHAM
Clwyd
LL11 3AR
(01978) 790266
S Byrne

8 Chancery Court
Lion Street
Hay-on-Wye
Herefordshire
HR3 5BP
(01497) 820152
Mr S Stocks

Abbey Grange Hotel
Horseshoe Pass Road
Lllangollen
Clwyd
LL20 8DD
(01978) 860753

Abbey Hotel
Llanthony
Abergavenny
Gwent
NP7 7NN
(01873) 890487

Afon Gwy
28 Bridge Street
Chepstow
Gwent
NP6 5EZ
(01291) 620158
Mrs R Jenkins

April Spring Cottage
Nantmawr
Oswestry
Shrops
SY10 9HL
(01691) 828802
J Richardson

Ardwyn
26 Church Street
Kington
Herefordshire
HR5 3BE
(01544) 231103
J and M Price

Ashburne House
Bridge Street
Chepstow
Gwent
NP6 5E -
(01291) 625747
Mr M Evans

Assisi
The Buckstone
Staunton
COLEFORD   Glos
GL16 8PD
(01594) 836900
Mrs J Hockey

Bache Farm
New Radnor
Presteigne
Powys
LD8 2TG
(01544) 350680
Mrs M Hardwick

Beacons View
91 Hereford Road
Monmouth
Gwent
NP5 4LA
(01600) 713591
Mrs J Emblen

Bear Hotel
Salop Road
Oswestry
Shrops
SY11 2NR
(01691) 652093

Beaufort Hotel
Beaufort Square
Chepstow
Gwent
NP6 5EP
(01291) 622497

Beeches
New Road
Montgomery
Powys
SY15 6UJ
(01686) 668663
H Thomas

Belmont House
Hay-on-Wye

Herefordshire
HR3 5DA
(01497) 820718
W P Gwynne

Bottom Farm
Penrhos
Raglan
Gwent
NP5 2DE
(01600) 780216
Mrs M Watkins

Bridge End Hotel
Mill Street
Llangollen
Clwyd
LL20 8AN
(01978) 860634

Brockweir Country Inn

Brockweir
Glos
NP6 7NG
(01291) 689548

Brompton Hall
Brompton
Churchstoke
Powys
SY15 6SP
(01588) 620544
Mrs H M Wallace

Brook Cottage
Norton
Skenfrith
Abergavenny   Gwent
NP7 8UB
(01600) 750319
Mrs J Finn

Bryn Clwyd
Waen
Bodfari
Clwyd
LL16 4BT
(01745) 710357
Mrs G Parry

Bryn Derwen Hotel
Abbey Road
Llangollen
Clwyd
LL20 8EF
(01978) 860583

Bryn Howel Hotel

Llangollen
Clwyd
LL20 7UW
(01978) 860331

Bryngele
4 Ash Grove
PRESTATYN
Clwyd
LL19 9DW
(01745) 886514
Mrs V Roberts

Brynhonddu
Pandy
Abergavenny
Gwent
NP7 7PD
(01873) 890535
C White

Bucks Head House
School Farm
Upper Hergest
Kington
HR5 3EW
(01544) 231063
Mrs E Protheroe

Burton Hotel
Mill Street
Kington
Herefordshire
HR5 3BQ
(01544) 230323

Burton House
St James Square
Monmouth
Gwent
NP5 3DN
(01600) 714958
Mrs B Banfield

Buttington View
Hope
Welshpool
Powys
SY21 8JD
(01938) 552295
D Jones

Bwlch Uchaf
Llanbedr DC
Ruthin
Clwyd
LL15 1YF
(01824) 780229
Iris Gates

Cae Bryn
North Road
Llanymynech
Powys
SY22 6HB
(01691) 830655
R Edwards

Cambridge Cottage
19 Church Street
Kington
Herefordshire
HR5 3BE
(01544) 231300
M and G Hooton

Castle Guest House
4 Bridge Street
Chepstow
Gwent
NP6 5EY
(01291) 622040
LT and P Cherrington

Castle Hotel
St Peters Square
Ruthin
Clwyd
LL15 1AA
(01824) 702479

Cayo Guest House
74 Vale Street
Denbigh
Clwyd
LL16 3BW
(01745) 812686

Cefn y Fedw Farm

Trevor
LLANGOLLEN   Clwyd
LL14 1UA
(01978) 823403
Mrs S Roberts

Chapel House
Trelystan
Leighton
Welshpool   Powys
SY21 8HX
(01938) 580476
C Owens

Church Farm Guest Ho
Mitchel Troy
Monmouth
Gwent
NP5 4HZ
(01600) 712176
R Ringer

Church House   *
Forden
Welshpool
Powys
SY21 8NE
(01938) 580353
Mrs S Bright

Church House   **
Church Road
Kington
Herefordshire
HR5 3AG
(01544) 230534
Mr A Darwin

Cinderhill House
St. Briavels
Lydney
Glos
GL15 6RH
(01594) 530393
Mrs G Peacock

Cliffe Point
Pant
Oswestry
Salop
SY10 9RB
(01691) 830356
Mr & Mrs R K Marsh

Clun Farm
High Street
Clun
Craven Arms
Shrops
SY7 8JB
(01588) 640432
M Lewis & C Lewis

Clwyd Gate Inn & Motel
Llanbedr DC
Ruthin
Clwyd
LL15 1YF
(01824) 704444

Cobweb Cottage
Belle Vue Place
Steep St
Chepstow
Gwent
NP6 5PL
(01291) 626643
Mrs Warren

Court Robert
Tregaer
Nr Raglan
Gwent
NP5 2BZ
(01291) 690709
Mrs J Paxton

Craignant Lodge
Selattyn
Oswestry
Shrops
SY10 7NS
(01691) 718229
K M Jones

Crown House
Church Street
Clun
Craven Arms   Shrops
SY7 8JW
(01588) 640780
J Bailey and R Maund

Curfew House
5 Bridge Street
Chepstow
Gwent
NP6 5EY
(01291) 628532
Mr & Mrs Peckham

Cwm Cole
Llanfair Waterdine
Knighton
Powys
LD7 1TU
(01547) 520357
J and A Lewis

Cwmgilla
Knighton
Powys
LD7 1PG
(01547) 528387
M Davies

Dinbren House
Dinbren Road
LLANGOLLEN
Clwyd
LL20 8TF
(01978) 860593
J Lewis

Dolbedwyn
Newchurch
Kington
Herefordshire
HR5 3QQ
(01497) 851202
Mrs A Williams

Dragon Hotel
Montgomery
Powys
SY15 6PA
(01686) 668359

Drewin Farm
Cwm
Churchstoke
Montgomery   Powys
SY15 6TW
(01588) 620325
Mrs C Richards

Dunfield House Centre
Stanner Road
Kington
Herefordshire
HR5 3NN
(01544) 230563

Elgar House
16 Elgar Close
Oswestry
Salop
SY11 2LZ
(01691) 661323 /
(0585) 171112
Mr D Harding

Empton Farm
Lower Hergest
Kington
Herefordshire
HR5 3ES
(01544) 230153
Mrs A James

Esgairlygain
Llangynhafal
Ruthin
Clwyd
LL15 1RT
(01824) 704047
Mrs I Henderson

Eyarth Station
Llanfair DC
Ruthin
Clwyd
LL15 2EE
(01824) 703643
J Spencer

Fernleigh
Hardwick Road
Cusop
Hay-on-Wye
HR3 5QV
(01497) 820459
W M Hughes

Fferm Catrin
Marian
Trelawnyd
Prestatyn   Clwyd
LL19
(01745) 571606
Mrs Y S Walker

Ffynnon Berth
Clwyd Gate
Llanferres
Mold   Clwyd
CH7 5TA
(01824) 780298
E M Davies

Ffynnon Beuno
Tremeirchion
St Asaph
Clywd
LL17 0UE
(01745) 710475
E Pierce

Fron Deg
Llanbedr DC
Ruthin
Clwyd
LL15 1U -
(01824) 702931
Mrs E Dalrymple

Fron Haul
Sodom
Bodfari
Clwyd
LL16 4DY
(01745) 710301
G M Edwards

Gales of Llangollen
18 Bridge Street
Lllangollen
Clwyd
LL20 8PF
(01978) 860089

Golden Lion
Four Crosses
Llanymynech
Powys
SY22 6RB
(01691) 830295
E Pritchard

Gorffwysfa
Llanfair DC
Ruthin
Clwyd
LL16 2UN
(01824) 702432
Mrs J Horrocks

Graygill
Staunton
Coleford
Glos
GL16 8PD
(01600) 712536
Mr & Mrs Bond

Great House
Newchurch
Kington
Herefordshire
HR5 3QF
(01544) 370257
Mrs Betty Lloyd

Great Tre-rhew Farm
Llanvetherine
Abergavenny
Gwent
NP7 8RA
(01873) 821268
Mrs A Beavan

Greystones
Brompton
Churchstoke
Powys
SY15 6SP
(01588) 620393
Mrs G Ferguson

Gumma Farm
Discoed
Presteigne
Powys
LD8 2NP
(01547) 560243
Mrs A Owens

Hafren   **
38 Salop Road
Welshpool
Powys
SY21 7EA
(01938) 554112 /
(0831) 183152
P Shaw

Haimwood
Llandrinio
Llanymynech
Powys
SY22 6SQ
(01691) 830764
J Nixon

Hawarden House Hotel
15 Victoria Road
Prestatyn
Clwyd
LL19
(01745) 854226

Hazelhurst Guest H'se
Gloucester Road
Tutshill
Chepstow Gwent
NP6 7DB
(01291) 622266
M Hughes

Hendre Farm House
Hendre
Monmouth
Gwent
NP5 4DJ
01600 740484
Mrs P Baker

Hendre*
Bear Street
Hay-on-Wye
Hereford
HR3 5AN
(01497) 820439
B and B Bentley

Hendy Isa
Valle Crucis Road
Llangollen
Clwyd
LL20 8DE
(01978) 861232
Mrs E Lloyd Jeffreys

Hill House Farm
Church Bank
Clun
Craven Arms
Shrops
SY7 8LP
(01588) 640729 /
640325
C Jones

Hillcrest Guest House
Hill Street
Llangollen
Clwyd
LL20 8EU
(01978) 860208
Mrs J Lloyd

Holmleigh
Monmouth Road
Tintern
Gwent
NP6 6SG
(01291) 689521
Mrs M Mark

Hospitality
Vyrnwy Bank
Llanymynech
Shrops
SY22 6LG
(01691) 830427
Mrs C Fahey

Hurst Mill Farm
Clun
Craven Arms
Shrops
SY7 0JA
(01588) 640224
Mrs J Williams

Ivydene Cottage
High Street
St Briavels
Lydney   Glos
GL15 6TD
(01594) 530699
Mrs C Routledge

Jasmine Cottage
Brook Street
Hay-on-Wye
Herefordshire
HR3 5BQ
(01497) 821168
R Jones

Kentigern Arms
High Street
St. Asaph
Clwyd
LL17 0RG
(01745) 584157

Kilverts
The Bull Ring
Hay-on-Wye
Herefordshire
HR3 5 - -
(01497) 821042

King's Head Hotel
Welsh Street
Chepstow
Gwent
NP6 5LL
(01291) 623379

Larkey Lodge
The Cwm
Knighton
Powys
LD7 1BT
(01547) 529011
Mrs J Walton

Lawn Farm
Newcastle-on-Clun
Craven Arms
Shropshire
SY7 8PN
(01588) 640303
Mrs V Lewis

Lion Hotel

Llanymynech
Powys
SY22 6EJ
(01691) 830234
R and J Beeston

Little Brompton Farm
Montgomery
Montgomeryshire
SY15 6HY
(01686) 668371
Mrs G Bright

Llanerch Farm
Pandy
Abergavenny
Gwent
NP7 8EW
(01873) 890432
J Ilkin

Lower Dolwilkin Farm
Knucklas
Knighton
Powys
LD7 1PT
(01547) 528249
D Bebbington

Lower Hardwick House
Hardwick Hill
Chepstow
Gwent
NP6 5PT
(01291) 622162
E Grassby

Lower Trelydan
Farmhouse
Guilsfield
Welshpool
Montgomeryshire
SY21 9PH
(01938) 553105
Mrs S Jones

Lynwood
Llanigon
Hay-on-Wye
Herefordshire
HR3 5PU
(01497) 820716
Mrs O Davies

Manor House Hotel
Well Street
Ruthin
Clwyd
LL15 1AH
(01824) 704830

Milebrook House Hotel
Milebrook
Knighton
Powys
LD7 1LT
(01547) 528632

Mill House Farm
Llanvihangel Ystern
Llewern
Monmouth
Gwent
NP5 4HN
(01600) 780468
K Anders

Millend House
Nr. Newland
Coleford
Gloucestershire
GL16 8NF
(01594) 832128
Mrs A Tremlett

Moat Farm

Welshpool
Montgomeryshire
SY21 8SE
(01938) 553179
Mrs G Jones

Montrose
Weston Lane
Oswestry
Salop
SY11 2BG
(01691) 652063
Mrs D Leggatt

Newcastle Hall
Newcastle on Clun
Craven Arms
Shropshire
SY7 8QL
(01588) 640350
P M Reynolds

Norville
Hardwick Road
Cusop
Hay-on-Wye, Hereford
HR3 5QX
(01497) 820162
Mr M W Murphy

Oak Cottage
St Briavels Common
Lydney
Glos
GL15 6SJ
(01594) 530440
Mr and Mrs W P J
Watts

Oaklands Guest House
Llangollen Road
Trevor
Llangollen   Clwyd
LL20 7TG
(01978) 820152
A Dennis

Oakmere
Regent Street
Lllangollen
Clwyd
LL20 8HS
(01978) 861126
J G Knibbs

Offa's Mead
The Fence
St. Briavels
LYDNEY   Glos
GL15 6QG
(01594) 530229
Mrs J Lacey

Olchon Cottage Farm
Turnant Road
Longtown
Herefordshire
HR2 0NS
(01873) 860233
Mrs I Pritchard

Olchon Court
Llanveynoe
Longtown
Herefords
HR2 0NL
(01873) 860356
Mrs J Carter

Old Black Lion
Lion Street
Hay-on-Wye
Herefordshire
HR3 5AD
(01497) 820841
Mr J Collins

Old Mansion House
Bridge Street
Knighton
Powys
LD7 1BT
(01547) 528248
M Price

Old Mill Inn
The Candy Valley
Llanforda
Oswestry   Salop
SY10 9AZ
(01691) 657058

Old School
Bronygarth
Oswestry
Shrops
SY10 7NB
(01691) 772546
J Bampfield

Old Time
29 High Street
Bishop's Castle
Shropshire
SY9 5BE
(01588) 638467
Mrs J Carroll

Oldcastle Court Farm
Pandy
Abergavenny
Gwent
NP7 7PH
(01873) 890285
O Probert

Ostrich Inn
Newland
Coleford
Glos
GL16 8NP
(01594) 833260

Park Hotel
Pandy
Abergavenny
Gwent
NP7 8DS
(01873) 890271
W and F Gal

Parva Farmhouse Hotel
Tintern
Chepstow
Gwent
NP6 6SQ
(01291) 689411
D and V Stubbs

Pedlar Corner
Colliery Road
Chirk
Clwyd
LL14 5PB
(01691) 772903
L and B Berry

Pen y Dyffryn Hall Hotel
Rhydycroesau
Nr Oswestry
Shrops
SY10 7DT
(01691) 653700
M Hunter

Pen y Graig
Tremeirchion
St Asaph
Clwyd
LL17 0UR
(01745) 710253
P Jackson

Pen-Y-Bryn Farm
Boderw
St Asaph
Clwyd
LL17 0LF
(01745) 583213
Mrs B Williams

Pendine Guest House
6 Bridge Street
Chepstow
Gwent
NP6 5EY
(01291) 623308
T & C Jones

Pentre Cottage
Pentre
Chirk
Wrexham   Clwyd
LL14 5AW
(01691) 774265
S Vant

Pentwyn Farm
Brilley
Whitney-on-Wye
Herefordshire
HR3 6HW
(01497) 831337
Mrs V Price

Penyclawdd Farm
Llanvihangel Crucorney
Abergavenny
Gwent
NP7 7LB
(01873) 890591
Mrs A Davies

Pilleth Court
Whitton
Knighton
Powys
LD7 1NP
(01547) 560272
Mrs H Hood

Plas Offa
Chapel Lane
Trefonen
Oswestry   Shrops
SY10 9DX
(01691) 653440
Mrs J Barber

Plas Offa Farm
Whitehurst
Chirk
Wrexham   Clwyd
LL14 5AN
(01691) 773760
P Mullen

Plas Penucha
Caerwys
Mold
Clywd
CH7 5BH
(01352) 720210
Mrs N Price

Plough Hotel
40 Market Street
Knighton
Powys
LD7 1EY
(01547) 528041
Mrs S Scotford

Quarry House
Newcastle on Clun
Craven Arms
Shrops
SY7 8QJ
(01588) 640774
R Woodward

Railway Inn
Forden
Welshpool
Powys
SY21 8NN
(01938) 580237
GG & JM Thomas

Raven Farm
Llandegla
Nr Wrexham
Clwyd
LL11 3AW
(01978) 790224
Mr Surrey

Red Lion House
16 Drybridge Street
Monmouth
Gwent
NP5 3AD
(01600) 713633
Mrs B Frost

Rest for the Tired
6 Broad Street
Hay-on-Wye
Herefordshire
HR3 5DB
(01497) 820550
J and M Thomas

Rhos Rhudd
Pandy
Abergavenny
Gwent
NP7 8DW
(01873) 890703
L Bray

Rhydspence Cottage
Whitney-on-Wye

Herefordshire
HR3 6EU
(01497) 831595
Mrs M L Phillips

Rhydspence Inn
Rhydspence
Whitney-on-Wye
Herefordshire
HR3 6EU
(01497) 831262

Riverside Hotel
Cinderhill St
Monmouth
Gwent
NP5 3EY
(01600) 715577 /
713236

Rosedale
Cusop
Hay-on-Wye
Herefordshire
HR3 5RF
(01497) 820804
Mrs J Jenkins

Roughsedge House
26-28 Marine Road
PRESTATYN
Clwyd
LL19 7HD
(01745) 887359
Mrs Y Kubler

Royal Oak Hotel
The Cross
Welshpool
Montgomeryshire
SY21 7DG
(01938) 552217

Royal Oak Inn
Church St
Kington
Herefordshire
HR5 3
(01544) 230484

Saith Daran Farm
Llandegla
Nr Wrexham
Clwyd
LL11 3BA
(01978) 790685
Mrs P Thompson

Scatterford Farm
Newland
Gloucestershire
GL16 8NG
(01594) 836562
J & S Benson

Severn Farm
Welshpool
Powys
SY21 7BB
(01938) 553098
J Jones

Severn View
Pool Quay
Welshpool
Powys
SY21 9JS
(01938) 590464
Mrs A Kellaway

Spring Cottage
Wern
Weston Rhyn
Oswestry
SY10 7LH
(01691) 650293
J and D Andrews

Springhill Farm
Clun
Craven Arms
Shrops
SY7 8PE
(01588) 640337
I Evans

St. Edward's Guest Ho
69 Marine Road
PRESTATYN
Clwyd
LL19 7HA
(01745) 853994
Magda Leightley

Sun Cottage
Pentre
Chirk
Wrexham   Clwyd
LL14 5AW
(01691) 774542
Mrs B Little

Sun Inn
High Street
Clun
Craven Arms
SY7 8
(01588) 640277

Swan Hotel
Church Street
Kington
Herefordshire
HR5 3AZ
(01544) 230510
Mr G Johnston

Sycamore House
Newland
Coleford
Gloucestershire
GL16 8NJ
(01594) 834895
Mrs B Hancock

Tan House Farm
Newland
Coleford
Glos
GL16 8NP
(01594) 832222

The Barn
Old Barland
Presteigne
Powys
LD8 2SH
(01547) 560402
Mr and Mrs Smith

The Benchmark
21 Church Street
Kington
Herefordshire
HR5 3BE
(01544) 230298
J and D Cresswell

The Boar's Head Hotel
Church Street
Bishop's Castle
Shropshire
SY9 5AE
(01588) 638521

The Butchers Arms
Clearwell
Coleford
Glos
GL16 8JS
(01594) 834313

The Cabin Restaurant
High Street
Presteigne
Powys
LD8 2BA
(01544) 267068
Mr and Mrs Duggan

The Castle Hotel *
The Square
Bishops Castle
Shrops
SY9 5BN
(01588) 638403

The Coach H'se Hotel
Park Road
Ruthin
Clwyd
LL15 1NB
(01824) 704223

The Crown Inn
Newcastle-on-Clun
Craven Arms
Shropshire
SY7 8QL
(01588) 640271

The Crown Inn **
Walton
Presteigne
Powys
LD8 2PY
(01544) 350663

The Fish N Game
Redbrook
Nr Monmouth
Gwent
NP5 4LZ
(01600) 713612

The Fleece House
Market Street
Knighton
Powys
LD7 1BB
(01547) 520168
Mrs D Simmons

The George Inn
East Street
St. Briavels
Lydney   Glos
GL15 6 -
(01594) 530228

The Grange   *
Capel y Ffin
Abergavenny
Gwent
NP7 7NP
(01873) 890215
The Griffiths Family

The Half Moon
Llanthony
Abergavenny
Gwent
NP7 7NN
(01873) 890611

The Halfway House Inn
Tal-y-coed
Monmouth
Gwent
NP7 8TL
(01600) 780269

The Hand
Llandegla
Nr Wrexham
Clywd
LL11 3AW
(01978) 790337
Mr Carlisle

The Hand Hotel
Church Street
Chirk
Nr Wrexham
LL14 5EY
(01691) 773472

The Hand Hotel **
Bridge Street
Lllangollen
Clwyd
LL20 8PL
(01978) 860303

The Harp Inn
Old Radnor
Presteigne
Powys
LD8 2RH
(01544) 350655

The Hawthorns
Weston Lane
Oswestry
Salop
SY11 2BG
(01691) 657678
E M Roberts

The Herbert Arms
Chirbury
Montgomery
Powys
SY15 6BG
(01938) 561216

The Hollies
Birch Hill
LLANGOLLEN
Clwyd
LL20 8LN
(01978) 869037
Mrs S M Stubbs

The Knighton Hotel
Broad Street
Knighton
Powys
LD7 1BL
(01547) 520530

The Lanterns
19 High Street
Knighton
Powys
LD7 1AT
(01547) 528922
Mrs S M White

The Lilacs
Dingestow
Monmouth
Gwent
NP5 4DZ
(01600) 740686
Mrs A E Clark

The Manor House
Pool Road
Montgomery
Powys
SY15 6QY
(01686) 668736
Mrs B D Williams

The Mill
Lloyney
Knighton
Powys
LD7 1RG
(01547) 528049
W and J Davies

The Old Brick Guest
House
7 Church Street
Bishops Castle
Shrops
SY9 5AA
(01588) 638471
P Hutton

The Old Farmhouse
Woodside
Clun
Craven Arms
Shrops
SY7 0JB
(01588) 640695
R H and M Wall

The Old Post Office
Llanigon
Hay-on-Wye
Herefordshire
HR3 5JQA
(01497) 820008
Mr E Moore & Ms L
Webb

The Old Rectory **
Tintern
Chepstow
Gwent
NP6 6SG
(01291) 689519
Mrs M Newman

The Old School
Llangollen Road
Trevor
Llangollen   Clwyd
LL20 7TL
(01978) 820412
Mrs P Pepper

The Old Vicarage
Bryn Howel Lane
Trevor
LLANGOLLEN   Clwyd
LL20 7YR
(01978) 823018
Mrs J M Wooolley

The Pentre
Trefonen
Oswestry
Shrops
SY10 9EE
(01691) 653952
Mr & Mrs Gilbert

The Royal George
Tintern
Chepstow
Gwent
NP6 7EN
(01291) 689205

The Skirrid Mountain
Inn
Llanvihangel Crucorney
Abergavenny
Gwent
NP7 8DH
(01873) 890258

The Swan at Hay
Church Street
Hay-on-Wye
Herefordshire
HR3 5DQ
(01497) 821188

The Three Pigeons Inn
Graigfechan
Ruthin
Clwyd
LL15 2EU
(01824) 703178

The White House Hotel
Rhuallt
St. Asaph
Clwyd
LL17 0AW
(01745) 582155

The Willows
St. Mary's Road
Hay-on-Wye
Herefordshire
HR3 5EB
(01497) Day 820387
Evening 820174
J and J Morris

Three Firs
High Pant
Nr Oswestry
Shrops
SY10 8LB
(01691) 831375
Ms A I Noblet

Tinto House
Broad Street
Hay-on-Wye
Herefordshire
HR3 5DB
(01497) 820590
Mrs M Ratcliffe

Traeth Ganol Hotel
41 Beach Road West
PRESTATYN
Clwyd
LL19 7LL
(01745) 853594
Mr C Groves

Treloyvan Farm
White Castle
Llantilio Crossenny
Abergavenny   Gwent
NP7 8UE
(01600 780478)
S and S Watkins

Tresco
Nr Redbrook
Monmouth
Gwent
NP5 4LY
(01600) 712325
Mrs M Evans

Tresi-Aur
Brookfield Road
Welshpool
Powys
SY21 7 PZ
(01938) 552430
Mrs B W Davies

Troy Lodge

Monmouth
Gwent
NP5 4HX
(01600) 715098
AL and AB Bennett

Tudor Farmhouse Hotel
Clearwell
Coleford
Glos
GL16 8JS
(01594) 833046

Two Hoots Guest H'se
4 Bod Hamer
Cwm
Nr. DYSERTH   Clwyd
LL18 5SL
(01745) 570226
Jill Tong

Ty Newydd Farm
Pandy
Abergavenny
Gwent
NP7 8DW
(01873) 890235
Mrs J Evans

Ty'n y Ffordd Isa
Bodfari
Denbigh
Clwyd
LL16 4DB
(01745) 710273
Mrs R Cahill

Ty'n y Llidiart
Llandegla
Wrexham
Clwyd
LL11 3AF
(01978) 790236
J Robinson

Ty-Brith
Pentrecelyn
Ruthin
Clwyd
LL15 2- -
(01978) 790279
Rhiannon Jones

Tyersall
St. Briavels
Lydney
Glos
GL15 6RT
(01594) 530215
Mrs J Morgan

Tyn Celyn Farmhouse
Tyn Celyn
Tyndwr
Llangollen   Clwyd
LL20 8AR
(01978) 861117
Mrs J Bather

Tynllwyn Farm

Welshpool
Powys
SY21 9BW
(01938) 553175 /
553054
Mrs F Emberton

Under Hill Farm
Trefonen
Oswestry
Shrops
SY10 9DR
(01691) 653687
Mrs G M Jones

Upper Sedbury House
Sedbury Lane
Sedbury
Chepstow, Gwent
NP6 7HN
(01291) 627173
Mrs C Potts

Woodcroft
Lower Meend
St Briavels
Lydney   Glos
GL15 6RW
(01594) 530083
Mrs M Allen

Valley House
Raglan Road
Tintern
Gwent
NP6 6TH
(01291) 689652
A Howe

Woodwinds
Discoed
Presteigne
Powys
LD8 2NW
(01547) 560302
J M Ambridge

Wain Wen
Gladestry
Kington
Herefordshire
HR5 3NT
(01544) 370226
M Lloyd

Wye Avon
Dixton Road
Monmouth
Gwent
NP5 3PR
(01600) 713322
D Cantrell

Wellingtonia Cottage
Norton
Presteigne
Powys
LD8 2EU
(01544) 260255
Mrs M Hobley

Wye Barn
The Quay
Tintern
Gwent
NP6 6SZ
(01291) 689456
J Russill

Wern Fawr
Llangynhafal
Ruthin
Clwyd
LL15 1RT
(01824) 703165
M McDonald

Ye Olde Anchor Inn
Rhos Street
Ruthin
Clwyd
LL15 1DX
(01824) 702813

Wesley House
West Street
Knighton
Powys
LD7 1EN
(01547) 520296
M D Roberton

York House
Cusop
Hay-on-Wye
Herefordshire
HR3 5QX
(01497) 820705
P and O Roberts

Willow Cottage
19 Station Road
Knighton
Powys
LD7 1DT
(01547) 528060
Mr R Potts

Campsites

Campsites are listed in alphabetical order:

Bacheldre Watermill Camp'g Park
Churchstoke
Montgomery
Powys
SY15 6TE
(01588) 620489
Mrs J Ripley

Beeches Farm
Tidenham Chase
Chepstow
Gwent
NP6 7LZ
(01291) 689257
Mrs M Cracknell

Bridge Caravan & Campsite
Dingestow
Monmouth
Gwent
NP5 4DY
(01600) 740241
Mr S Holmes

Bridge End
Buttington
Welshpool
Powys
SY21 8SR
(01938) 552249
Mrs B M Pryce

Church Cottage
Llanvetherine
Abergavenny
Gwent
NP7 8RG
(01873) 821475
Mrs E A Caldicott

Court farm
Llantillio Crosenny
Abergavenny
Gwent
NP7 8SU
(01600) 780288
Mrs S Nugent

Little Bank
Pool Quay
Welshpool
Powys
SY21 9JS
(01938) 590505
Mrs S Jones

Llyn Rhys Farm
Llandegla
Wrexham
Clwyd
LL11 3AF
(01978) 790627
L Hughes

Memorial Hall
C/o Mrs S Byrne
2 The Village Llandegla
Nr Wrexham
LL11 3AR
(01978) 790266
Mrs S Byrne

Minffordd
Llanbedr
Ruthin
Clwyd
LL15 1TS
(01824) 707169
Mrs S Betts

Monmouth Caravan & Camp Park
Rockfield Road
Monmouth
Gwent
NP5 3BA
(01600) 714745
Mr S J Brown

Monnow Bridge Caravan Site
Drybridge Street
Monmouth
Gwent
NP5 3AD
(01600) 714004
Mrs M Murray

Panpunton Farm
Knighton
Powys
LD7 1TN
(01547) 528597
Mrs E G Williams

Penoffa Farm
Evenjobb
Presteigne
Powys
LD8 2PB
(01547) 560237
T F Evans

Radnors End Campsite
Hay-on-Wye
Herefordshire
HR3 5RS
(01497) 820780
Mrs Z M Davies

Rockbridge Park
Presteigne
Powys
LD8 2NF
(01547) 560300
R M Deakins

Station House Caravan Park
Bodfari
Denbigh
Clwyd
LL16 4DA
(01745) 710372
R S Hastings

The Cross Keys

Selattyn
Oswestry
SY10 7DN
(01691) 650247
P J Rothera

The White House Caravan Park
Rhuallt
St. Asaph
Clwyd
LL17 0AW
(01745) 582155
GG & J Jones

THE CROWN IS YOUR
SURE SIGN
OF WHERE TO STAY

HOTELS, GUESTHOUSES, INNS, B&Bs & FARMHOUSES

Throughout Britain, the tourist boards now inspect over 17,000 hotels, guesthouses, inns, B&Bs and farmhouses, every year, to help you find the ones that suit you best.

THE CLASSIFICATIONS: '**Listed**', and then **ONE to FIVE CROWN,** tell you the range of facilities and services you can expect. The more Crowns, the wider the range.

THE GRADES: **APPROVED, COMMENDED, HIGHLY COMMENDED and DE LUXE,** where they appear, indicate the quality standard provided. If no grade is shown, you can still expect a high standard of cleanliness.

Every classified place to stay has a Fire Certificate, where this is required under the Fire Precautions Act, and all carry Public Liability Insurance.

'**Listed**': Clean and comfortable accommodation, but the range of facilities and services may be limited.

ONE CROWN: Accommodation with additional facilities, including washbasins in all bedrooms, a lounge and use of a phone.

TWO CROWN: A wider range of facilities and services, including morning tea and calls, bedside lights, colour TV in lounge or bedrooms, 20% or more of bedrooms with private WC, bath or shower.

THREE CROWN: At least half of the bedrooms with ensuite WC and bath or shower, plus easy chair, full length mirror. Shoe cleaning facilities and hairdryers available. Hot evening meals available.

FOUR CROWN: At least 90% of the bedrooms with ensuite WC, bath and/or shower plus colour TV, radio and phone, 24-hour access and lounge service until midnight. Last orders for meals 8.30 pm or later.

FIVE CROWN: All bedrooms having WC, bath and shower ensuite, plus a wide range of facilities and services, including room service, all-night lounge service and laundry service. Restaurant open for breakfast, lunch and dinner.

THE LODGES

 The Lodges. If you are looking for somewhere convenient to stop overnight on a motorway or major road route the 'Lodge' **MOONS** are a sure sign of where to stay. The number of **MOONS (1-3)** will show the range of facilities and the quality grades are indicated by: **APPROVED, COMMENDED, HIGHLY COMMENDED OR DE LUXE.**

We've checked them out before you check in!

223

STOP PRESS

<u>Inside front cover</u> - "Other paths" should be a dash and dot repeated

<u>Inside rear cover</u> - exc = excluding, inc = including

see page 223 for Tourist Board Gradings.

<u>Page 33</u> - List of OS Sheets - add Sheet 126

<u>Page 117</u> - Norton Arms is now The Knighton Hotel

<u>Page 133</u> - Before point "Z", note Path is now over new stile to the West of cattle pens.

<u>1996 - Local Authority Changes</u>

With effect April 1996 there are a number of changes to the structure and boundaries of Welsh local authorities. The Welsh Office offered an A4 drawing of the new boundaries but were unable to say what the new Postal County's would be called. The Post Office is adopting a flexible policy and hadn't decided exactly how the changes were going to affect addresses. Their best advice was to ensure you include the Postal Town and Postcode in the address.

<u>Travel Help-Lines</u>

<u>Gwent</u> - Splits into 5 authorities. Blaenau Gwent County Borough Council will co-ordinate travel enquiries from new offices (still being built March 1996!). Meantime, try Ebbw Vale Civic Centre (01495) 350555.

<u>Powys</u> - New Powys Council will retain existing helpline.

<u>Clwyd</u> - Try Flintshire County Council (no number available as at March 1996).

Langton's Guides - Update Registration

To register for the Offa's Dyke Path Update (produced February/March), please complete and post this card (No stamp required).

Langton's Guides are registered under the Data Protection Act and no information will be passed to any third party.

Mr/Mrs/Ms/Miss (delete as appropriate) Initials   Surname

Address

Postcode

Please tell us where you bought this Guide?

What type of accommodation do you use?

Which walking magazine(s) do you buy, if any?

On a scale of 1-5 (5 = Excellent, 4 = Good, 3 = Satisfactory, 2 = Below expectation, 1 = Poor)

How do you rate our:

Routefinding maps -   Directions -   Location maps -   Facilities information -

Background/ historical information -   Overall rating -

How might we improve our guides?

Langton's Guides

LANGTON'S GUIDES
69 COMMON ROAD
WESTON COLVILLE
CAMBRIDGE
CB1 5NS